## Praise for *Curious Characters*

In this thought-provoking book, Lena-Sofia Tiemeyer leads the reader on a journey among ambiguous biblical characters and encourages us to question these ambiguities—and our responses to them. This book is highly relevant for the current world, perhaps more than ever: Rather than applying a binary judgment of good vs. bad, Tiemeyer acknowledges the Bible's complexities and then carefully engages them.

—**Zohar Hadromi-Allouche**, Trinity College Dublin

Lena-Sofia Tiemeyer shares her love of reading and of biblical characters. *Curious Characters* is a beautiful and thought-provoking book written in a personal voice. Written for a Christian lay readership, Tiemeyer's book introduces her readers to a wide range of literary retellings from both Jewish and Christian authors. These retellings open new ways of reading familiar stories and invite us to ponder new questions as we read. Lena-Sofia Tiemeyer is not afraid of questions and of leaving the answers open, which makes *Curious Characters* a very refreshing book.

—**Hanne Løland Levinson**, University of Minnesota, and author of *The Death Wish in the Hebrew Bible: Rhetorical Strategies for Survival*

With an international reputation and a wide range of publications, Professor Lena-Sofia Tiemeyer now brings her wealth of insight to a wider audience. Anyone curious about figures like the prophet Jonah (Is he an annoying grouch?), the princess Michal (Is she a hapless pawn?), or Noah (Why on earth does he get so drunk?) will appreciate this introduction to some surprisingly complicated biblical characters.

—**Keith Bodner**, Crandall University

# CURIOUS CHARACTERS

# CURIOUS CHARACTERS

## OLD TESTAMENT FIGURES WHO STILL SPEAK TO US TODAY

LENA-SOFIA TIEMEYER

FORTRESS PRESS
Minneapolis

CURIOUS CHARACTERS
Old Testament Figures Who Still Speak to Us Today



Originally published as *Mina bibliska vänner och jag* 2024 by Lena-Sofia Tiemeyer. Copyright Spricka förlag, a part of Inmedit AB, Hammarbacksvägen 93, 238 36 Oxie, Sweden.

31 30 29 28 27 26 25 1 2 3 4 5 6 7 8 9

Library of Congress Control Number: 2025023073 (print)

Cover design: Kris E. Miller
Cover image: Nadia Grossman-Bulighin, Lectură ("Reading"). Photographed at Art Safari 2024, Dacia Building, Bucharest. On loan from Octavian and Ilinca Brandeu collection

Print ISBN: 979-8-8898-3771-8
eBook ISBN: 979-8-8898-3772-5

# CONTENTS

# INTRODUCTION

## *People Like You and Me*

The Bible is God's speech to us. This statement has many dimensions and can be understood in several different ways. First of all, the Bible is God's address to us, preserved in book form. As Christians, we read the Bible in pieces, where each individual part testifies to God's love for us. We also understand each part as part of a larger whole that communicates God's love to us. When we say that the Bible is the word of God, we also mean that the texts we have in our Bibles today, both in terms of selection and content, are meant by God to be there.

On another level, we know that the Bible did not fall from heaven neatly packaged. We maintain, on the one hand, that the Holy Spirit guided not only the authors of the Bible as they wrote their books but also the people who selected which of them would be included in the canon of the Bible. On the other hand, we are aware that the Bible is written by humans. The Bible is not only God's word but also Israel's word. The Old Testament authors tell us about God's actions through the ages in relation to his chosen people, Israel, and the New Testament authors describe how God sent his only Son to save the world through the suffering, death, and resurrection of Jesus, and they discuss the implications of this for our lives.

We are also aware that there are significant differences between the various books of the Bible. A quick survey of the Old Testament, which is the focus of this book, shows that the authors of the different books describe God in complementary ways, emphasizing different aspects and dimensions. The authors of the Psalms depict Israel's worship of God. They show how the people of Israel worshipped God, and they have preserved the words Israel used to express their feelings of joy and sorrow. Other writers describe God's commands and point out what Israel should do to show their appreciation to God. What laws should they keep, how should they worship, and how should they treat their neighbors? The prophets constitute a third major group. They are called to be God's representatives on earth and to relay God's will in specific historical situations. Last but not least, a large number of other writers describe God in prose. They tell stories of how God walks with his people through times of war and peace, prosperity and hardship, and they testify to how the people of Israel act toward each other. This book is mainly concerned with this last group of texts.

## People Like You and Me

The authors of the Bible were people who lived in a world and in times that were very different from the world and times in which we live today. It is therefore wise to be cautious when approaching the stories of the Bible and to realize that the world of the Bible is not always like our world. The people we meet in the biblical stories can sometimes seem very strange and behave in ways that we find difficult to relate to. At the same time, they are people like us. They eat and sleep, they love and hate, they cry when they are sad and laugh when they are happy, they are jealous, greedy, generous, and forgiving just like us.

We may like some of these characters intuitively and wish we could get to know them, while we may find others unpleasant and perhaps even repulsive. We do not have to like every character in the Bible. It is perfectly feasible to say that we do not like a particular person or rather a particular characteristic of that person. Moreover, we do not all have to like the same characters because what one person finds interesting another may find annoying. I intuitively like Jonathan because he is an extremely verbal person, but it is quite possible that others think he babbles too much. I like Joseph because he gets on with things, while I fully understand that others may find his energy level exhausting. I am drawn to Jonah because he questions everything, but I realize that others may want to criticize him for the same reason.

One of the challenges when reading the Old Testament is that we often do not know who is the bad guy and who is the role model of the story. This makes it unclear whom to support. It is pretty clear that we are supposed to root for David in his fight against Saul. David is the lonely, hunted man on the run who nobly refuses to kill Saul despite repeated opportunities to do so. Yet other aspects of the David story undermine this impression. Saul is portrayed so tragically that most readers cannot help feeling at least a little sorry for him. In most cases, however, the biblical stories avoid telling us what to think and feel about what happens in the text. They refuse to take sides, leaving it up to us to decide who is the villain and who is the hero—if they exist at all. This can lead to considerable frustration, especially when we are also dealing with texts that are thousands of years old and come from a culture very different from our own. Could the Bible not have given us a little more guidance? We feel that we risk reading the stories "incorrectly" and missing clues in the text which, had we understood them better, could have led us to simple and unambiguous answers.

Moreover, many stories lack a clear moral. Rather, they appear almost amoral, at least from our modern, Western perspective, in that they do not seem to advocate clear guidelines on what is right and wrong. This amorality, too, can lead to irritation and uncertainty. On a few occasions, the Bible shows its clear disapproval of someone's behavior. For example, we cannot help but agree with the prophet Nathan when he reprimands King David for committing murder and adultery. In most cases, however, the biblical stories do not provide any guidance on how we should feel and think about what is happening in the text. No one tells us whether a person is acting rightly or wrongly. Instead, we are left to ponder and decide these things for ourselves. This again leads to hesitation and a feeling of inadequacy. Is Jael's assassination of Sisera in Judges 4 a morally flawless act? No, it probably is not. Our inner moral compass tells us not to invite people into our homes and then kill them, with or without tent pegs. At the same time, the story is about a war situation, and Sisera is a soldier on active duty. Can we count Jael's murder as an excusable and even justified act of war against an enemy soldier? Yes, this is a plausible interpretation, but it is not the only possible one.

This book will not provide any clear answers. It will not tell you whether Jael's behavior is ethically defensible. Nor is this the aim of the book. Instead, it will draw on the feelings of ambivalence and hesitation that we feel when we read the stories in the Bible. It will insist that it is up to us, the readers, to decide whether a character is right or wrong. Strictly speaking, what matters is not the answer but, to paraphrase the Swedish poet Karin Boye, the journey. The biblical stories raise questions, and these questions are there to be discussed. We can learn much from the stories in the Bible precisely because they require us to take a stand. To return to Jael, her story forces us to ask what we would have done in her situation. Would we also have killed Sisera if we were in her shoes? Is it right to kill an enemy if it means giving our loved ones a chance to survive? Is it right to resort to unorthodox methods if they lead to victory? Or is Jael's behavior reprehensible because she does not play by the rules? In short, do the ends justify the means or not? The Bible does not give answers, but it wants us to take a stand.

A potential challenge with this kind of reading concerns the inspiration of the Bible and our view of its authority. How can we readers decide how a divinely inspired story should be interpreted, and with what authority do we make these decisions? Do we even have the right to pass judgment on the characters in the Bible? Should we not just accept their behavior and act likewise? The difficulty with this approach is precisely that we do not know whom to emulate and whose example we should shun like the plague. In the case of King David and Nathan, it is obvious that we should not murder and commit adultery. And yet we know that already, even before reading about David's behavior toward Uriah and Bathsheba, because it is written in the Ten Commandments (Exod 20:13–14). Rather, it is the unclear narratives that grab our attention. It is cases like Jael's that are interesting precisely because they are so opaque.

I do not think it is problematic to reconcile a high view of the Bible with interactive Bible reading. We show respect for the biblical texts precisely by taking them seriously and spending time and energy entering their world, getting to know their characters, and reflecting on their behavior. We discover that most biblical characters are neither good nor bad, but instead complex and three-dimensional individuals like you and me. Sometimes their baser sides predominate and sometimes their better ones. For example, Joab, King David's nephew and later commander, is one of the Bible's more violent characters, and many of us may feel uneasy about this man who takes up the sword more often than necessary. For example, he kills Saul's former commander, Abner, in a private vendetta, despite the fact that this man had sided with David and contributed to the peace between David and the few surviving members of Saul's family (2 Sam 2:13–3:21; 3:27). He also chooses to cooperate with David to carry out the murder of Uriah (2 Sam 11:14–25). At the same time, even Joab has laudable moments, especially when he dares to go against David's explicit orders and executes Absalom after his rebellion against David (2 Sam 18:5, 11–22). Although I am rarely in favor of violence, Joab's actions in this particular case show both foresight and political savvy. Killing a rebel is a necessary evil in an unstable political situation, something that even David is forced to recognize in the end (2 Sam 19:1–8).

As already mentioned, the stories in the Bible are very old and were written in a different culture that sometimes has very different norms compared with ours. Does this not mean that our modern evaluation of the behavior of biblical characters risks being anachronistic? How can I, on the basis of my own values, understand and even pass judgment on them? Would it not be more respectful to accept that I do not understand everything? Yes and no. I absolutely believe it is important to recognize that there are nuances in the text that we do not understand and may even misunderstand because of our different values and preconceptions. At the same time, I maintain that the Bible is able to transcend these limitations. Even if I do misunderstand a text, I can still learn something, but perhaps more about myself than about the original message of the text. Besides, this is God's word we are talking about, and I firmly believe that it can speak to us today. We need not fear that we are violating the biblical text when we relate to it on our own terms. We do not have to think someone is good just because we think we should because we think the author would have wanted us to. As you can see, it all gets rather convoluted if we go down that route. Rather, we can trust our feelings. The Bible evokes our involvement, our empathy, and sometimes even our anger, and it is precisely these qualities that make it so endlessly fascinating.

Some stories are more upsetting than others, and some characters capture our interest more than others. This is very personal. Depending on our own experiences and personality, we are drawn to some biblical stories while finding others less interesting. In this book, I have chosen nine characters that fascinate me personally. My hope is that these people will capture your interest too. I have deliberately selected people who live through events we may experience ourselves and whose feelings we may understand and share. The seemingly disengaged Noah, childless Sarah, bullied Joseph, grieving Naomi, vulnerable Ruth, depressed Saul, divided Jonathan, neglected Michal, and rebellious Jonah. Stories about people like you and me.

## Reading the Old Testament as Literature

The Bible contains many different kinds of texts—legal texts, poetry, prophecy, proverbs, and above all stories. Our focus here is on the last category. The narrative texts of the Bible—and here I am speaking primarily of the stories in Genesis, Exodus, Joshua, Judges, Ruth, 1–2 Samuel, 1–2 Kings, Ezra, Nehemiah, Esther, and Jonah—can be read as literature. By that statement I mean that these texts have a plot and are filled with main and supporting characters who interact with God and with each other. When we read novels, short stories, poems, or go to the theater or cinema, we are invited into a narrative world that resembles our own world but at the same time differs from it because it is about people other than ourselves. Stories allow us to understand the world around us and our fellow human beings in a unique way. They take us out of ourselves and make us look at the world through someone else's eyes. Reading stories gives us a better understanding of other people's situations. We can imagine how someone else experiences a situation and mirror ourselves in that person. Stories enrich us by making us question how we would have acted if we were in a similar situation. When I read about Sarah, I identify with her and imagine how I would have reacted if I had been her. How does it feel to wait, month after month, to get pregnant, only to be equally disappointed every time your period comes? When I read about Saul, I ask myself, shuddering with horror, how I would have felt had God rejected me. When I read about Jonah, I am confronted with the question of whether I would have followed God's call to travel to the capital of my enemy's country or instead tried to escape. The answer is not obvious, but the stories help me to broaden my horizons and imagine what it is like to be someone else.

Reading the stories of the Bible as just stories says nothing about their historicity. It is perfectly possible to read Genesis and focus on the portrayal of Noah in the biblical text while maintaining that Noah was a historical figure. One does not exclude the other. In this book, however, we will only look at the first aspect, that is, how a given character is presented in the text. We will focus on the behavior of the characters, both toward God and their fellow human beings, in the text and see how these characters relate to each other. This is important when we start to speculate. When we think about what, for example, Michal feels when Saul forces her to marry Palti (also called Paltiel) or when she is reunited with David and realizes that he already has five other wives, it is not the historical woman we are speculating about but Michal in the biblical text.

This is in line with my view of the Bible. I believe that it is the biblical text that is inspired, not the underlying historical situation. For example, when we read that Saul is offended when he hears the people praising David (1 Sam 18:8), I assume that this is a reflection of the literary character in the text. At that moment, I think it unlikely that the author has insight into the emotional life of the historical Saul. At the same time, I believe that the same author, inspired by God to write about Saul, wants to convey something important about his situation. Furthermore, when I read about David and Jonathan meeting alone and talking in 1 Samuel 20, I assume that it is the literary characters who do so. At the same time, I assume that the author is not lying in the bushes eavesdropping on their private conversation. It is, of course, entirely possible that the historical figures of the same names behaved exactly like their namesakes in the biblical text, thought like them, and felt like them. However, this possibility is not the focus of my discussion.

My literary focus can, to some extent, be compared to the study of Jesus's parables. When I read about the Good Samaritan, the focus is on this literary character. It is irrelevant whether there was a historical person who behaved as the Samaritan did. He comes to life in Jesus's parable, and it is the parable, as told by Jesus, that is inspired. I can identify with the Samaritan and realize that I should act in a similar way toward my neighbor. I can also reflect on the behavior of the other characters and try to understand them. Why did the Levite and the priest not stay? Were they prejudiced and selfish or just scared? Moreover, what would I have done in their place? Would I really have stopped to help, or would I have hurried on, worried and afraid, so as not to be ambushed myself on the barren and completely deserted stretch between Jerusalem and Jericho? As above, it is entirely possible that there was a Good Samaritan who lived his life outside the parable, but Jesus's story is no more or less relevant if that were the case. It is important in its own right.

Good literature is characterized by telling something that is important and true and relevant. It contributes to my understanding of the world around me and gives me greater insight into my own behavior. I read literature to get to know people and understand their behavior. Sometimes I think I learn more about my fellow human beings by reading a novel than by meeting them in real life. In a novel, I get to know their thoughts and feelings, while these are often hidden from me in real life.

## Reading the Old Testament with and Without Preconceived Ideas

A text does not have only one meaning. This statement may be obvious to some people and overwhelming to others. It is common to talk about the difference between authorial intent, that is, the message an author wanted to convey when writing their text, and reader experience, that is, what readers over time have understood the text to be about.

## Reading the Bible with the Author

Some people insist that the most important thing is to understand what the author of a text wanted to say. I tend to agree. If we do not take into account when a text was written, we can easily misunderstand a number of things. On a linguistic level, we can misunderstand words and expressions. For example, is an expression meant as a metaphor or should it be read literally? One of my favorite examples is the description of the woman in Song of Songs 4. I suspect it is meant to be read metaphorically. When the text says that the woman's teeth are a flock of ewes coming out of the bath, most readers intuitively realize that this description should not be taken literally. Furthermore, the fact that all the sheep have twins probably means that none of the teeth are missing but that they are all still in the mouth. At the same time, we make a lot of other assumptions, which are also intuitive but based on our own perception. Most people hopefully assume that the text is talking about white rather than black sheep, simply because we perceive white, and thus healthy, teeth to be more attractive than black ones. At the same time, I know that my knowledge is too limited to understand the imagery in its entirety. I assume that a neck resembling the tower of David is a beautiful neck, but since I have never seen said tower, it must remain a conjecture. In the end, I am forced to throw in the towel and admit that I do not understand what the tower of David has to do with the neck.

In other cases as a reader, I am less confident in my ability to correctly understand a biblical text. These texts were written so long ago by people I know nothing about and whose purpose is obscured by the passage of time. For example, we do not know who wrote 1–2 Samuel and what exact message these authors wanted to convey. Some scholars consider the books to be propaganda about David, while others are more open to the idea that they are what we might call "serious entertainment," that is, a text that seeks to entertain readers but at the same time convey something important about the behavior of God and humanity in this era of Israel's history. I want to understand, but I also know my limitations.

## The Bible and the Reader

Others argue that once a text leaves the author's hand and lands in the reader's, it is no longer tied to what the author wanted to say but becomes what the reader makes of it. A published book no longer belongs to the author but to those who read it. An author cannot complain and say, "I didn't mean it like that when I wrote it," but must accept that once the work has left the printing presses, they have lost the authority to determine how people understand it.

Some books quickly become obsolete. Libraries around the world regularly decide to get rid of books that no one reads anymore. A mediocre, ten-year-old crime novel can easily become boring. If it does not have the power to convey something universal and timeless, that little "extra" that turns it into literature, it falls into oblivion. That little extra turns out not to be an extra at all but something essential. Some crime novels will never go out of print. I am uncertain how many times I have read Dorothy L. Sayers's *Gaudy Night.* I reread it not because I want to know "who did it" but because it speaks to me on a deeper level. I identify, as always, with Harriet Vane and her struggle for integrity and the right to self-determination. This is literature doing what literature is supposed to do, which is both to entertain and challenge us to create new ways of thinking.

Sometimes a book needs to be rewritten or, as is often said in academic contexts, readdressed in order to remain relevant. It may be that the intended readership no longer understands it or for other reasons cannot absorb the original text. They are no longer fascinated by it in the same way as previous generations were, perhaps because their own life situations are so different. This loss of relevance often leads to a debate between those who want to keep the original version and those who fight for a new, updated version. To draw a Swedish analogy, there are many today who would like to see a new film production of Astrid Lindgren's beloved book *Bröderna Lejonhjärta* (hereafter, *The Brothers Lionheart*) so that today's children can relate to it. At the same time, there are just as many who think it would be sacrilegious to replace the old one. The book itself will always be in our libraries. I cannot see any librarian worthy of the name willingly getting rid of it. Its visual interpretation, that is, the film, is updated, but the book is always there, in the background, for those who want to read the original.

The Old Testament texts present a similar case. To return to 1–2 Samuel, it is not always easy to determine what message the authors wanted to convey. At the same time, we know that the stories of Saul and David have been preached in many different ways throughout the ages and have been rewritten to speak to the preacher's audience. This rewriting has already started in the Bible itself. The books 1–2 Chronicles are in many ways a rewriting of 1–2 Samuel. The same stories are told, but the perspective is different. Some characters are no longer present (Jonathan and Michal are two good examples) while other events have been added (David, for example, makes a lot of speeches in 1 Chronicles). At the same time, 1–2 Samuel remain in the Bible, and generation after generation constantly return to them for inspiration and strength, as well as to be confronted and challenged by their often difficult and, in many respects, troubling ideas.

## Interpretive Communities

This leads us to the concept of the interpretive community. The meaning of a text is not stable. Instead, it is influenced by our preconceptions and expectations. It also changes from time to time and from place to place. When we open our Bible, we usually know not only what we will find but also what we think about it. This statement may seem cryptic. How can we know what we are going to read and what we will think of it before we read it? The answer often lies in what we call our interpretive community. Our social and religious context determines what the Bible should mean and, at the same time, sets limits on what it should not mean. We all come to the Bible with preconceptions. What sets us apart is our background.

If we have grown up going to a Christian Sunday school and other children's groups in Church, we usually have a rather naive view of the contents of the Bible. God loves us and wants us all to be well. We have also learned which stories in the Old Testament are important. We sometimes talk about a canon within the canon. A good example of this is found in Christian children's Bibles. There is an almost canonical selection of stories from the Old Testament that every child who has grown up in a Christian community knows: Adam and Eve, Noah's ark, Joseph and his coat, Moses floating on the Nile, Ruth in the cornfields, David and Goliath, Daniel in the lions' den, and Esther at court. These stories are furthermore retold in a particular manner that emphasizes God's providence and care and, last but not least, they are transformed into child-friendly versions. This is obvious when teaching children. No sane person would think of telling their Sunday school class about Noah's drunkenness, Joseph's experiences of sexual abuse, Moses's circumcision, Ruth's escapades on the threshing floor, David's gathering of Michal's bride price, and so on. However, this selection and sanitization lead to many Christians being shocked when they encounter these stories in their entirety as adults. It also often results in them rarely being taught in any greater detail. In this way, we create a canon within the canon where only certain stories, and only narrated in a certain way, are heard from the pulpit.

Others come from a more secular context and may have encountered the notion that God, especially in the Old Testament, is a belligerent and misogynistic God who seems more interested in carrying out acts of violence than showing love. In a way, they have heard all the stories that the Church hardly ever talks about. At the same time, they often display a lack of understanding of the literary and historical context of the stories. They relate to the biblical texts as if they were written today and criticize, for example, their depictions of war without recognizing the vulnerable position of historical Israel in the shadow of first the Neo-Assyrian and then the Neo-Babylonian empires. Furthermore, laws from Leviticus are stripped of their social context and consequently misinterpreted with the sole aim of proving the misogynistic and racist nature of the Old Testament.

## The Importance of a Text in the Canon

Our interpretive community is closely linked to our canon. Our interpretation of a single biblical text is very much influenced by what other texts we consider to be part of our Bible. I mentioned above that the Bible is God's word to us, both in its content and its selection. The Protestant canon contains sixty-six books: thirty-nine in the Old Testament and twenty-seven in the New Testament. This canon represents the books that we consider to be inspired by God and that give us guidance about God's will for our lives. Moreover, we Christians often maintain that the books in the canon have a common function of holding together and correcting misinterpretations of the various individual texts: One text in the canon sheds light on another text. Each text is part of a larger whole, and each piece contributes to the message of the whole. At the same time, the whole helps us to see what each piece may mean.

However, several factors complicate this claim and require us to have a more nuanced discussion. We know that it took centuries for the church to decide which books should be included in the Christian canon. We likewise know that there is no consensus among Christians worldwide as to how many books are actually in the Old Testament. It is never less than the Protestant thirty-nine books, though. This has a major impact on how we interpret the

Bible. If the whole guides us as to the meaning of each individual part, then it is important to consider which books are part of the whole.

This difference is most marked when we compare Christian and Jewish readings of the Bible. A Christian interpretation of an Old Testament text often allows New Testament material to determine what that Old Testament text should (and should not) mean. Similarly, later Jewish traditions often govern how Jews interpret the individual texts of the Old Testament (or rather the Hebrew Bible, which is a more appropriate name in a Jewish context). This becomes very important when we read an Old Testament text. Do we intuitively choose an interpretation that is in line with what the New Testament preaches, and do we feel most comfortable with a reading of an Old Testament text where the New Testament has the last word? Alternatively, are we willing to let the Old Testament speak for itself, and are we prepared to embrace an interpretation that rests solely on the immediate literary context of the story in the Old Testament? These questions become relevant when we think about Noah and Abraham, among other characters. How do we decide how to interpret the Old Testament text if we detect a potential conflict between the Old and New Testament portraits of these two characters?

## Interpretive Communities (Again)

Returning to the question of interpretive community, we shall find, as I have said, that whether we are Jewish or Christian makes a big difference to how we interpret an Old Testament text. First, the selection of Old Testament texts preached on Sundays in churches is not the same as those read on Saturdays in the synagogues of the same country. That Jews and Christians do not know the same texts was something I learned pretty quickly during my studies at the Hebrew University of Jerusalem. It often happened that I, alone among all the students in the classroom, was ignorant of a particular story. Occasionally, the opposite happened: I knew a text that most of the others in the class had never read before. I realized that I knew my Bible only as long as I hung out with other Christians. Among my Jewish friends, I turned out to be quite ignorant.

Second, we shall notice that Jews and Christians often have different approaches to the biblical stories. While Christians emphasize certain aspects, Jews will emphasize others. This difference is partly due to differences in our respective canons. Here Noah provides a good example. Jewish Bible interpreters tend to understand Noah's conduct in dialogue with the thirty-nine books of the Hebrew Bible and later rabbinic traditions. Noah will thus be compared to other biblical characters such as Abraham (Gen 18:20–33) and Moses (Exod 32:10–14), who find themselves in similar situations. Several Jewish exegetes throughout the ages have thus emphasized that Noah prays for his contemporaries: Just as Abraham and Moses pray that God would change his mind and not send the planned destruction on Sodom and Israel, Noah prays that God will not send the flood.

Christian biblical interpreters, on the other hand, have often maintained that Noah is preaching repentance to the people around him when he builds the ark. This interpretation derives from the New Testament, especially from 2 Peter 2:5, where Noah is described as a "preacher of righteousness," and from 1 Peter 3:20, where the people are described as recalcitrant. In other words, the portrait of Noah in the Old Testament is complemented by the portrait of Noah in the New Testament, and the result is a composite picture in which Noah urges the people to repent. The material in the New Testament is not unambiguous, however, as other biblical texts, such as Matthew 24:37–39, indicate that the people of Noah's time do not know that the flood is coming.

Neither intercessory prayer nor preaching are found in the Noah story—they have been read into the text—but what is important in this context is precisely our interpretive community. We are taught to understand the biblical texts from a certain perspective and in accordance with a certain canon. This is something we bring from home, from our culture, and from our religious context. In other words, we are all part of an interpretive context, and this context shapes our preunderstanding of what the Bible says. It is almost impossible to read the Bible without preconceived ideas.

## Reading the Bible Through Literature

However, preconceived ideas are there to be confronted and challenged. This is the main purpose of this book. Using modern novels, short stories and poetry, we shall read a selection of biblical texts from different (Jewish, Christian, secular) perspectives. None of these works, which I have chosen to call *retellings*, claim any kind of divine inspiration. Rather, they represent people's thoughts and questions about the biblical text. They illuminate, question, challenge, and criticize the biblical texts from a deeply human point of view. These different approaches may nevertheless help us to discern, and eventually perhaps even work through, our own preconceptions. Sometimes the retellings may even depart from the explicit meaning of the biblical text and allow the biblical characters to act in alternative ways. Even this can be helpful to us, however, because we are then challenged to consider whether the real behavior of the biblical characters (that is, what the biblical text says) is to some extent counterintuitive or otherwise surprising.

Finally, we will find that different narrators focus on different aspects of the text. As mentioned earlier, there is a marked difference between Jewish and Christian writers, both in terms of focus and interpretive choices. It is interesting to note that while Jewish writers are almost obsessed with King Saul, and poet after poet ponders his thoughts and feelings as he walks to his death on Mount Gilboa, Christian retellers are relatively uninterested in him. At the same time, there is a considerably deeper interest in Joseph among Christian novelists than among their Jewish counterparts. In parallel, it appears that female retellers, perhaps for natural reasons, tend to favor female Bible characters to a larger extent than male retellers do. I do not mean to make a qualitative distinction between different interpretations and maintain that one way is better than the other. Quite the contrary! Even so, when reading it is always worth noticing a narrator's interpretive community while thinking further about how their respective backgrounds affect their choices and influence their understanding of and empathy for certain characters. My choice of characters to discuss in this book, as mentioned above, naturally reflects my personal interests and emotional involvement. Some characters simply fascinate me more than others. At the same time, this fascination can probably be explained by my upbringing and what I have experienced during my life.

The aim of retellings is never to replace the Bible. Rather, these contemporary writers use the biblical texts to help us reflect on God's role and will in our lives. Sometimes they can make us uncomfortable, as they question and criticize an interpretation that we, given our own interpretive community (our church, parish, family, etc.), are used to seeing as the only right one. In other cases, they can give us an "aha!" moment in that their retelling sheds new light on a text. We suddenly discover new interpretive possibilities in texts that we, until now, had thought could only mean the one thing that we were used to seeing. In further cases, it can fundamentally change the way we understand a biblical text. What all these different scenarios have in common is that they constitute encounters with the biblical texts. These encounters will affect us, and that, in turn, will hopefully lead us to discover new aspects of the Bible and become more nuanced readers of the texts. My hope is that we all gain an enriched and deepened understanding of God's word and what he wants to say to us.

## Reading the Old Testament as a Starting Point for Theological Discussion

The Bible's openness to different interpretations and the idea that it does not have only one single meaning can be both a relief and a challenge. How can we relate to God's word if it is not eternal and unchanging? I maintain, however, that it is both eternal and at the same time changeable, in the sense that each new reader must figure out what God wants to communicate through his word in terms that are relevant to us today. If we focus only on what the author of the text wanted to convey, we easily end up in historical research. The biblical text becomes a museum that we enter, look around in for a while, and then leave. If our whole interest is centered on what the original authors wanted to communicate to their contemporaries, where do we place ourselves in the text? Most of us do not belong to the people of Israel, live in the ancient Near East, or share the hardships that Israel had at that time. God has promised never to drown his creation again (Noah), most of us do not have to lie about our marital status when traveling to Egypt (Abraham and Sarah), and the Neo-Assyrians do not pose a military threat to our country (Jonah). Therefore, to a very large extent, we need to recontextualize the texts if we want them to remain relevant to us.

Biblical theologian and exegete John Barton insightfully writes that when we read the biblical texts, we must assume that the people in the Bible function in much the same way as we do: They have the same kinds of feelings, experiences, and needs as we do. Furthermore, the reason we can learn from the biblical stories is that their characters are real in the sense that we can relate to them in the same way we do to people around us. We are correct when we try to make the biblical characters understandable to us, assuming that we can share their feelings and understand their motives in light of our own experiences. Barton goes a step further when he insists that the difference between our relationships with real people and with fictional characters is relatively unimportant:

> We cannot get close to another person unless we see them as making a certain sort of sense, having a life history with something that could be called a plot, a personality with a certain Gestalt or shape to which we can relate. That is why, when we first meet someone, we directly or indirectly quiz them on who they are and where they have come from; and if we find ourselves drawn to them, we develop an intense interest in their total life history. Drawing a fictional character is an imitation of this process. But the point can easily be stood on its head, and we can say that getting to know another real person is a little like drawing a fictional character.[1]

If we put the emphasis on ourselves, the biblical text becomes a dialogue partner that we can challenge and be challenged by. We can reflect on the different meanings that the text can have and learn from others who have seen different things in the text than we have. Some aspects of the biblical stories are timeless and speak to us across the millennia. People are still bullied by their close family members (Joseph), people starve and lose loved ones (Naomi), more people than ever are choosing migration and experiencing alienation in a new country (Ruth), and far too many people feel that they must choose between two people, yet simultaneously also fearing that they are letting both down (Jonathan).

This interaction and discussion may lead to a deeper understanding of God and our relationship with him. As mentioned above, many of the texts in the Bible are neutral—too neutral for many people's liking—and this neutrality can leave us with a sense of dissatisfaction, uncertainty, and even discontent. We as readers are not given enough information to know what to think and feel about a biblical character. To revisit the story about Jael, am I supposed to agree with Jael, consider her behavior to be good, and act in the same way in a similar situation? Or should I rather distance myself from her behavior and condemn her actions? A literary reading does not provide clear answers, but it does raise important questions that can form the basis of further conversations in sermons, Bible studies, and among friends. It is unlikely that all readers will feel the same way, and that is not the goal. It is in the tension between the different interpretations that we can find theological truths. This tension forces us to confront the text deeply and honestly and to take it seriously. What does it want to tell us, and how can we deal with this message? It is the collective interaction with the text that provides greater theological insight.

In the end, we will not be able to say what the narrative biblical texts are about. We will not be able to clarify and isolate their single, simple, and unambiguous message. There is no such thing, nor is it worthwhile trying to find it. Instead, after pondering the stories, we shall hopefully have reached a deeper understanding of them. They will form a starting point for us to work out how we, prayerfully and with God's guidance, may relate to a particular theme. The individual biblical texts thus become catalysts for a more mature approach to ethical dilemmas, a deeper understanding of ourselves, and a closer relationship with God.

In the background of this discussion is the realization that many Old Testament texts are deeply problematic because of their often misogynistic attitudes and the impression that they endorse violence. Similarly, their portrayal of God as the originator and sustainer of many of these attitudes is a recurring issue in many discussions of the Old Testament and its relevance to us today, whether we are Jews, Christians, or embrace some other worldview. This book does not intend to defend these serious aspects in any way. On the contrary, many, if not most, of the retellings we shall look at refer precisely to this problem.

Nor is my aim to hide away the difficult texts of the Bible and hope that no one will discover them. Instead, I want to highlight their troubling aspects, so that together we may find ways of dealing with the issues responsibly. The intention is to reach a deeper insight into the biblical texts and a better understanding of them. The solution is not to cut out the difficult texts but to stare them in the face, wrestle with them, and relate to them in ways that both listen to and dare to criticize what is being described. In some cases, it is evident that the biblical authors did the same: No authorial reading of Amnon's rape of Tamar in 2 Samuel 13 should doubt that the Bible rejects Amnon's act of violence. In other cases, it is the inherent ambivalence of the text that may lead to a fruitful ethical discussion. As mentioned above, it is unclear how the author relates to Jael and her murder of the enemy who visits her home in Judges 4. The answer is not given, but it is the journey, that is, the pondering of the text and the discussion it evokes, that is worthwhile.

I have deliberately chosen not to focus on God as the main character. To do so would have resulted in a very different book, where the choices to affirm or criticize God's actions would have been central. Rather, my focus is on those texts where God is one of several characters, and where we can reflect on the interaction between God and humanity.

## Reading the Bible Is Equal to Reading for Pleasure

I do not like it when my students ask if something will be in the exam in the implicit sense that if it is not in the exam, there is no point in learning it. Similarly, I have difficulty with a type of biblical reading where the text is reduced to examples that we should either try to emulate or, more often, not follow. My objection is not to the search for examples per se but because such an attitude sometimes has a tendency of reducing God's word to a textbook. It takes away the beauty, excitement, and pleasure of reading. I do not have time to stop and enjoy the story because I feel like I am constantly thinking about how to use it.

A textbook is rarely fun to read, I think most people would agree. I discovered this early on as a teenager. I have always loved history, but most of my historical knowledge has been absorbed through novels rather than in the classroom. Also, school history lessons tended to focus on the development of the sewing machine and the industrial revolution (important in its own right, I know), whereas at that age I preferred to hear about political intrigue, romantic entanglements, and dynastic battles. I still find the Wars of the Roses interesting (especially as retold by Philippa Gregory). I read Anna Sparre's *Farväl amiral* (Farewell admiral) and learned about Kristina Gyllenstierna's defense of Stockholm against the Danish King Kristian II, I ploughed through Elsi Rydsjö's books and gained a whole new understanding of the hardships of the defeated Caroleans in the Siberian prison camps. Being an academic at heart, after reading the novels, I often checked in the encyclopedia standing in the living room about how much of what was written was really true. More recently, I have also enjoyed Shona MacLean's detective stories set in seventeenth-century Aberdeen, Scotland, and Oliver Pötzsch's sometimes rather gruesome murder histories set in seventeenth-century Bamberg, Bavaria.

So, let us not reduce the Bible to a textbook, but instead let us preserve it as literature that we can enjoy. We will not learn less for that but rather more. Let us read the Bible for pleasure and allow ourselves to be fascinated by the world that opens up before us when we turn the pages. Let us not read the Bible primarily to use it but to enjoy the privilege of listening to it and partaking in its marvelous content. As Mikael Tellbe writes in his book *Vad menar vi med att Bibeln är Guds ord?* (What do we mean when we say that the Bible is the word of God?), let us read the Bible with empathy, let us identify with and see ourselves in its characters, and let us make their stories our stories.[2]

## Some Practical Things and Several Words of Thanks

I have chosen to discuss my selected biblical friends in canonical order, beginning with Genesis and ending with Jonah, but this arrangement is not important from a reader's perspective. On the contrary, it is perfectly possible to read the chapters in a different order. Furthermore, each chapter constitutes a separate unit and can thus be read independently. It should be said, though, that the three chapters about Saul and his two children Jonathan and Michal form a larger, loosely connected narrative that can advantageously be read in order.

I am a biblical scholar and therefore read the Old Testament in its original language, Hebrew. However, I have chosen to use the New Revised Standard Version (NRSV) translation in this book because it remains close to the biblical text and reflects recent scholarly insights. In the few cases where the choice of translation is relevant, I shall compare the NRSV with other English translations. In a few rare cases, I have preferred to translate the biblical text myself, not because there is anything wrong with the extant translations, but because I want to emphasize something special that would otherwise not be clear.

The Old Testament usually portrays God as a male character. He is a king, shepherd, warrior, and so forth. Furthermore, Hebrew always uses masculine pronouns and verb forms in connection with God. At the same time, there are a number of metaphors that describe God in traditionally female terms: Psalm 110:3 and Isaiah 42:14 liken God to a woman in labor, Isaiah 66:13 portrays God as a mother comforting her child, and Hosea 11:3–4 describes God as a parent teaching their children to walk, to name a few examples. Despite this variation, I have chosen to refer to God as *he* and *him* because this is in line with how the majority of biblical texts imagine God. This decision also has to do with my feeling for language: I find it clumsy not to be able to use pronouns when referring to God. I apologize if this annoys anyone.

In the case of the literary texts I discuss, I have chosen to quote the original text only if the book or poem is in English. Otherwise, I have either used existing translations, as in the case of Thomas Mann's classic novels about

Joseph, or translated the text myself. In the case of poetry, I have included the original text, as so much of the beauty of the poem is lost when moving from one language to another, though I provide translations next to the original text. For novels and other works, however, only the translation is included.

I would like to take this opportunity to thank my two friends, Zohar Hadromi-Allouche and Sygal Amitay, who helped me with the translation of Shaul Tchernichovsky's poems about King Saul. Tchernichovsky's Hebrew, a fascinating mix of biblical Hebrew, later rabbinic Hebrew, and very early modern Hebrew, is incredibly beautiful but sometimes a little too difficult for me.

Last but not least, I would also like to express my gratitude to a number of people who have read and commented on earlier versions of this book and pointed out lots of typos and other sloppy mistakes—those that remain are entirely my own responsibility. Many thanks go to my husband Andreas, who is (almost) always willing to read and then both praise and criticize my work; my friends and colleagues Greger Andersson, Maria Brolin, Stefan Green, Åsa Molin, and Mikael Tellbe at ALT School of Theology; and my friends Emma, Charlie, and Elias Cronberg, Ulrika Josefsson, and Ulf Wilnerzon Thörn in my local congregation, Sörbykyrkan, in Örebro. They have all helped me to make this a better book. A big thank you also goes to Bengt Rasmusson at Spricka förlag who heard me speak at a conference in Linköping about Jonathan and Jonah in literature, encouraged me to write a book about them and my other biblical friends, and then faithfully and patiently supported me throughout the writing process. For the English version, I am indebted to Amy Bender and Dorothy Plummer, who proofread my translation, and to Carey Newman at Fortress Press who enthusiastically welcomed my project. Thank you so much!

CHAPTER ONE

# Noah

## *Obedient God Fearer or Callous Commissary?*

NOAH IS ONE of the most enigmatic figures in the Bible. He is described in Hebrews 11:7 as a hero of faith: "By faith Noah, warned by God about events as yet unseen, respected the warning and built an ark to save his household; by this he condemned the world and became an heir to the righteousness that is in accordance with faith." Even so, I do not always find it easy to connect with this image of Noah when I read about him in Genesis 6–9. One of the most complicated aspects of Christian interpretation of the Old Testament is whether we should let the Old Testament speak for itself or whether we should adapt the Old Testament image to the interpretation advocated by the New Testament. In other words, how much should we let Hebrews 11:7 influence us when we read Genesis 6–9? Should we follow the lead of Hebrews 11 and relate to the Old Testament Noah as a hero of faith? In this chapter, we shall take a closer look at Noah, focusing on how he is portrayed in the Old Testament. At the same time, we shall ask whether this Noah can be understood as "moved with godly fear" (as the American Standard Version has it) and what it means that he "built an ark to save his household." Last but not least, what exactly does it mean that he "condemned the world"? In the end, it may not be that difficult to reconcile the Old and New Testament images of Noah.

From a literary perspective, the flood story in Genesis 6–9 is not one of the better-written stories in the Bible. It consists almost entirely of long speeches, and there is much repetition. In addition, the characters are never described, and they do not show any emotions. I often feel like I do not really get to know the people in the story, and I do not get a sense of who Noah really is. It is as if he lacks personality. All he does is build an ark in accordance with God's command.

At the same time, the story affects me because of what is described. Who can remain unmoved when reading about the end of the world? Furthermore, the scarcity of details encourages the reader to want to know more about Noah and the people around him. The sparse descriptions almost force us to speculate about what is not in the text. For example, we may begin to wonder exactly what kinds of sins the people around Noah have committed. What sorts of atrocities have Noah's contemporaries been involved in that make them deserve to be drowned in the abyss? Noah's reaction to God's command to build the ark leads to other questions. What makes him blindly obey God, when other people in similar situations, such as Abraham and Moses, seek to convince God to change his plans and show mercy instead of anger? Personally, I cannot help but think about what happens to the people and animals who are not in the ark when the flood comes. Maybe it is my morbid imagination, but I keep imagining the drowning people and animals clinging to trees and other floating objects in vain attempts to survive. Finally, what do Noah and his family members feel when they realize that they are the only survivors? Do they feel guilty about being alive or relieved to have survived? Has their faith been strengthened by being preserved, or are they unable to maintain faith in a good God in the face of the many dead?

## Background

Before we plunge into the biblical story world, it is useful to know a little about the literary background of the flood narrative. As mentioned in the introduction, the focus of this book is on the stories of the Bible. Having said that, I have nothing against the existence of a historical flood. In my view, it is quite possible that the biblical flood narrative preserves the memory of a historical event. What I am interested in here, though, is not the history behind the Bible but the history in the Bible. One issue does not contradict the other, but we should keep them separate. My focus is on the Bible's portrayal of Noah and his actions, and I maintain that it is the words of the Bible that should form the basis of any theological discussion.

The biblical story of Noah is part of a larger literary treasure trove of similar stories that flourished in Mesopotamia (present-day northern Syria, Iraq, and Kuwait) and the Levant (present-day southern Syria, Lebanon, Jordan, Israel, and Palestine). The best-known Mesopotamian versions of the flood stories are found in the so-called *Epic of Gilgamesh* and *Atra-Hasis*. In these texts, Noah's counterpart is called Utnapishtim. Noah and Utnapishtim fulfil the same role: They build an ark and survive on board it with their family.

At the same time, the Mesopotamian and biblical texts differ in several important respects. According to the former, there are several gods: one who warns Noah and one who sends the flood. In the *Epic of Gilgamesh*, Utnapishtim is warned by the god Ea. Ea has learnt that the god Enlil has decided to send a powerful flood that will drown the world. To survive the disaster, Ea instructs Utnapishtim to build a boat so that a limited number of people and animals can survive. Everything then goes according to plan: Utnapishtim follows Ea's directive, Enlil sends the flood that lasts six days and seven nights, after which the ark is stranded on Mount Ararat. After another seven days, Utnapishtim releases a sequence of birds to explore whether water still covers the earth. He first sends a dove, which returns to the boat, and then a swallow, which also returns. Finally, Utnapishtim sends a raven, and when it does not return, it is seen as a sign that the flood is receding and that the earth is once again habitable. Utnapishtim then makes a sacrifice to the gods, who enjoy the fragrance of the offering. The story ends with Utnapishtim becoming immortal. *Atra-Hasis* contains a similar story.

The biblical flood story, preserved in Genesis, has much in common with the Mesopotamian stories in the *Epic of Gilgamesh* and *Atra-Hasis*. At the same time, we should not see this as a straightforward adoption of the story by the Bible's authors. Rather, the biblical story is an independent work that shares many literary motifs but also reflects Israel's faith and distinctiveness. Instead of multiple gods being involved, the Bible's version makes it clear that it is the God of Israel who is responsible both for sending the flood and for presenting Noah with the possibility of surviving it. In many ways, the biblical version is a polemic against the Mesopotamian texts in that it explains the flood in a way that is in line with the Bible's overall theology of justice, sin, and grace. The stories also differ in their respective explanations of why the flood occurred. According to the *Atra-Hasis*, the flood is an attempt at population control: Overpopulation is a problem which the gods "solve" by sending a flood that effectively reduces the number of people. In the *Epic of Gilgamesh*, Enlil's decision to send the flood seems completely unjustified and exemplifies the precarious situation of humanity in the hands of the gods. These explanations for the flood stand in stark contrast to the one given in the Bible, where God's decision to drown the earth is a just punishment for sin and violence.

The question, however, is whether the Bible's theological explanation is satisfactory. Can we agree that the sins of humanity justify God's decision to destroy his creation? We will ponder these questions together with a number of novelists. Without further ado, let us now enter the world of literature.

## Narratives

I am not alone in my thoughts and questions about the Bible's flood narrative. Rather, most biblical scholars wrestle with the theological challenges posed by God's decision to drown his creation, and every solid biblical commentary discusses them. At the same time, the discussions can easily become so abstract that they do not affect us to the degree that they rightly should. To really experience the flood story in a concrete and tangible way, we shall therefore use four novels that retell the biblical text. Along with these literary creations, we shall enter the narrative world of the Bible and reflect on the motives, feelings, and thoughts of the different characters. These books also enable us to experience the flood story as something that could happen to us, here and now, which in turn helps us to understand the scale of the disaster.

**Marianne Fredriksson** (1927–2007) was a Swedish novelist. Many of her books, including the trilogy *Paradisets barn* (Children of paradise), are based on stories from the Bible. Her novel *Syndafloden* (The deluge) is aimed at adult readers but is also accessible to young adults. It follows the structure of the biblical text and centers on Noah and his family, but it also incorporates material from the Mesopotamian flood stories mentioned above, which are preserved in *the Epic of Gilgamesh* and *Atra-Hasis*.

*Syndafloden* (Wahlström & Widstrand, 1993).

**Madeleine L'Engle** (1918–2007) was an American author best known for her books for children and young adults. Her fantasy novel *Many Waters* (part of the same universe as L'Engle's best-known book *A Wrinkle in Time*), is written for young adults from an explicitly Christian perspective. L'Engle's two main characters, twin brothers Dennys and Sandy, have traveled back in time and arrived just before the flood story begins.

*Many Waters* (Bantam Doubleday Dell, 1986).

**Geraldine McCaughrean** (b. 1951) is a British author of mainly young adult fiction. Her children's book *Not the End of the World* follows the structure of the biblical story but begins when Noah and his family have just entered the ark and closed the door.

*Not the End of the World* (Oxford University Press, 2004).

**Anne Provoost** (b. 1964) is a Flemish-speaking Belgian author. Her novel *In the Shadow of the Ark* is intended for young adults but is also accessible to older readers. It is mainly set in the time before the flood, but its final chapters deal with the time on board the ark.

*In the Shadow of the Ark*, trans. John Nieuwenhuizen (Arthur A. Levine, 2004). Originally published as *De arkvaarders* (Querido, 2001).

## Noah's Ethical Dilemma

Noah is called righteous in Genesis 6:9: "These are the descendants of Noah. Noah was a righteous man, blameless in his generation." The temporal aspect is important: When and among whom was Noah righteous? The NRSV brings out the emphasis in the original Hebrew text that Noah was righteous "in his generation." This wording hints at the possibility that Noah, in a different time and compared to other people, would not have been counted as righteous. This small but important nuance offers us an opportunity to reevaluate Noah and thus a way out when wrestling with the Bible's portrait of him. Many Jewish exegetes, who often read the Bible in its original language, argue that Noah's righteousness is not a fact but a relative description: "Among his contemporaries he was righteous" but, by implication, if he had been contemporary with, say, Moses, he would be counted among the sinners.

After introducing Noah, Genesis 6:11 describes how God sees the earth becoming more and more corrupt and filled with violence: "Now the earth was corrupt in God's sight, and the earth was filled with violence." The focus is not only on humans. The whole earth is full of violence and therefore all creation, including animals, should be punished. This reading raises questions about God's justice, as only humans have knowledge of good and evil (Gen 3:5–6). Why does God choose to punish animals, who cannot control their behavior, along with sinful humanity?

The Bible further tells us that God instructs Noah to build an ark and gives him detailed plans regarding its appearance (Gen 6:13–21). At the same time, there is no information on how Noah should practically go about the task. Can eight people—assuming the whole family helps—actually build a vessel of this size and with the capacity to house wild and domestic animals together? Does Noah even know how to do carpentry?

Noah's only response is tacit consent: "Noah did this; he did all that God commanded him" (Gen 6:22). This verse, and the similar one in Genesis 7:5, creates unease. What kind of *mensch* (a person of integrity, morality, and dignity) does not protest? How can Noah just stand there and do nothing while God describes his planned act of mass destruction? Noah's behavior stands in stark contrast with other characters in the Bible who are willing to dialogue with God and often succeed in thwarting God's destructive plans. The most famous examples are Abraham, who intercedes on behalf of the (potentially existing) righteous people of Sodom (Gen 18), and Moses, who prays for sinful Israel (Exod 32:9–14). In all three cases (Noah, Abraham, and Moses), God confides in a human being and, in a sense, invites them to oppose him. It is not going too far to say that, after all, God wants to be contradicted. The later written prophets act in a similar way. God shares his plans with his prophets, and the prophets intercede between God and Israel. The classic example is found in Ezekiel 22:30, where God looks for an intercessor but unfortunately finds none: "And I sought for anyone among them who would repair the wall and stand in the breach before me on behalf of the land, so that I would not destroy it; but I found no one."

Moses manages to do just that in Exodus 32:9–14, with the result that God decides not to destroy Israel:

> The Lord said to Moses, "I have seen this people, how stiff-necked they are. Now let me alone, so that my wrath may burn hot against them and I may consume them; and of you I will make a great nation."
>
> But Moses implored the Lord his God, and said, "O Lord, why does your wrath burn hot against your people, whom you brought out of the land of Egypt with great power and with a mighty hand? Why should the Egyptians say, 'It was with evil intent that he brought them out to kill them in the mountains, and to consume them from the face of the earth'? Turn from your fierce wrath; change your mind and do not bring disaster on your people. Remember Abraham, Isaac, and Israel, your servants, how you swore to them by your own self, saying

> to them, 'I will multiply your descendants like the stars of heaven, and all this land that I have promised I will give to your descendants, and they shall inherit it forever.'" And the Lord changed his mind about the disaster that he planned to bring on his people.

Noah, however, does nothing. When we compare Noah's inertia with the actions of Abraham and especially Moses, Noah is weighed and found wanting. Why does Noah not take responsibility for his fellow human beings? Does God really mean for Noah to keep the news of the coming destruction to himself, or is it rather God's hope that Noah will pray for the people around him and consequently try to persuade God to refrain from carrying out his decision and instead preserve his creation? Alternatively, is God's purpose that Noah will go out and preach repentance so that the people around him can return to God and, as a result, reverse God's deliberate destruction (cf. Jer 18:7–10)? The biblical Noah, however, chooses neither of these paths. Instead, he just stands there and obeys orders.

In this respect, Noah becomes the model of the good but passive man who does not protest. To quote the philosopher John Stuart Mill's inaugural speech at the University of St Andrews, Scotland (1867): "Let not any one pacify his conscience by the delusion that he can do no harm if he takes no part, and forms no opinion. Bad men need nothing more to compass their ends, than that good men should look on and do nothing. He is not a good man who, without a protest, allows wrong to be committed in his name, and with the means which he helps to supply, because he will not trouble himself to use his mind on the subject."[1] Obedience, in this case, may thus seem to have less to do with faith and more with unbelief. What kind of relationship does Noah have with God if he does not dare to protest? This question is very much for us readers too: What does it say about our image of God when we elevate Noah's obedience to something good? A responsible reading of the Bible takes the bull by the horns and questions Noah's (and God's) behavior.

This brings me back to Hebrews 11:7, which describes Noah as being "filled with holy fear" (my translation) when he builds the ark. What does that really mean? Fear of God (*yir'at adonai*) is, as we know, "the beginning of knowledge" (Prov 1:7; 9:10) and thus something positive. The equivalent expression in the New Testament is often "fear of God" (φόβος θεοῦ, as in 2 Cor 7:1). The expression used here in Hebrews, however, is a rarer one that is found only here as a verb in the New Testament (εὐλαβέομαι; it is attested as a noun in Heb 5:7; 12:28; and as an adjective in Luke 2:25; Acts 2:5; 8:2; 22:12). In the New Testament it usually means to show respect and reverence. The verb form is also used in the Greek translation of the Old Testament (the Septuagint), where it means not only "to honor" (Jer 5:22; Nah 1:7; Prov 2:8) but also "to fear" someone (Deut 2:4; 1 Sam 18:29; Job 13:25; Dan 4:5).

So, I wonder if there is not something interesting hidden in the text of Hebrews as well. Of course, we should always remember that God is a holy God, and that he is therefore dangerous. C. S. Lewis says it best in *The Lion, the Witch and the Wardrobe* when Mr. Beaver replies to Lucy that of course Aslan is dangerous—but he is good (69): "'Safe?' said Mr. Beaver; 'Don't you hear what Mrs. Beaver tells you? Who said anything about safe? 'Course he isn't safe. But he's good. He's the King, I tell you.'" At the same time, I am tempted to think that Noah may be a little too reverent or perhaps even a little too afraid of God. Abraham and Moses are surely also terrified when they stand before God and argue for the people's survival, but they still dare to come to God with their doubts. So, Hebrews puts its finger on something important when it describes Noah acting in holy fear. It makes us think about the balancing act of relating to God as both holy and immanent.

Many later biblical interpreters, both Jewish and Christian, have noticed and pondered Noah's actions or rather lack of action. What should he have done when he heard God's message? Although there is no strict boundary between Jewish and Christian interpretations, Jewish interpreters tend to argue that Noah prays for his neighbors while Christian interpreters more often insist that Noah preaches repentance. I have regularly seen this reinterpretation in Sunday schools throughout my country. The final lines of Lydia Lithell's well-known Swedish children's song "If I Were a Little Mouse" (You may laugh, but I do not, because I know that in the end, / Only those who believe in the Lord and live in the ark will be saved), reflects an innate conviction that the people around Noah know that the flood is coming and that they have a choice to believe, or not to believe, in God. Even the little mouse has a choice, as the first stanza of the song makes clear: "If I were a little mouse, I would live in Noah's house." It is implied that if the mouse so desires, it has a given place on the ark. What the song does not make clear, however, is that this mouse will then take the place of another mouse, as only two little mice are offered a chance at life.

## To Warn or Not to Warn

Many contemporary retellings of Genesis 6–9 question and problematize Noah's behavior. They require us to engage with the situation and challenge us to take a stand. Would we choose to join Noah and help him build the ark, or would we join the people around him? Would we try to do what Noah explicitly does not, that is, save more people and animals than our immediate family? These retellings ponder whether Noah will try to smuggle more people onto the ark to save their lives, whether he will preach repentance to show God that people deserve a second chance, whether he will argue with God and try to change his mind, or whether he will, as in the Bible, calmly and unassumingly obey in silence.

Madeleine L'Engle's book, *Many Waters*, is careful to point out that Noah and his family warn their neighbors of the coming flood disaster. Noah himself clearly states that the people have a right to be warned: "They have a right to be warned. To prepare. And who knows—if they repent, then perhaps El will not send the flood" (286). The people in L'Engle's book respond by laughing at Noah's warning. They ridicule him and his family, throwing both stones and scraps of food at them (220–222), behavior that in turn absolves Noah of responsibility. He has done his human duty and warned them; now it is up to them to decide how to react. Noah's behavior also relieves God of some of the responsibility. God has warned the people through Noah and can now send the flood with a (relatively) clear conscience.

L'Engle's description is probably inspired by 2 Peter 2:5, where Noah is portrayed as a preacher of righteousness: "And if he did not spare the ancient world, even though he saved Noah, a herald of righteousness, with seven others, when he brought a flood on a world of the ungodly" and 1 Peter 3:20, which describes the people's refusal to listen: "Who in former times did not obey, when God waited patiently in the days of Noah, during the building of the ark, in which a few, that is, eight people, were saved through water."

Marianne Fredriksson chooses a different approach to Noah's passivity in the Old Testament. In the biblical story, Noah is given detailed instructions on how the finished ark should look, but we as readers never get to see how he actually carries out the work in practice. I would not even be able to build an ark out of Lego pieces if the only instruction I had access to was God's instruction in Genesis 6:14–16. Fredriksson fills the gap in the biblical text by making Noah a shipbuilder with his own shipyard. This shipyard is also located in an independent area with diplomatic immunity. Noah thus has the professional competence required as well as the necessary seclusion to build the ark without too much external interference. At the same time, Fredriksson's Noah abdicates responsibility for selecting the survivors. In a conversation with his wife, Naema, Noah exclaims that he refuses to make these choices:

> Sensing Noah's anger, Naema put her hand over his:
> "What are you going to say?"
> "That if God has decided to drown the people, He himself can choose those to be saved. I refuse to make that choice." (122; my translation)

Rather, the selection is made naturally. Some people leave the shipyard when they notice that Noah has lost interest in building ordinary boats. Others hear about Noah's building project and voluntarily seek him out. Noah himself welcomes all who want to join and sees no conflict between his welcoming attitude and God's commands.

L'Engle's and Fredriksson's respective Noahs depict a man with whom we readers can easily identify and even look up to. He is a fellow human being who is trying to do the right thing in a very difficult situation, and he chooses to interpret God's commands in a generous way that mitigates the cruelty of the situation. At the same time, these two portraits of Noah are studies in what we might call "benevolent exegesis." The authors' additions transform Noah into a recognizable and compassionate *mensch*.

In sharp contrast to L'Engle and Fredriksson, Anne Provoost and Geraldine McCaughrean choose instead to adhere strictly to the Bible's portrait of Noah and, moreover, to draw out its inexorable consequences. Their respective Noahs do exactly what the Bible says, resulting in an extremely unlikable character. Provoost's Noah (or "the Builder" as he is called in *In the Shadow of the Ark*) withholds knowledge of the coming flood from those around him. He understands God's words in Genesis 6:18 as a narrow decree that the ark can only hold eight people: "But I will establish my covenant with you; and you shall come into the ark, you, your sons, your wife, and your sons' wives with you." Provoost has Re Jana, the book's narrator, and her father act as Noah's opposites. They have been driven from their home by the rising waters of the neighboring rivers. Re Jana's father, an experienced shipbuilder, joins Noah's shipyard and becomes one of his most important employees. In one of several discussions with Noah, Re Jana's father insists that Noah has a moral obligation to his fellow man. Noah should either preach repentance or try to mediate between God and humanity to prevent the coming flood: "If all those people must be punished, is it not only right that they be warned?" Noah disagrees and replies that "The calamity itself is the warning" (217). To really hammer home the message, Provoost later has the people repent and make amends—all without Noah's help. Instead, it is Re Jana's father who takes the initiative:

> And my father set the example in showing contrition. He was amongst the first to don sackcloth and get rid of his last belongings. [. . .] Some of the people in the shipyard listened to his advice and followed his example. [. . .] The Builder witnessed the display of penance and said, "You are sacrificing, you are doing what you have always done for your old gods. If you were really contrite, you would not only cut off your hair, but also change your hearts. But you only cut off your hair." (245–246)

Rather than welcoming the initiative, Provoost's Noah chooses to devalue the people's penance. It simply does not fit with his perception of reality. Provoost herself does not comment on the honesty of Re Jana's father's intentions; perhaps it is just an attempt to survive.

Provoost's Noah further assumes that in order to keep God's decree, the true purpose of the ark must be kept secret. Otherwise, if the people around learned of the coming flood, they would all want a place on the ark, which in turn would lead to unprecedented chaos in defiance of God's will. Noah and his sons therefore deceive everyone around them, including their own relatives who help them guard the ark. They also keep quiet about the true nature of the building project before their hired construction workers. Soon, however, the people begin to grasp that disaster is imminent, and they assume—quite naturally, given that most of them are actively involved in the construction of the ark—that they will have their rightful places on board (135). The warriors, who guard the ark in order to prevent "unauthorized persons" from entering it, try to explain that they are not chosen, but the people refuse to believe them (229–230). The situation culminates just before the ark is closed when the warriors themselves realize that they too have been deceived and will be excluded:

> Under the gangway lay warriors. Many had been killed by the fall. Of those who had stood below, some died because the storm hurled rocks against their heads or drove sharp pieces of wood through their bodies. They were the lucky ones: They perished quickly and from a cause they could, in their final moments, comprehend. Those who were still alive now were gripped by despair. The notable, the distinguished, the warriors, the tradesmen, they all rushed the ark. They hit its sides with their fists, they pressed against the bow like dogs. And the children, all those boys and girls who used to hang around the ship hoping to be given a pitch doll, they screeched like animals. (268)

All this leads most readers to develop no sympathy for Noah and his family and instead begin to hope for a different ending to that found in Genesis.

The situation is again different in McCaughrean's novel *Not the End of the World*, yet it shares the negative portrayal of Noah and his family with Provoost's book. Although the novel begins when Noah and his family enter the ark, there are flashbacks to earlier times. There are several hints to the secrecy surrounding the construction project. McCaughrean's narrator, Noah's non-biblical daughter, Timna, describes how the people around their family were systematically kept in the dark about the real purpose of the ark:

> Every day during the building they came and stood about asking, "What is it for?" "What are you doing?" "Are you all mad?" [. . .] Then Japheth would start to explain: "It's father . . . He's found out that . . ." But the other brothers would cough, or shout loudly for the mallet bag, or drop something down from the decking and tell Japheth to bring it back up to them. "Remember," Shem would mutter. "We keep ourselves to ourselves and our mouths shut." (2–3)

McCaughrean's story lacks room for both grace and repentance. Noah follows God's command blindly and literally. The ark only holds eight people, so therefore everyone else must be denied a place. To firmly reinforce this harsh message, McCaughrean describes in detail the slow death of humanity.

When the flood comes, the people refuse to give up: "It should have been over in a flash. If it had to happen, it should have been quickly over. [. . .] But people are so resilient. They put up such a struggle" (15). They cling to logs and other floating objects to stay alive: "The water boiled with people. They were swimming, or clutching on to logs, doors, cartwheels. Animals, too, were swimming among them—dogs and horses, cattle, goats. The sky was full of displaced birds, circling, circling, with nowhere to land" (7–8). When they discover the ark, the drowning people rejoice and expect to be rescued on board. Blinded by their literal understanding of God's command, however, Shem and Ham dash the poor people's hopes when they push them away as they cling to the sides of the ark.

> Hands were clinging to the hull, the hands of swimmers who had somehow managed to find a grip on the rough timber. Ham was in a frenzy, rolling like a drunkard from end to end of the deck yelling, "Get off! Get off! Leave go! It's too late, I told you! It's your own faults!" Fearless, implacable as ever, Shem swung out from the ship's rail by one hand, wielding his stave, dislodging people from the hull in the same way you might swat horseflies off the flanks of your horse. [. . .] Japheth—the youngest—had crammed himself between the aviaries, fingers in his ears, his eye sockets full of rain; curled up, crumpled up. Great silver bubbles swelled from his nose and mouth as he wept, so that he looked to be several fathoms down and drowning. (8–9)

In other words, Noah's eldest sons commit premeditated murder to preserve Noah's (and God's) vision of a new society cleansed of evil, and Noah's youngest son is so traumatized he can barely function. The irony is palpable. McCaughrean's Timna goes on to describe how, a few days later, the bodies are floating in the water: "Today I went out on deck—to get away from the dreams. And there they all were: the people I had dreamt about, floating in the water. Face-down, face-up. The eddies rolled them over and over like restless sleepers who couldn't get comfortable on the lumpy water. A camel must have got itself tangled up in vegetation and drowned. Suddenly its carcass broke free and breached like a whale right alongside the ship, all bloated. Its legs wheeled over ever so slowly, rigid . . ." (16).

The above four novels are all based on Genesis 6–9. They read the biblical narrative carefully but at the same time challenge it by turning its message on its head. Fredriksson and L'Engle transform Noah into a recognizable and compassionate human being in order to uphold the statement of Genesis 6:9 while taking into account the complementary picture of Noah in 1–2 Peter. In contrast, Provoost and McCaughrean take the reference to Noah's obedience in Genesis 6:22 and 7:5 to its bitter end. Are some of these narratives more biblically faithful than the others? This depends entirely on how we define the term *biblically faithful* and to which canon we relate. If the definition is a retelling that reflects the content of the specific biblical text as closely as possible, then the latter two retellings fall into that category. There is no evidence in Genesis that Noah either prays for his neighbors or preaches repentance. He fulfils God's command verbatim and seemingly without emotion. If the definition of biblical fidelity is a rewriting of the biblical texts in line with the Christian canon's pervasive message of God's love, mercy, and compassion, then surely a certain amount of rewriting is required for Noah to fit that mold. Writer and reader must work together to transform the passive Noah, who does not lift a finger to help his fellow human being, into a compassionate man who acts to save those around him. To use a New Testament image, Noah must be transformed from being a man who thinks it is perfectly acceptable to stone the sinner to a man who recognizes his own sin, refuses to cast the first stone, and gives the sinner a second chance (John 8:7).

## To Save or Not to Save More People

The biblical text tells us that only eight people survive the flood; only Noah and his immediate family are standing saved on Mount Ararat when the water begins to recede. Most novelists choose to challenge this picture by asking a series of questions. First, can humanity really continue with so few individuals?

Fredriksson's account is distinguished here by its focus on the survival of human civilization. She chooses to follow the *Epic of Gilgamesh* rather than the biblical story in that she allows more people than Noah's immediate family on board the ark. In addition to his wife, sons, and daughters-in-law, Noah includes a blacksmith, potter, weaver, farmer, herb gatherer, ropemaker, and carpenter. He also rescues the art of writing and the cultural treasures of poetry, music, and art. In Fredriksson's hands, the flood story is less about the survival of the animal kingdom and more about preserving human knowledge.

All her protagonists are therefore not just individuals but also types. The idea is that the people who survive the disaster are the bearers of all the characteristics of humanity. The reader encounters a diverse and highly varied cast of characters, including extroverted and introverted people, with different sexual orientations, interests, talents, and knowledge. Some are artistic, others practical, some musical, others literate. The whole of humanity is to be preserved in all its richness and diversity. In other words, Fredriksson turns the Bible's vision of a new beginning into an attempt to preserve what is good about what already exists.

Other authors also toy with the idea that more people survive the flood than the Bible tells us. To push the boundaries of the biblical story and challenge us as readers, L'Engle chooses to give Noah a daughter, Yalith. Her presence creates both tension and conflict and invites a deeper engagement with the theological message and inherent ethical issues of the flood story. Much is centered on Dennys's and Sandy's love and concern for Yalith. The two brothers, who have traveled back from our own time to the time before the flood, grew up in a Christian home and are familiar with the biblical story. They therefore know that no character named Yalith will be among the survivors on board the ark. Does this mean that El (God) will let Yalith die, or will he save her in another way?

> Anoher silence. Then Sandy asked, "Do you think we could take Yalith with us?"
>
> Dennys did not answer for a while. Then: "No, I don't think so. We're not supposed to change history."
>
> "But she'll drown."
>
> "I know. I love her too." [. . .]
>
> "A lot of people are going to drown. Would you mind changing history if it would save Yalith?" [. . .]
>
> "I understand that floods and other disasters happen. But if this flood is really being sent by El . . ."
>
> Sandy said, "If it's being sent by El, then I don't like El, not if Yalith is going to drown." (270–272)

L'Engle ultimately chooses to save Yalith by allowing her, like Enoch, to be taken from the earth by God (Gen 5:24). Dennys and Sandy watch as the seraph Aariel, on behalf of El, takes Yalith into his arms: "Ariel wrapped her in his creamy wings, glittering with gold at their tips. Then he held her only with his arms, lifted and spread the wings, beat with them softly, and then rose into the air, up, up. They watched until all they saw was a speck of light in the sky, as though from a new star" (297).

McCaughrean is the one who most clearly invites her readers to consider whether more than Noah's immediate family survives the disaster. This strategy, in turn, makes us reevaluate Noah's narrow and noninclusive values. First, like L'Engle, McCaughrean chooses to give Noah a daughter, Timna. Timna serves as the author's critical voice, primarily questioning the patriarchal values of the flood narrative. McCaughrean then introduces two more people. Timna, after several days aboard the ark, finds a tree branch wedged against the sternpost. A boy, Kittim, clings to it with one arm while holding an infant with the other. Timna, Japheth, and Japheth's wife, Zilla, defy Noah's prohibition and hide the refugees inside among the turtles. After some more time, Noah and his family see another ship approaching. On board is a couple who reach out to Noah, offer them food, and express their willingness to share bread with them. Yet Noah and his sons respond only with arrows. The stranger conveys his grief and disappointment: "'In the day of disaster, people should be close,' he said, with an air of saddened disappointment. 'We see you—our heart lifts! Alone we are too few. God made us to live as the rooks not as the crows, not like the crows.' He gave a dejected shrug, called to his daughter to keep low, helped his wife down into the well of the boat, and they began adjusting the empty sails" (90). At the end of her retelling, McCaughrean defies Noah's decision to save only eight people one last time when she allows Timna, along with the stowaway Kittim, to set off on a dark night on a raft toward an uncertain future.

Provoost, too, challenges us by saving more people on board the ark. Rather than adding a daughter, like L'Engle and McCaughrean, Provoost chooses to give Ham two wives. Provoost's narrator, Re Jana, falls in love with Ham and later becomes the mother of his child, while Ham's wife is barren. Re Jana survives, thanks to Ham, who hides her on board. Meanwhile, her father is left to die along with the rest of humanity, despite the fact that it is his shipbuilding skills that made the construction of the ark possible. Re Jana concludes that survival is random; a place on the ark depends on personal relationships rather than a person's inherent goodness and moral merit.

## The Flood Story and the New Testament

Before concluding the discussion of Noah's responsibility, let us return for a moment to Hebrews 11:7. According to this verse, Noah "built an ark to save his household," a description that is entirely consistent with the Old Testament picture of Noah: Noah chooses to save his own family while the rest of humanity perishes. Again, I am struck by how the picture of Noah in Hebrews fits with that in Genesis 6–9—but also how this description is not as positive as I first assumed. Another biblical passage grabs my attention, namely Jesus's words in the Sermon on the Mount: "For if you love those who love you, what reward do you have? Do not even the tax-collectors do the same? And if you greet only your brothers and sisters, what more are you doing than others? Do not even the Gentiles do the same?" When I read Genesis 6–9 together with Hebrews 11:7 and Matthew 5:46–47, Noah is just doing what any other human being would do, no more and no less. His decision to "save his household," well, that is what any tax collector or pagan would do, but God's demand for humanity seems to be higher.

Many may wish that the story of Noah ended in Genesis 9:19, when everyone comes out of the ark, and God makes a covenant with all living things. Unfortunately, it continues instead, leaving Noah with one of the most embarrassing endings in the Bible. Noah plants a vineyard, gets drunk, and ends up naked in his tent for his male relatives to see. Any Swede who knows their Carl Michael Bellman knows this, although I sincerely hope that most Swedish children who plod through the song "Old Noah" on the recorder do not have any idea of what the song is really about. I will not discuss either Bellman or Genesis 9:20–26 in detail here, but I cannot help but wonder about the reasons for Noah's inappropriate behavior. The biblical text says nothing about why Noah chooses to act as he does, but I wonder in the back of my mind if it might not be that he is trying to drown his guilty conscience in wine (see Provoost, 362). Perhaps Noah is drowning his guilt at having survived when so many others died? Perhaps he seeks oblivion in drunkenness when the guilt of not having saved more people becomes overwhelming? This interpretation, which comes out clearly in Darren Aronofsky's 2014 film *Noah*, is, at least in my view, a psychologically possible interpretation.

## God's Ethical Dilemma

Genesis 6:5 describes how "The Lord saw that the wickedness of humankind was great in the earth, and that every inclination of the thoughts of their hearts was only evil continually." This situation, in turn, causes God grief and lays the foundation for his decision to destroy the earth: "And the Lord was sorry that he had made humankind on the earth, and it grieved him to his heart" (Gen 6:6). God's statement and subsequent decisions are difficult to understand for several reasons. First, what does it mean that God "was sorry" for having done something? The Hebrew word here, *niham* (נחם), is used in situations when God changes one of his previously made decisions. Most often, this verb indicates God's grace. In other words, God has previously planned to punish Israel but instead, because of his mercy, decides to change his plans (cf. Amos 7:3, 6). Here, however (and in 1 Sam 15:11, in the case of Saul's kingship), the situation is reversed: God mourns that what he had in mind did not quite turn out as he intended.

Together, the biblical passages mentioned above paint a picture of God that I find deeply attractive. God not only has a single, inescapable plan for our lives but adapts it to our actions.

> At one moment I may declare concerning a nation or a kingdom, that I will pluck up and break down and destroy it, but if that nation, concerning which I have spoken, turns from its evil, I will change my mind (*niham*) about the disaster that I intended to bring on it. And at another moment I may declare concerning a nation or a kingdom that I will build and plant it, but if it does evil in my sight, not listening to my voice, then I will change my mind (*niham*) about the good that I had intended to do to it. (Jer 18:7–10)

I remember how relieved I was as a teenager when I discovered this. I had become so entangled in the issue of predestination. A well-meaning youth leader had said that God had a spouse planned for us all. Rather than interpreting this statement as reassuring, however, I was completely taken aback as I began to wonder what would happen if my intended spouse did not listen to God. Would I have to live unmarried for the rest of my life because the other person (that is, the one God had chosen for me) messed up, did not listen to God, and went and married someone else? It all felt deeply unfair. It took me quite a while and a lot of robust counseling from other, more insightful, youth leaders, before I understood how deeply wrong my view of God was. Yes, he has a plan for our lives, but it is adapted and reshaped as we go along based on our decisions, both right and wrong.

Back to Noah, Genesis 6 does not paint a picture of an omniscient deity (unlike, for example, 1 Chron 28:9 and Jer 1:5). Rather, the focus is on a God who is displeased with humanity. According to the flood story, God is disappointed with the wickedness of humans. He had hoped that they would act differently. At the same time, the question is up in the air whether God's decision may be changed. God's declaration that he will destroy the earth may be seen as an invitation to prayer. Elsewhere in the Bible, for example in Amos 7:1–6, God tells Amos that he will destroy Israel. Amos immediately responds with intercession, which in turn leads to God changing his mind (again *niham*). Does God expect Noah to react in the same way as Amos does later? Does God want an interlocutor who can give him a reason to change his mind one more time and show mercy instead of causing destruction? Is Noah perhaps meant to respond with robust dialogue rather than with "holy fear"?

> This is what the Lord God showed me: he was forming locusts at the time the latter growth began to sprout (it was the latter growth after the king's mowings). When they had finished eating the grass of the land, I said, "O Lord God, forgive, I beg you! How can Jacob stand? He is so small!" The Lord relented (*niham*) concerning this; "It shall not be," said the Lord. This is what the Lord God showed me: the Lord God was calling for a shower of fire, and it devoured the great deep and was eating up the land. Then I said, "O Lord God, cease, I beg you! How can Jacob stand? He is so small!" The Lord relented (*niham*) concerning this; "This also shall not be," said the Lord God. (Amos 7:1–6)

Just as God shows Amos what is to come, God gives Noah a revelation "about events as yet unseen," as Hebrews 11:7 emphasizes. Here, however, the Old Testament and the New Testament differ in their assessment. While Hebrews praises Noah for taking God's word seriously, believing in the reality God shows him and building the ark, Genesis would probably have preferred Noah to go one step further. Taking God's word seriously and acting in faith means not only obeying God's word but also entering into a dialogue with God about it.

## An Insufficiently Evil World and Insufficiently Good Survivors

At the same time, God's decision to destroy his creation poses an ethical dilemma, regardless of God's possible expectation that Noah would protest. It is possible, at least in theory, to escape the difficulty by describing the people around Noah as so utterly rotten that God sees no other way out than total destruction. Interestingly, however, none of our four chosen authors goes down that route. Instead, they decide to address the eternal question of whether innocent suffering is not only permitted but also instigated by God. They highlight the ethical question posed by the flood story rather than trying to resolve it. Moreover, all four authors agree that the disaster is ultimately a failure: The flood worsens rather than improves humanity.

Fredriksson's retelling is closest to the biblical text in its description of a world where people commit all kinds of evil. Evil is symbolized by, on the one hand, the totalitarian state North, which has murdered its clergy and abolished its religious cult, and on the other hand, the thriving trading city South, whose prosperity is based on slave labor. At the same time, Fredriksson emphasizes that both states contain decent and honest people. Noah's sons' wives represent both states. Ham's wife, Nin Dada, is the daughter of a rich scribe from the South, while Shem and Japheth's wives, Kreli and Milcah, come from the North. The shipbuilder Haran's thirteen-year-old son puts their feelings into words: "'I can't bear to see all the slaves. They have never really lived, and now they will die when the flood comes. It's so unfair . . . I think God should give the ship . . . and salvation to them.' No one had a word of comfort or explanation" (286; my translation). Later, while in the ark, Noah watches the survivors struggle with their faith and their image of God: How could God, whose goodness they had all trusted until now, make such a drastic decision? At the same time, they also struggle with their human relationships: The people, with their very different personalities, do not have an easy time as they try to get along during these long, agonizing days trapped on the ark. They worry about the future and wonder how they will be able to live in the new world with their survivor's guilt and rootlessness. They lack context and a past in God's new creation after the destruction. After the flood, when both kingdoms have perished, Fredriksson's Noah walks heavily up the hillside to "meet his God and answer without clearing his name or explaining himself" (341). Noah begins his long speech to God by insisting that the flood has failed:

> "You have kept your promise. We have been brought alive to a new land. I did not keep my end of the bargain, however. I never sought the pure in heart that You intended to save. The people who are with me on the ark are as people are, weak and false. [. . .] Also on board is the jealousy that pits brother against brother. I don't know if my sons have committed adultery, but harlotry has occurred on the middle deck during the difficult time when You took away the light from us. We also have brought hatred and envy. There have been moments when people have come close to gouging each other's eyes out. The liar is in our midst, boasting and evil gossip abound on board."
>
> He paused again before saying, "'Pride and anger I myself bring to the new life."
>
> There was still no sign that God was listening, and when Noah continued, the voice was harsh: "I do not defend myself, but sometimes I think that my crimes are small in comparison with Yours. [. . .] You killed thousands. [. . .] We get to live our cut-off lives, without roots and connections. The difficult memories and the guilt of having survived will follow us and our children for generation after generation. The people will never trust You again." (342–343; my translation)

Instead of curing human evil, the flood has led to more evil, as humanity has forever lost their faith in God and his goodness.

L'Engle also portrays an evil and rotten society. In the oasis where Noah lives, there are a number of rather unsavory characters. When they find Dennys, dehydrated and badly burned by the sun, they choose to throw him in a rubbish dump instead of giving him water and medical attention (46). This behavior, however, is a far cry from the total evil portrayed in Genesis 6:5. Furthermore, alone among the quoted authors, L'Engle does not touch to any great extent on the question of undeserved suffering. It is found to some extent in Dennys's and Sandy's concern for the fate of Yalith, with whom they are both slightly in love.

> "You can't let Yalith drown in the flood."
> "Why not?"
> "Yalith is good. I mean, she is really *good*."
> Alarid bowed his head. "Goodness has never been a guarantee of safety." (277)

In other words, even good people are subject to suffering.

Finally, L'Engle also touches on the futility of the flood. Although the overarching message of the novel is God's love combined with human trust and faith in him, L'Engle challenges God's actions when it ultimately becomes clear that the world after the flood has not become a better place than it was before:

> "Anyhow"—Sandy's voice was flat—"it didn't work."
> "What didn't work?"
> "The flood. Wiping out all those people, and then starting all over again. People are taller, and we do even worse things to one another because we now know more."
> Dennys took the palm frond out of Sandy's hand. "I wouldn't choose Ham and Anah to repopulate the world, if I were doing the choosing."
> "Oh, they're not that bad," Sandy said. "And Shem and Elisheba are all right. Not terribly exciting. But solid. And Japheth and Oholibamah are terrific."
> "Well. What you said. It didn't work." (197–198)

Despite his lack of heroic qualities, however, L'Engle's Ham proves to be more righteous than the twins are willing to admit. When Noah insists that God has told him to bring his wife and their sons and daughters-in-law on board the ark, his sons protest. Ham even offers to give up his place for the sake of his sister, Yalith, when he realizes that she has no place on the ark:

> Shem protested. "But it's going to be a big boat, Father! Surely there's room for more than just the eight of us. [. . .]

> "I don't believe any of this," Ham said. "But if it should come to pass, I will give my place on the Ark to Yalith." (249)

Unlike L'Engle and Fredriksson, where Noah and his family, despite their weaknesses, still represent the good guys, Provoost and McCaughrean deconstruct the moral of the story. They make Noah and his family stand for evil, while the decent people, who rightly should have been the survivors, perish. Provoost's book as a whole focuses on issues of good and evil, as it questions how a merciful God can be capable of selecting some people who will survive while allowing others to be killed. Provoost has Re Jana's father insist that the people who participated in the building of the ark are people of good will and thus not representatives of a morally depraved humanity:

> "Only those who are righteous will be spared, the Builder said. I have been wondering what that means for us. Have we not cared for your mother all that time? Have we not taken in an orphan child, the child of nomads, with no manners? Are we not hardworking people who are content with what we get for our work? And all those other men, the tradesmen who use their utmost skill, the artists who put their very soul into every vault, into every arch they polish and every image they carve." (149)

Re Jana describes her shock when she comprehends that they will die in the flood. Re Jana puts things into perspective when she challenges Ham to reflect on his own given place on the ark. Would not a truly good person give their life for their fellow human being (cf. L'Engle)?

> "What is this?" I asked when we stood apart from the others. "What are you planning? Will whoever stays behind die? Is that what it means not to be of the elect? Is being righteous the same as staying alive?"
>
> He stared ahead and said not a word.
>
> "If you were righteous, you would now be giving up your places. You would be giving them up to the children, the lame, and the feeble-minded! What do they have to atone for? For the injustice you

> have created? You choose yourselves a woman and make her righteous. You reject another woman and make her an outcast." (127–128)

Finally, Provoost's Re Jana joins L'Engle's Sandy and Fredriksson's Noah in observing that no change seems to have occurred in humanity after the Flood.

Like L'Engle and Provoost, McCaughrean also highlights the difficulties surrounding God's selection. Why is Noah's family saved and not others? Noah's daughter Timna ponders her own fate: "A lucky escape then. I am much luckier than most. Luckier than any other child on Earth, in fact. God wept and his tears have drowned the world. But first He reached out and plucked me and my family to safely. So why can't I lift up my heart in praise? I must be so ungrateful, so thankless" (10). McCaughrean's focus is on people's experiences during their days on the ark. What really happens during those months of confinement while all life around them perishes? Her description offers the reader a dark vision of surviving humanity. She has Noah's wife exclaim that the survivors on the ark are not exactly the pride of humanity, given the way they have behaved toward each other. If a place on the ark had been based on moral merit, other people should have survived too. If not, God's plan is just a big mistake: "And if survival is down to merit, there must have been better than us. Seeing the way we behaved towards our fellow men. You were quite right, Timna. There must be others. There are too many flaws in God's plan unless there are" (159). In the end, we can conclude that no retelling accepts God's behavior. Is it even possible for us readers not to condemn genocide, not to mention universal holocaust? To paraphrase the words of Rabbi Irving Greenberg, writing about the Holocaust, "No [biblical retelling] should be made that would not be credible in the presence of [drowned] children." Although our modern society is aware of the symbolic value of ancient myths, modern retellings of the same myths require us to scrutinize them and question their value system.

## The Rainbow

The story of the flood (but not of Noah) ends with God's promise never to drown humanity again (Gen 9:1–18) and the sign of God's promise is the rainbow in the sky. I have been thinking a lot about the rainbow, especially during the COVID-19 pandemic. In many windows in Scotland, where we lived in the spring of 2020, many children drew a rainbow and put their drawings in the window. I saw many such drawings on my daily, responsibly-completely-alone bike rides around Aberdeenshire. The rainbow is a sign of hope, but it is also a sign that all is not well.

> God said, "This is the sign of the covenant that I make between me and you and every living creature that is with you, for all future generations: I have set my bow in the clouds, and it shall be a sign of the covenant between me and the earth. When I bring clouds over the earth and the bow is seen in the clouds, I will remember my covenant that is between me and you and every living creature of all flesh; and the waters shall never again become a flood to destroy all flesh. When the bow is in the clouds, I will see it and remember the everlasting covenant between God and every living creature of all flesh that is on the earth." (Gen 9:12–16)

We see the rainbow in the sky and trust that God will not send a flood again. At the same time, the rainbow reminds us of the biblical story where God undeniably sent a flood that drowned almost all of humanity. Sometimes I wonder if we can understand the rainbow as an outstretched hand and a prayer for forgiveness. According to the biblical text, it is not a reminder for us but for God: "When I bring clouds over the earth and the bow is seen in the clouds, I will remember my covenant that is between me and you and every living creature of all flesh." God uses the rainbow to remember what he has done and then promises never to do again.

* * *

Genesis 6–9 raises deep theological questions but provides few answers. These questions have been noted by biblical interpreters throughout the ages and are brought to prominence in many contemporary literary retellings. At the forefront is God's autocratic decision to destroy all life on earth in his disappointment with its evil. It is an accepted notion that God's omnipotence, justice, and love have difficulty coexisting. Some aspect seems to have to give way in order to explain the situation in which we live. In Genesis 6–9, God exercises his power and authority by destroying the earth, showing very little of his grace and mercy. God chooses to let justice triumph as he punishes sin with death. This, in turn, raises questions about mercy and innocent suffering.

Noah's behavior in the flood story raises further theological questions. When is obedience good, and when is it bad? All the Old Testament writers agree that Israel should obey God's commands, worship only him, and be faithful and loyal to him in all they do. At the same time, a thread runs throughout the Old Testament that questions blind obedience. God, who created humans in his image (Gen 1:26), does not require Israel to carry out God's commands without understanding and without thinking. Rather, Israel is invited to have fellowship with God and to learn to see the situation from his point of view. Furthermore, God desires interlocutors. He wants to create the world together with humanity, where humanity is set to multiply and rule the earth (Gen 1:28). This vision is in stark contrast to Noah's actions, as Noah rather chooses not to engage God in dialogue but instead to carry out his command uncritically.

With all this in mind, how can we reflect theologically on Genesis 6–9? First of all, I think it is important not to reduce the story of Noah's ark to a child-friendly story of God saving the animals. He does not save all the animals—he preserves two of every unclean species and fourteen of every clean species. Instead, I want to encourage us all to step into the Bible's narrative world, identify with its characters, and dare to ask ourselves how we would have acted in that situation. Would we have obeyed orders, built the ark, and saved (only) our family? I hope not. Rather, I trust that most of us would have sided with our fellow human beings and tried to save more than our immediate family members, even though this would have meant disobeying God's specific command. Would we have turned in an unauthorized person hiding in the hold, or would we have chosen not to betray the stowaway? I further dare to hope that most of us would have prayed for our fellow human beings and tried to get God to reconsider and not send the flood.

A broader theological reflection concerns our view of the Bible. In our reflections we can, on the one hand, choose to emphasize the mercilessness of the biblical Noah. Our approach then becomes a reaction to what is written in the Bible, and our task is to consider how we can relate to this. Is Noah's reaction a reasonable reaction, is it a Christian reaction, and is it a reaction that we should seek to emulate? What does it mean to obey God and how do we know what is God's will? If our whole being screams that God's will in this case is ethically indefensible, that genocide is always wrong no matter how prone to violence God's creation is, then yes, we must reject Noah's behavior.

On the other hand, we have the possibility to re-create and contextualize Noah's obedience so that it becomes acceptable in our eyes. At the same time, we choose to read aspects into the biblical text that are not there. We interpret the Bible in a way that we find ethically defensible: Noah must have prayed for the people, and he must have preached repentance, otherwise, to quote Lindgren's Jonathan in *The Brothers Lionheart*, "He is not a human being, but just a bit of filth" (46). He is then no better than the people around him in his generation who were condemned to perish in the waters of the flood. Noah must become better than what the biblical text says he is in order to uphold the Bible itself. We must deconstruct the text so that its message does not disintegrate before our very eyes.

CHAPTER TWO

# Sarah

## *Posh First Wife or Helpless Victim?*

WHAT LITTLE THE Bible tells us about Sarah is found as scattered comments in Genesis 12, 16–18, 20–21, and 23. We know nothing about her background. Yet her name, Sarah, which means mistress, makes me think of a woman of royalty. So, I choose to see her as a queen: beautiful, proud, and determined.

This focus on Sarah leads to an incomplete portrait of Abraham. For me, Abraham is a man with many good attributes but unfortunately also many bad ones. Like you and me, in other words. I admire Abraham for his faith in Genesis 12. Likewise, I am deeply impressed by his behavior when he intercedes for the people of Sodom in chapter 18. Had I chosen to focus on Abraham, my discussion would certainly have resulted in a considerably more nuanced portrait of him, where all his different sides would have been observed. As it is, I shall only discuss Abraham insofar as his actions affect Sarah, and it is unfortunately precisely in that relationship that Abraham's behavior is sometimes reprehensible. Abraham is a man we can admire in many ways, but his unpleasant characteristics are prominent in his role as Sarah's husband.

The story of Sarah can be likened to a minefield where things below the surface can explode at any moment. Sarah, more than any other woman in the Bible, is associated with involuntary childlessness. Do we dare to walk this minefield and examine whether God allows some families to despair as they long for a child? There are also many other stones that we would rather not turn over. Abraham, praised in Galatians 3:6 and Hebrews 11:8–19 for his assurance of faith, shows throughout Genesis how he doubts God's promise of heirs and how Sarah suffers as a direct result thereof.

Finally, the story of Sarah contains what many would probably call the worst story in the Bible, namely how Abraham shows himself capable of killing their own son. If there is any text in the Bible that should never, and I really mean never, be made a theological model, it is this text, which, to cite Søren Kierkegaard, evokes *Fear and Trembling* (*Frygt og Bæven*—a title probably derived from Phil 2:12). What is our duty to God and to our neighbors? Can a father decide what God's will is without consulting his child and its mother? In such a case, is obedience to God ever ethically defensible?

Both Sarah and Abraham change their names during the course of the story, from Sarai and Abram to Sarah and Abraham. Sarai and Sarah seem to be two forms of the same name, and both mean *princess* in Hebrew and in Akkadian, the language spoken in Babylon until the first millennium BCE. However, there is another possibility, namely that the first form, Sarai, means *barren* and *sterile*, which fits Sarah's situation for most of her adult life. Despite this name change, I shall consistently use the latter pair of names for the sake of simplicity.

## Narratives

Sarah's fate has fascinated many novelists and poets, and my ongoing dialogue with the biblical texts about her is greatly influenced by their work. Here, we will reflect more deeply on how these authors struggle with the questions raised by the story of Sarah and the people around her. How do they understand Sarah's relationship with God, her husband Abraham, her servant Hagar, and her son Isaac?

**Edna Afek** (b. 1943) is an Israeli Jewish writer and professor at the David Yellin College of Education, Jerusalem.
"שרה היתה" (Sarah was), in *Does David Still Play Before You? Israeli Poetry and the Bible*, ed. David C. Jacobson (Wayne State University Press, 1997), 178–181.

**Orson Scott Card** (b. 1951) is an American author who belongs to the Church of Jesus Christ of Latter-day Saints (Mormonism). He is best known for his science fiction novels.
*Sarah* (Bookcraft, 2000).

**Amir Gilboa** (original name Berl Feldmann) (1917–1984) was an Israeli Jewish poet. He was born in Ukraine and immigrated to the then British Mandatory Palestine in 1937. Much of his poetry deals with his war experiences as a soldier in the Israeli army. See also what he writes about Saul in chapter 5.

"שרי" (Sarai), in *Does David Still Play Before You? Israeli Poetry and the Bible*, ed. David C. Jacobson (Wayne State University Press, 1997), 188–191.

**Anita Goldman** (b. 1953) is a Swedish Jewish author and journalist. Her book about Sarah has great psychological depth and shows a good understanding of human nature. The characters of the Bible come to life in her prose, and we can sympathize and identify easily with them.

*Den sista kvinnan från Ur* (Litteraturfrämjandet, 1988).

**Marek Halter** (b. 1936) is a Jewish writer born in Poland. He and his parents barely escaped the Warsaw Ghetto during World War II and ended up in Russia and Uzbekistan. After the end of the World War II, they immigrated to France. His retelling contains a wealth of material not found in the biblical story. Some is found in Jubilees 12:12–14, a book written just before 100 BCE, as well as in later classical Jewish narratives (Midrash, a kind of "fan fiction" that embellishes the biblical stories and fills in narrative gaps). In these works we find, for example, the idea that Terah, Abraham's father, serves as a priest to the Babylonian gods (Numbers Rabbah 19:1; 19:33) and makes idols (Eliyahu Rabbah 6, Eliyahu Zuta 25) that Abraham then destroys.

*Sarah: A Heroine of The Old Testament* (Bantam, 2004).

**Yehudit Kafri** (b. 1935) is an Israeli Jewish author and poet. Her best-known work is the historical novel *Codename: Zosha* (published in 2003 and available in English translation), based on the life of Zofia "Zosha" Poznańska.

"בראשית" (In the beginning), in *Does David Still Play Before You? Israeli Poetry and the Bible*, ed. David C. Jacobson (Wayne State University Press, 1997), 216–217.

**Carolina Klintefelt** (b. 1973) is a Swedish author and writer best known for her children's books *Siarbarnet* (The seer child) and *Boken mellan världarna* (The book between worlds). She has previously worked as an editor for the magazine *NOD* and for the daily Christian newspaper *Dagen*.

"Förkastad, sedd," in *Och Gud skapade människan*, ed. Magnus Sundell (Libris, 2014), 101–117.

**Shin Shifra** (1931–2012) is the pseudonym of the Israeli Jewish poet, writer, and academic Shifra Shifman Shmuelevitch. She is best known for her translations of Mesopotamian poems and other literary works from Sumerian and Akkadian into Hebrew (with the Assyriologist Jacob Klein, professor emeritus from Bar-Ilan University, Ramat Gan). She has also written children's books in Hebrew that retell Mesopotamian texts.

"יצחק" (Isaac), in Dalia Marx, "Where Was Sarah? Depictions of Mothers and Motherhood in Modern Israeli Poetry on the Binding of Isaac," in *Mothers in the Jewish Cultural Imagination*, eds. Marjorie Lehman, Jane L. Kanarek, Simon J. Bronner (Littman Library of Jewish Civilization, 2017), 255–281.

## Sarah's Childhood in Ur

Genesis 11:27–30 tells us about Sarah's background but does not give us much information: "Now these are the descendants of Terah. Terah was the father of Abram, Nahor, and Haran; and Haran was the father of Lot. Haran died before his father Terah in the land of his birth, in Ur of the Chaldeans. Abram and Nahor took wives; the name of Abram's wife was Sarai, and the name of Nahor's wife was Milcah. She was the daughter of Haran the father of Milcah and Iscah. Now Sarai was barren; she had no child." When we read this, we assume that Sarah, as well as Abraham and his family, was born in Ur, which was a city state in southern Mesopotamia. This city, considered one of the oldest in the world, was located where the Euphrates and Tigris Rivers flow into the Persian Gulf. Cuneiform tablets and other archaeological remains—temples, musical instruments, jewelry—indicate that Ur was a powerful trading center with a rich culture. This assumption further suggests that Sarah should not be seen as a typical nomadic woman but as a city dweller. Although the text says nothing about her level of education, her urban background challenges us to consider the extent to which she is aware of and, as a young person, perhaps even participates in Ur's cultural and ritual ceremonies.

The only thing we know about Sarah when we meet her in Genesis is that she is barren and thus has not given birth (Gen 11:30). There is no indication in the biblical text itself that God has caused Sarah's barrenness. Being childless is not only a sadness for those who long for children; in many societies, it is also a social disgrace, especially in patriarchal societies where a woman's worth is measured by her capacity to bear sons. Childlessness may also be a source of economic hardship. If you do not have children, who will take care of you in your old age? Without children, you may be forced to starve. At the same time of course, childlessness may be the only thing keeping you alive at a time when childbirth is one of the leading causes of death among women. So, not having children means a lonely and shameful life but also a relatively healthy one. Sarah, unlike the other women in the gradually growing group of people around Abraham, is not worn out by perpetual childbirth and breastfeeding but has both her figure and her health intact.

For some reason, Abraham's immediate family decides to leave their hometown of Ur and head east to Harran, another important trading center with considerable political and cultural significance. Harran was located in what is today the borderland between Turkey and Syria, near the sources of the Euphrates and Tigris rivers. "Terah took his son Abram and his grandson Lot son of Haran, and his daughter-in-law Sarai, his son Abram's wife, and they went out together from Ur of the Chaldeans to go into the land of Canaan; but when they came to Haran, they settled there. The days of Terah were two hundred and five years; and Terah died in Haran" (Gen 11:31–32). Sarah is not allowed to make herself at home in Harran, however, for God has other plans for her and her husband's life. They will travel further south, via Shechem and Bethel, eventually reaching their final destination in the Judaean wilderness (Gen 11:5–9) and the grove of Mamre outside Hebron (Gen 13:18).

## Sarah's Mesopotamian Life

As I said, the Bible tells us nothing about Sarah's background. We are therefore free to speculate. Is she an ordinary Babylonian woman, or is she part of Ur's nobility? Many novelists give Sarah a privileged background. While Abraham's family belongs to the fringes of Ur, Sarah is at the center of Mesopotamian society, both socially and religiously. Moreover, it is very common in literary retellings to link Sarah's Mesopotamian background with her barrenness. The Bible itself does not give us any information about Sarah's background, and the only information we have about her barrenness is Genesis 16:1–2a, which only shows Sarah's own understanding of the situation: "Now Sarai, Abram's wife, bore him no children. She had an Egyptian slave-girl whose name was Hagar, and Sarai said to Abram, 'You see that the Lord has prevented me from bearing children; go in to my slave-girl; it may be that I shall obtain children by her.'" Another interesting phenomenon is that several authors associate Sarah with Inanna/Ishtar, the Mesopotamian goddess of fertility, love, and war, and her cult. Inanna is the Sumerian name and Ishtar the Akkadian name of this goddess. This connection is not entirely intuitive, as Ishtar's temple complex of Eanna was located in Uruk and not in Ur. In addition, the association is somewhat ironic, since Sarah, more than any other biblical person, is associated with barrenness rather than its opposite.

In her book *Den sista kvinnan från Ur* (The last woman from Ur), Anita Goldman places Sarah in the temple of Ishtar. As the daughter of its high priestess, Sarah has a deep knowledge of plants and their healing properties. This comes in handy in her life with Abraham, as she often acts as midwife to the much less knowledgeable nomadic women of Canaan. At the same time, Sarah's background and expertise contribute to her vulnerability and isolation as the other women both fear and look down on her because of her foreign customs. Her attempts to help the women avoid unwanted pregnancies and find ways to reduce sexual violence are not well received by either the men or the women. Sarah refuses to be subdued, but the pain is there, as is the sadness when she observes that the God of Israel does not seem to care much about women. Their main task in life is to bear sons, with no thought for what pregnancy after pregnancy does to a woman's body.

Orson Scott Card, in his book *Sarah*, similarly chooses to give Sarah a high position in society when he makes her the descendant of a now deposed royal family. She meets Abraham while living in what Card calls "northern Ur," that is, Harran, where she, along with her immediate family, lives a comfortable but hidden life. Card also chooses to associate Sarah with the cult of Ishtar. Unlike Goldman, who portrays Sarah's background positively as something that gives Sarah important knowledge, Card represents it as a sin in her life. According to him, Sarah's connection to Ishtar is a contributing factor to her barrenness.

Marek Halter likewise links Sarah to the cult of Ishtar and also finds a link between this cult and Sarah's barrenness in his book *Sarah: A Heroine of the Old Testament*. In Halter's case, however, Sarah's barrenness is the cause of her becoming one of Ishtar's priestesses and not, as in Card's book, its effect.

At an early age, in order to avoid an unwanted marriage, Sarah chooses to eat herbs that stop her periods. Unfortunately, Sarah does not realize the full power of these herbs. She suffers permanent repercussions—her "moon blood" ceases completely—making her an excellent priestess who can serve Ishtar full-time without sharing her time with husband and children. Abraham recognizes her barrenness when he later rescues her from Ur, just before its fall to the Gutians, a group of Zagros hill tribes that posed a threat to the southern Mesopotamian city states between 2200 and 2100 BCE. He trusts, however, that God will sort it all out in due course and fulfil his promise of heirs to him.

## Sarah's Absence of a Summons

As mentioned earlier, Abraham is always at the center of God's call and God's promises. It is unclear whether Sarah knows anything at all about God's intentions for her. In the biblical texts, God always speaks only to Abraham.

Halter clearly shows how God's lack of direct communication with Sarah leaves her vulnerable. She is always forced to rely on Abraham's version of God's speech. The final straw that breaks the camel's back is when God also starts talking to Hagar. Broken by jealousy, Sarah asks Abraham to choose between herself and Hagar, with the result that Hagar leaves. When Hagar returns four days later, filled with her experience of God's presence and speech, Sarah reacts violently and jealously: "'Lies!' Sarai thought. 'She's the one who humiliates me. I'm her mistress, and she treats me like a handmaid. Who would believe it? And now Abram's god speaks to her! More lies. A fable she's invented to seduce Abram. Oh, yes!'" (195).

Similarly, in his poem "שרי" (Sarai), the Israeli poet Amir Gilboa chooses to emphasize Sarah's lack of calling. God calls Abraham to leave Ur; he never calls Sarah. In Gilboa's hands, this becomes a motif for Sarah's rootlessness and sense of meaninglessness. The journey from Ur, via Harran, to Canaan never becomes Sarah's journey. She is just trailing along, with no clear goal or meaning to her journey: "A long way she went. Over mountains and in valleys. Mountains upon mountains she left behind her and still she walks and walks. She embarked at sunrise ninety years earlier [. . .] On her way, during ninety years she conceived in her imagination generations of great grandchildren, grandchildren, fathers, and grandfathers. [. . .] But she did not bear even one son in her arms that she could bring close to her heart" (189–190). The dream of Canaan is never Sarah's dream, and the dream of a God-given people as stars in the sky (Gen 15:5) is never her vision. Like Abraham, she wants descendants who live on, but the focus is on the people—a child in her arms—rather than a future nation. Sarah arrives at the end of the poem when she gives birth to Isaac. For her, the destination is not the land of Canaan but motherhood.

## Sarah's Stays in the Harems of Powerful Men

Abraham and Sarah leave Harran and eventually arrive in Canaan and, more specifically, the Judaean wilderness. Life there is no bed of roses, however. Famine strikes several times, hitting them and their flocks hard. As a result, they are forced to take refuge in other places.

### Visit to Egypt

The first time that famine strikes, Abraham and Sarah go to Egypt: "Now there was a famine in the land. So Abram went down to Egypt to reside there as an alien, for the famine was severe in the land" (Gen 12:10). In Egypt, a different kind of danger awaits Sarah, namely, joining Pharaoh's harem. One of the Bible's more amusing verses is Genesis 12:11a where Abraham, after who knows how many years of marriage, notices that his wife is beautiful: "When he was about to enter Egypt, he said to his wife Sarai, 'I know well that you are a woman beautiful in appearance;'" Yet according to Abraham, Sarah's beauty poses a deadly threat to both her and Abraham:

> "And when the Egyptians see you, they will say, 'This is his wife'; then they will kill me, but they will let you live. Say you are my sister, so that it may go well with me because of you, and that my life may be spared on your account." When Abram entered Egypt the Egyptians saw that the woman was very beautiful. When the officials of Pharaoh saw her, they praised her to Pharaoh. And the woman was taken into Pharaoh's house. And for her sake he dealt well with Abram; and he had sheep, oxen, male donkeys, male and female slaves, female donkeys, and camels. (Gen 12:11b–16)

This text is frightening in many ways. I do not want to minimize in any way the real danger that the journey to Egypt poses to Abraham and his loved ones. Famine is a terrible thing and people in such a life-threatening crisis are often prepared to compromise their principles and do almost anything to survive. When faced with the choice between starving to death and subjecting themselves and their family members to humiliating experiences, most people choose the latter, despite all that this choice entails. Nor should we underestimate the utter vulnerability of Abraham and Sarah as strangers in Egypt trying to find food and how easily they could be exploited by ruthless people seeking their own gain.

Despite this, Abraham is portrayed as a selfish coward who, fearing for his life, sacrifices Sarah's well-being without a second thought. Abraham's words "so that it may go well with me because of you" (Gen 12:13) emphasize his focus on his own well-being. This is not a selfless declaration of love "in sickness and in health" but an excuse to save his own skin at the expense of others, in this case Sarah. Abraham allows his wife to end up in Pharaoh's harem where she is likely forced to have sex with Pharaoh. In the meantime, Abraham seems to be doing quite well with his sheep and cows, slaves and slave girls, donkeys and camels. What would you choose if you were Abraham? Abraham is also lying to Pharaoh. There is nothing in the text so far to suggest that Abraham and Sarah are related in any way. Furthermore, even if that were the case (Gen 20:12), it does not excuse Abraham's behavior. Lies might be excusable if they save lives, like the midwives' lies in Exodus 1:15–21, which saved a large number of innocent children from death, but not if they are for personal gain.

God seems to be on Sarah's side, however, as he allows Pharaoh and his court to suffer severe plagues: "But the Lord afflicted Pharaoh and his house with great plagues because of Sarai, Abram's wife" (Gen 12:17). Pharaoh is predictably furious with Abraham when he discovers Abraham's deceitful behavior, which has resulted in Pharaoh taking an already married woman into his harem. He immediately orders Abraham to take his belongings, including his wife and all the livestock and servants he has hidden away, and leave the country. "So Pharaoh called Abram, and said, 'What is this you have done to me? Why did you not tell me that she was your wife? Why did you say, "She is my sister," so that I took her for my wife? Now then, here is your wife; take her, and be gone.' And Pharaoh gave his men orders concerning him; and they set him on the way, with his wife and all that he had" (Gen 12:18–20). A nasty end to a sad story—I wonder how this affects Sarah and Abraham's marriage? Probably not for the better, I guess. What scars might

Sarah's (probable) experience of sexual abuse in Pharaoh's harem have left on her soul? Thankfully, one might say, she was not at risk of becoming pregnant. Yet the question of a possible pregnancy makes Abraham's behavior even more inexcusable. Think for yourselves, God has promised that he will make Abraham into a great nation (Gen 12:2). To ensure the fulfilment of that prophecy, it is probably not the smartest thing for Abraham to let his wife spend time in Pharaoh's bed. Abraham's behavior is a disgrace, not only to Sarah but also to God and his promises. Alternatively, did Abraham coldly reckon with Sarah's barrenness when he exposed Sarah and Pharaoh to his deception? Is the nonexistent risk of an "unwanted" pregnancy the reason for Abraham's behavior? Or, and now I'm treading where angels fear to tread, does Abraham doubt his own ability and hope for a "wanted" pregnancy? Perhaps we should not speculate too much in that direction.

Thanks to Pharaoh's gifts, Abraham is now a rich man (Gen 13:2). Lies and deceit seem to pay off. He and his family live a nomadic life, moving their cattle around the Judaean wilderness in search of fertile pastures. It is a harsh life in the barren terrain, which leads to disputes not only between Abraham and Lot but also with other shepherds in the area (Gen 13:3–7). Too many goats and sheep can upset the delicate harmony between the grazing the animals need and what nature can offer. It is possible that Abraham's newfound wealth will ultimately lead to more rather than fewer economic problems.

## Visit to Gerar

Many years later, in Genesis 20, Abraham decides, for unclear reasons, to go to Gerar. We then get a repeat of Abraham's earlier behavior toward Pharaoh (Gen 12), when Sarah again ends up in the harem of a powerful man: "From there Abraham journeyed towards the region of the Negeb, and settled between Kadesh and Shur. While residing in Gerar as an alien, Abraham said of his wife Sarah, 'She is my sister.' And King Abimelech of Gerar sent and took Sarah" (Gen 20:1–2). This is obviously a crux, as this visit to Gerar is late in the story of Sarah. Already in chapter 18 we read that both Sarah and Abraham are old and Sarah complains that she feels so worn out (vv. 11–12). Thus, if we accept a linear chronology, we must assume that Abimelech found Sarah attractive regardless of her advanced age. I am not one to argue with that.

The text contains a larger moral challenge, however, which is associated with Abraham's behavior. Seeing that Abraham repeats the attempt to make powerful men believe that Sarah is his sister rather than his wife, then unfortunately we must draw one of two conclusions. Either Abraham is a particularly dimwitted man, as he seems to have learned nothing from his mistakes. Should the man, who was forced to flee Egypt with his tail between his legs because he lied about his and Sarah's marital status, not have grasped by now that it is not a good idea to put Sarah through this again? Or, and perhaps worse, Abraham comes across as a calculating man. He learned the first time that there was financial gain in passing Sarah off as his sister and realizes that it might be worth a try to repeat the feat. Moreover, there is evidence that he teaches his son Isaac to do the same. Genesis 26 is in many ways a repetition of Genesis 20, with Isaac playing the role of Abraham and Rebekah playing the role of Sarah.

The most serious issue, however, concerns Abraham's relationship with God. Abraham's behavior in Genesis 20 reflects his deep distrust of God. God's messenger had already assured him in Genesis 18:10, two chapters earlier, that Sarah would have a child when the messenger returned a year later. Should Abraham then not do everything possible to make sure that Sarah's son is really his own and not the son of the king of Gerar?

Most biblical scholars resolve the situation by seeing the stories in Genesis 12 and 20 as two parallel versions. The same applies to the story in Genesis 26 about Isaac, Rebekah, and the king of Gerar, which is seen as an additional, third version. Alternatively, it is possible to assume that chapter 20 reflects an event earlier in the chronology of the Abraham story.

Returning to the biblical text, we read how God once again needs to save Sarah. This time, thankfully, she does not have to have sex with Abimelech: "Then God said to him in the dream, 'Yes, I know that you did this in the integrity of your heart; furthermore it was I who kept you from sinning against me. Therefore I did not let you touch her'" (Gen 20:6). Enough is enough, at least for me, when Abraham once again passes the burden onto Sarah: "And when God caused me to wander from my father's house, I said to her, 'This is the kindness you must do me: at every place to which we come, say of me, He is my brother'" (Gen 20:13). If you want to show me love, lie so I can save my skin and get lots of cattle and other riches (vv. 14–16) while subjecting you to forced sex. I am sorry, Abraham, but I am not impressed by your reasoning.

## Sarah: Victim or Femme Fatale?

The difficulties with the stories in Genesis 12 and 20 about Sarah's enforced time with Pharaoh and the king of Gerar are obvious. Here the question arises again as to what characterizes a biblically faithful interpretation. On the one hand, if the goal is to describe Abraham's behavior in a way that corresponds to the exact content of the Bible, it is difficult to avoid portraying him as a selfish and irresponsible man. On the other hand, if the goal is to maintain the positive appreciation of Abraham in later traditions, other measures are required.

An obvious way around the dilemma is not to retell Genesis 12 and 20. One could say that Hebrews 11:8–12 is at the forefront of this kind of interpretive strategy. This text chooses to emphasize Abraham's good points while omitting his journey to Egypt.

> By faith Abraham obeyed when he was called to set out for a place that he was to receive as an inheritance; and he set out, not knowing where he was going. By faith he stayed for a time in the land he had been promised, as in a foreign land, living in tents, as did Isaac and Jacob, who were heirs with him of the same promise. For he looked forward to the city that has foundations, whose architect and builder is God. By faith he received power of procreation, even though he was too old—and Sarah herself was barren—because he considered him faithful who had promised. Therefore from one person, and this one as good as dead, descendants were born, "as many as the stars of heaven and as the innumerable grains of sand by the seashore."

The result is that Abraham remains a hero of faith and thus a good role model for us. A number of modern writers take the same approach. Goldman, for example, never mentions Abraham and Sarah's journey to Egypt, which results in her portrayal of Abraham being more positive than the one in the Old Testament.

Those who dare to embark on this figurative morass, tend to merge Genesis 12 and 20 (in line with most biblical scholars), thus allowing Sarah to experience only one stay in a harem rather than two. Card chooses this path. In addition, and in my opinion more maliciously, Card's Abraham subjects Sarah to "gaslighting," that is, a form of manipulation where the intention is to make a person doubt their own perceptions and question their memories. Sarah is initially very angry with Abraham when he calls her his sister, accusing him of putting her in danger and prioritizing his own well-being before hers. Abraham admits that they are in danger and asks Sarah to trust in God, which does not calm Sarah down but makes her even angrier and more afraid of both God and her husband. Later, however, she understands how dangerous the situation is for Abraham and is prepared to do anything to prevent him from being killed. Card thus allows Abraham to invalidate Sarah's feelings and makes her doubt her own experience:

> The thought of Abram murdered was unbearable. At once her anger at God was swept away in fear for her husband. Do whatever you must to me, she prayed silently, but let no harm come to Abram. (68)

> O God of Abram, she prayed. Forgive my selfishness in resenting the deception thou didst urge upon us, and my vanity in thinking I was wise in the ways of a royal house. I will bear whatever burden thou placest upon me, but keep my husband safe. (73)

Talk about internalization. Abraham puts Sarah in danger and Sarah takes the blame. Abraham manipulates Sarah so that she, the real victim, adopts and accepts the perpetrator's, namely Abraham's, perception of reality. In addition, the reader who identifies with Sarah is led to believe that a good wife should be like Sarah toward her husband.

Card's retelling of Sarah's time in Pharaoh's harem is also so sanitized and unhistorical that the whole story becomes slightly ridiculous. Pharaoh proposes marriage to Sarah, and, although he is disappointed when she declines his offer, he respects her refusal. In this way, Sarah is never forced to have sex with Pharaoh and therefore never risks becoming pregnant by anyone other than Abraham. Moreover, this maneuver serves to exonerate Abraham: He was right to lie about Sarah's status as her virtue was never at risk. What nonsense!

Halter's novel, *Sarah: A Heroine of the Old Testament*, presents a more interesting picture with more depth; yet it also blames Sarah in a different way. Halter's Pharaoh neither forces himself on Sarah nor seduces her. Rather, it is Sarah who seduces him with her dance and her beauty. Sarah wants him and enjoys having sex with him. Then the next morning, when Pharaoh realizes that Sarah is Abraham's wife, he proves to be a better person than both Sarah and Abraham. He explains to Sarah that he is not in the habit of killing people in order to marry their widows: "'You were mistaken, you and your husband. Pharaoh isn't going to feed you to the crocodiles. As my father wrote, "Do not be wicked. Feed the poor man, for a rich people does not rise in revolt—Become great and lasting through the love that you leave behind." Repeat those words to Abram'" (258). Both Sarah and Abraham receive a severe rebuke. Pharaoh further accuses them of not trusting the god they speak so highly of:

> "Why?" he screamed again. "Why lie to me like that?"
>
> "Because Abraham was afraid you would kill him to make me your wife. And I, too, was afraid you would kill him."
>
> Pharaoh gave a nasty laugh, as if he spat. "Afraid?"
>
> "Yes, afraid of Pharaoh."
>
> Pharaoh sneered. [. . .] "So, Abram's God Most High isn't mighty enough to protect you against fear?" Sarah lowered her eyes without a reply. (256–257)

Halter clearly shows that neither Abraham nor Sarah passes the test. Their joint act reflects not only their contempt for Pharaoh but also their unbelief in God.

## An Awkward Love Triangle

Sometime later, God again promises Abraham children, and Abraham believes God's promise, which is credited to him as righteousness (Gen 15:4–6). However, God does not mention Sarah by name when promising Abraham heirs. On the one hand, it is reasonable to assume that Sarah, as the only wife mentioned so far in the biblical text, is the intended mother. On the other hand, this is a so-called argument from silence, that is, an implicit conclusion based on something that has not been explicitly said. It is also unclear how much Sarah knows about God's promise, as God seems to communicate solely with Abraham. The only time Sarah hears anything about it is when she eavesdrops (Gen 18:1). Even though Genesis 21:1 mentions that God has not forgotten his promise to Sarah, it is uncertain whether Sarah has actually received this information: "The Lord dealt with Sarah as he had said, and the Lord did for Sarah as he had promised" (Gen 21:1). Sarah, who may or may not have been informed of God's promise of children, decides to take matters into her own hands. Her thoughts in Genesis 16:2 suggest the latter. Instead of knowing that Abraham has been promised children by God, Sarah seems to be of the erroneous opinion that her childlessness is God's doing. According to Sarah, God has, for some inexplicable reason, made her barren.

> Now Sarai, Abram's wife, bore him no children. She had an Egyptian slave-girl whose name was Hagar, and Sarai said to Abram, "You see that the Lord has prevented me from bearing children; go in to my slave-girl; it may be that I shall obtain children by her." And Abram listened to the voice of Sarai. So, after Abram had lived for ten years in the land of Canaan, Sarai, Abram's wife, took Hagar the Egyptian, her slave-girl, and gave her to her husband Abram as a wife. (Gen 16:1–3)

Sarah's behavior here leaves much to be desired. Here Sarah subjects another woman, Hagar, to something she herself has been subjected to, namely being forced to have sex with a man she has not chosen. Sarah's behavior may be acceptable in its original social context and can perhaps even be understood as an expression of her desperation, but that does not make it excusable when we read it in the light of our own modern values.

Sarah's plan is thwarted when Hagar not only becomes pregnant but also, as a direct result, begins to look down on Sarah. Sarah has now lost not only her husband to another woman, but also her handmaiden's respect. I have often wondered if Sarah actually hopes that Abraham would not agree to her proposal. Could it be that, deep in her heart, Sarah would rather hear Abraham say that there is only one woman for him and that is Sarah herself? Being an incurable romantic, I am disappointed in Abraham. However, perhaps I should not expect too much from a man who had previously allowed his wife to become part of Pharaoh's harem.

Sarah, scorned, betrayed, and humiliated, takes her revenge on Hagar and punishes her for her rebellion. Abraham is beyond her reach as she is dependent on him. Here too, God is on Sarah's side. When Hagar escapes, she is rescued by God's angel, but the angel also commands her to return to Sarah and submit to her authority (Gen 16:6–9). Eventually, Ishmael is born, and Sarah is forced to watch the child of her husband and Hagar grow and flourish. What shame and anguish for Sarah, and it is all self-inflicted.

## Women Mistreat Other Women

Sarah and Hagar's relationship turns the spotlight on how women treat other women. The biblical story does not provide examples of good role models. Rather, it paints a tragic picture of women's behavior in a patriarchal world where everything is focused on a woman's ability or inability to provide heirs for her husband. Sarah and Hagar are not sisters working together; they are rivals fighting each other to the death. There is no way to tell who is right and who is wrong in this battle; they are both losers.

Goldman highlights this tragedy when she describes how Sarah, the chief's wife, behaves condescendingly toward Hagar. Hagar is Sarah's property to be treated as Sarah sees fit and whose purpose in life is to serve Sarah. Hagar has no intrinsic value. Sarah makes the decision to have a child through Hagar without any regard for Hagar's own well-being. The scene where she prepares Hagar to have sex with Abraham shows Sarah's coldness toward Hagar but also her own desperation. Hagar herself is insecure and afraid:

> Hagar leaves, once again rebuffed, again commanded. She doesn't know whether to be scared or happy. Abraham, the great powerful man, the awe-inspiring man, how will she . . . what will he do . . . will it hurt . . . how will she dare to take off her dress, the shame will kill her . . . and he, his . . . oh no . . . and Sarah's coldness, sharp as a knife blade . . . if she could only ask someone, someone old and wise, like Mother Mamre . . . or run and talk to her friends . . . but, no, she dares not go anywhere, only straight into her part of the tent. (75; my translation)

Later, however, after suffering through the sex act, Hagar notices that something has changed. There has been a power shift between her and Sarah. This feeling is reinforced when she realizes that she is pregnant. Now she has something Sarah does not, and a sense of triumph sets in: "She doesn't look up at Sarah from below, with a quick, watchful look. She looks straight at Sarah and although she must stretch her neck to reach the other's height, she does not lose her dignity. Thus the women stand and measure each other, and Sarah knows that she must scrape together every ounce of self-respect so that the defeat will not be total" (88; my translation). Sarah, for her part, feels the defeat in the depths of her heart. When Abraham has sex with Hagar, Sarah cries out her sorrow in the arms of a friend (77), and when Sarah finds out about Hagar's pregnancy, her age catches up with her, and she is transformed, literally, from being the most beautiful woman in the tribe to becoming a bent old woman (88–89).

In her short story "Förkastad, sedd" (Rejected, seen), Carolina Klintefelt similarly chooses to depict Hagar's vulnerability, shame, and pain when Abraham lies with her, but then also her pride when she discovers that she has something that Sarah does not have, namely a child in her womb. Klintefelt's Hagar describes how Sarah feels compelled to demonstrate her power over her by beating her but that her son turns out to be worth all the shame and humiliation: "And she saw it so clearly in the wife's sharp gaze: She doesn't like me! Should one have to put up with such things? Punished for carrying a child for others, for being young, for being forced into a life as a slave? No, no! She couldn't stand it; it was too much!" (111; my translation).

In the Bible, Sarah initiates the power shift between herself and Hagar. Several contemporary retellings ponder how much initiative Sarah really has. Edna Afek chooses to undermine the biblical narrative when she transforms the relationship between Hagar and Abraham into an extramarital affair. In her poem "שרה היתה" (Sarah was), Afek highlights Sarah's powerlessness as she watches Abraham spend more and more time with Hagar. Sarah, on the surface a gentle and obedient wife with a good heart, suffers in silence. She never confronts Abraham openly but secretly dreams of how she wants to get back at Hagar. It is only when she has a child of her own that she can let go of the situation. Her identity as a woman is no longer tied to her role as Abraham's wife but is based on herself and her role as Isaac's mother.

| | |
|---|---|
| Sarah was<br>soft and tender-hearted<br>but<br>a woman<br>submissive and cruel<br>and he—<br>with Hagar<br>always.<br>(178–181) | שרה היתה<br>רכה ורחמנית<br>אבל<br>אשה<br>כנועה ואכזרית<br>והוא—<br>אצל הגר<br>תמיד |

In a very different way, Card chooses to salvage Abraham and Sarah's reputations by, once again, placing the blame on a woman, this time on Hagar. Despite this, in my opinion, unfair blaming, there are redeeming aspects in Card's retelling that give the portrait of Hagar some depth. Sarah discerns that Hagar's behavior has its origins in her background. Hagar was captured and enslaved as a child. Her entire existence up to that point has been one of survival, leaving her unable to see Sarah's outstretched hand, when they first meet in Pharaoh's harem, as an invitation to mutual friendship. To gain her own advantages, Hagar constantly does what she thinks Sarah wants her to do. The same is true when Sarah asks her to bear a child for Abraham. Hagar immediately agrees, as she sees it as a way to gain more influence. As the mother of Abraham's son, she will be less dependent on Sarah. Once Ishmael is born, Hagar immediately seizes the opportunity to usurp Sarah's position. Sarah suffers when Abraham also seems to fall for Hagar's manipulation:

> "But she never was my friend, in her heart. That was just an act she put on. That's what I think now. Because the moment she had your child in her, she had the upper hand over me. Now she was the mother of your heir-to-be. And all her hatred can finally come out. Now the way for her to gain the most from this situation is to weaken me, so that she can rise above me in your eyes and the eyes of everyone else in the camp. And . . . it worked."
>
> "You really think she's that evil?" asked Abram.
>
> "No, I don't think she's evil," said Sarai. "I think she's a girl who had everything stolen from her as a child, and thinks that's how the world works—you take everything you can the moment you can get it. [. . .] It is not evil, it's survival. She's still struggling to survive." (243–244)

In line with his choice to have Sarah seduce Pharaoh, Halter links Sarah's time in Pharaoh's harem with Hagar's time in Abraham's tent. Just as Abraham was forced to suffer in the knowledge of Sarah's extramarital affair, Sarah will now suffer in the knowledge of Abraham's similar relationship with Hagar. Like her biblical namesake, Halter's Sarah initiates the contact, implicitly because she feels guilty about her seduction by Pharaoh and her enjoyment of it:

> Abram fell silent again, and looked for Sarai's eyes in the dim light. With the tips of his fingers, he stroked her lips gently. "You'll suffer," he whispered. "It won't be your child."
>
> "I'll be strong."
>
> "I'll be giving pleasure to Hagar. You'll suffer."
>
> Sarai smiled to hide the mist in her eyes. "I will know what you knew when we were in Pharaoh's palace." (289)

Sarah, however, does not realize what she is getting into and thus suffers all the pangs of jealousy when she hears through the tent canvas how Abraham and Hagar enjoy each other's intimacy. She suffers even more when Hagar begins to disregard her authority and when God speaks to Hagar, and even more when Ishmael is born and she is forced to observe Abraham's obvious love for his son (290–297).

## A Long-Awaited Pregnancy

Both Abraham and Sarah have doubted God's promise of a child, which so far has only led to negative consequences for all parties involved. Despite this, God shows renewed concern as he once again reiterates his promise that Abraham and Sarah will have a son:

> God said to Abraham, "As for Sarai your wife, you shall not call her Sarai, but Sarah shall be her name. I will bless her, and moreover I will give you a son by her. I will bless her, and she shall give rise to nations; kings of peoples shall come from her." Then Abraham fell on his face and laughed, and said to himself, "Can a child be born to a man who is a hundred years old? Can Sarah, who is ninety years old, bear a child?" And Abraham said to God, "O that Ishmael might live in your sight!" God said, "No, but your wife Sarah shall bear you a son, and you shall name him Isaac. I will establish my covenant with him as an everlasting covenant for his offspring after him. As for Ishmael, I have heard you; I will bless him and make him fruitful and exceedingly numerous; he shall be the father of twelve princes, and I will make him a great nation. But my covenant I will establish with Isaac, whom Sarah shall bear to you at this season next year." (Gen 17:15–21)

Again, it is not clear whether Abraham informs Sarah of God's renewed promise. Later, when God and his angels visit Abraham and Sarah in Mamre, Sarah seems surprised when, eavesdropping, she manages to hear the message that she will have a son:

> They said to him, "Where is your wife Sarah?" And he said, "There, in the tent." Then one said, "I will surely return to you in due season, and your wife Sarah shall have a son." And Sarah was listening at the tent entrance behind him. Now Abraham and Sarah were old, advanced in age; it had ceased to be with Sarah after the manner of women. So Sarah laughed to herself, saying, "After I have grown old, and my husband is old, shall I have pleasure?" The Lord said to Abraham, "Why did Sarah laugh, and say, 'Shall I indeed bear a child, now that I am old?' Is anything too wonderful for the Lord? At the set time I will return to you, in due season, and Sarah shall have a son." But Sarah denied, saying, "I did not laugh"; for she was afraid. He said, "Oh yes, you did laugh." (Gen 18:9–15)

Sarah reacts by laughing. She does not think she is capable of having sex with Abraham. She no longer feels particularly attractive, and Abraham is, as the text says, old too. So, Sarah laughs. Is it a mocking laugh, or a resigned laugh, or a laugh that shows disbelief, or maybe it is her sense of powerlessness or even anger that shines through? The situation is basically not funny at all but rather quite embarrassing, and I find it hard to understand God's ways here. Sarah has spent a lifetime oscillating between hope and despair. Month after month, she has hoped for a pregnancy, only to find out that her period has come—again and again and again. Then she goes into menopause. Now I do not know anything about Sarah's hot flashes and mood swings due to hormonal changes, but I can vividly imagine them. And then the whole misery starts all over again. Plus, the thought of pregnancy, with the possible accompanying pelvic girdle pain and acid reflux, when you are well past retirement age and neither Gaviscon nor Rennie have been invented yet, is a far from attractive scenario. Finally, I panic when I think of all the breastfeeding and sleepless nights once Isaac is born, although Sarah may have maids and wet nurses to help her. Are we really supposed to cope with such things in old age? So, I wonder in the back of my mind if all this is really necessary. Why can Sarah not be allowed to give birth a little earlier? Would that not be more merciful, rather than this prolonged mental and physical agony? What is God really trying to prove?

Goldman captures the grotesque aspects well when she describes Sarah's heavy, pregnant body and the other women's horrified fascination. The humiliation is complete. To be forced to endure a lifetime of pity and contempt because of your infertility and then to be made a spectacle is cruel.

> It was most difficult at the beginning, when the women moved aside at the well, almost imperceptibly, to make room for the chief's wife, the fat one. She looked grotesque, she knew it, she could see her ludicrous appearance reflected in their eyes, in their teasing looks. The women fell silent when she arrived and then someone asked how she was, and she answered curtly and saw how the youngest girls giggled. No one called her condition by its proper name. It was as if this monstrous stomach beneath the drooping old woman's breasts was such a haunting sight, so tasteless and disgusting, that one had to remain silent about it. (127; my translation)

Other (mainly male) authors choose not to deal with these biological aspects. Halter, who had previously held Sarah responsible for her barrenness, similarly makes her responsible for becoming fruitful. Heartbroken, crushed by her jealousy of Hagar, Sarah turns to God in prayer. She cries out her despair at God's silence, recognizes her own responsibility for her barrenness, and asks God to help her. And God hears her prayer. He allows Sarah suddenly to regain her fertility at the same time as she begins to age. She also regains her desire for her husband, who in turn tells her about God's promise of land and people. They share a good laugh and embrace each other. It is only later that Abraham and Sarah are visited in Mamre and are promised a son, but by then this son has already been conceived some time previously (304–307).

## One Father, Two Mothers, and Two Brothers

Sarah eventually becomes pregnant, and Isaac is born. Sarah is happy (Gen 21:6) and everything seems to go well for a few years. There is, however, a fly in the ointment and it is Isaac's older half brother Ishmael. The Hebrew text of Genesis 21:9 is very ambivalent, which is reflected in the differing translations of the NRSV and the NIV.

> But Sarah saw the son of Hagar the Egyptian, whom she had borne to Abraham, *playing with* her son Isaac. (NRSV)

> But Sarah saw that the son whom Hagar the Egyptian had borne to Abraham was *mocking*. (NIV)

Ishmael is playing (*tsachak*) with Isaac, a word game where the verb uses the same letters as those in Isaac's name. The question is why Sarah is so upset. Is she jealous of the boys' good relationship, an interpretation suggested by the NRSV, or is she angry because Ishmael does not play nicely with Isaac, an interpretation favored by the NIV? Both translations are possible, and both are in line with the Hebrew text. It is thus difficult to decide which of them is more likely. God again appears to be on Sarah's side. He commands Abraham to send Hagar away, but at the same time, when Abraham seems to hesitate, promises to take care of both Hagar and Ishmael (Gen 21:11–13).

Many writers have struggled to understand what is going on between the two brothers and how this in turn influences Sarah's decision to expel Hagar and Ishmael. Is Sarah acting responsibly to save her son, or is she overreacting out of unjustified jealousy? At one extreme is Card's novel in which he, as usual, blames Hagar. Full of jealousy, Hagar sees how the birth of Isaac has once again shifted the balance of power between her and Sarah. Until the birth of Isaac, she has been the mother of Abraham's only descendant; now she is once again relegated to second place. The game between Ishmael and Isaac is not an innocent endeavor but a veiled attempt at murder, in which a truly evil Ishmael, silently encouraged by his mother, almost tries to strangle the three-year-old little Isaac: "The soft laughter came from Ishmael. The screaming came from little Isaac. Ishmael had bound a long scarf around Isaac's open mouth, muffling his voice. And Ishmael held the end of the scarf like a tether, so that even though Isaac strained against it with all his might, he could not get away" (310). This atrocity effectively turns the reader's sympathies in Sarah's favor and excuses her decision to send Hagar and Ishmael away. God also helps, as his promise of a future for Ishmael makes it easier for Abraham to agree to expel his eldest son and leave him to face the dangers of the desert.

Goldman describes the ruthlessness of love in a more nuanced way. Sarah, filled with love for Isaac, is prepared to treat Hagar and Ishmael in an almost inhuman way in order to protect and preserve her child. Goldman chooses to interpret the word *play* in Genesis 21:9 as an expression of mockery (cf. NIV). Sarah sees how Ishmael teases Isaac and mocks him for his clumsiness, and she hits Ishmael as punishment (132–134). As Sarah lays hands on Ishmael, she perceives how much Hagar hates her, and this hate makes her cold. In order to protect Isaac from evil, these two people must be removed: "And since love is not only good and warm, but also protective, and since love must protect itself, secure those who are subject to its power, since love—once known and recognized—cannot imagine living without the beloved, so the essence of love is not only good, but also ruthless" (134; my translation). Abraham tries to reason with Sarah: "'You do not own Hagar,' he said, 'and she too is a human being'" (138), but Sarah has God on her side. Abraham, weak and fragile, fails to defend Hagar and Ishmael. He recognizes that this atrocity is unforgivable, but he lets it happen anyway. However, something in Abraham is destroyed that day, and his relationship with God will never be the same again (139). Sometime later, Abraham takes Isaac with him and sets out with wood for burnt offerings but without a sacrificial animal (141).

Klintefelt chooses the alternative path. Told from Hagar's perspective, Klintefelt's retelling highlights Sarah's unfounded jealousy. Hagar describes how Sarah cannot bear to see the boys together. There is no question of Ishmael wanting to hurt Isaac; instead, the two brothers play peacefully together. Hagar is also angry with Abraham and his apathy: "He had lifted the child onto her shoulders and given her a sack of water. He didn't even look her in the eye. The cruelty, the injustice, the powerlessness she felt all cried out within her. Why did he allow this, it was after all his own son? Why did he let the jealous one decide? And after all that he had whispered to her under the cover of night?" (113; my translation).

## Sacrificing a Child

The Bible does not mention Sarah after her decision to send Hagar away (Gen 21:9–12). Even so, there is no indication that she dies soon afterward. On the contrary, her death at the age of 127 is only reported in Genesis 23:1. Before we get there, we must endure one of the most infamous biblical texts ever, called in Jewish tradition "the binding of Isaac" and in Christian tradition "the sacrifice of Isaac." Both names convey a version of the text's message. Although Abraham "merely" binds Isaac to the altar, he also shows his willingness to sacrifice him. We read with increasing horror how father and son walk together toward Mount Moriah and how an angel saves Isaac at the last minute.

The sense of time in Genesis 21–23 is unclear. First, how old is Isaac at the beginning of chapter 22? Is he still a young boy who does not really understand what is happening, or is he a grown man actively participating in the journey toward his own death? Second, how close to death is Sarah at the end of chapter 22? Does she live on for several years in good health, or does she die almost immediately afterward?

The text is sparse and none of the characters show any emotion. Despite this, and perhaps because of it, the reader cannot help but speculate about what the various characters are thinking and feeling. The story evokes strong emotions in most people. Is Abraham doing the right thing in obeying God, or should he protest (as he does against God's decision to destroy Sodom in Gen 18)? Should Isaac, depending on his age of course, run away once he realizes the significance of the lack of sacrificial animals, rather than being complicit in his own death (an aspect which has contributed to the use of Gen 22 as a type for the suffering and death of Jesus in Christian tradition)? A grown-up Isaac could easily wrestle down a centenarian Abraham. Finally, does Sarah know what her husband has decided to do, or does Abraham choose not to inform his wife of his real intentions with her only, longed for child?

Genesis 22, like the earlier Genesis 6–9 (chapter 1), reflects on blind obedience. While God commands Abraham to sacrifice Isaac, it is the angel of the Lord who prevents him from doing so. Is God so shocked by Abraham's obedience that he is ashamed to show himself? Alternatively, is God angry with Abraham for not protesting? What does Abraham's test actually entail, and is it possible to determine whether he passes it or not? Is Abraham's blind obedience in fact a failure? Should Abraham not have known better than to believe that God requires human sacrifice? Is the ram, which Abraham ultimately sacrifices in place of Isaac, nothing but collateral damage, dying only because Abraham does not know God well enough?

Last but not least, what happened afterward? Is Isaac able to reconnect with his father after this shattering event, when he is forced to face the truth that Abraham chooses God over his own son? Or is the trauma too deep for the relationship to ever heal? There is a hint in the Hebrew text, where Abraham and Isaac "walk together" to Moriah but not afterward. The same question applies to Sarah. Is there any possibility for Sarah to trust her husband again after it turns out that he was prepared to sacrifice their son? Is there a link between chapter 22 and Sarah's death in chapter 23? Does Sarah die because she cannot live with the knowledge of Abraham's behavior?

## Sarah's Death

Goldman links Sarah's death to Abraham's willingness to sacrifice Isaac in Genesis 22. When Sarah notices that Abraham has gone off with Isaac, she goes mad with fear. The lack of sacrificial animals scares her beyond reason, and for the first time in her life she prays to God. In her prayer, she accuses him of his silence toward her and of his treatment of and power over Abraham. She herself was never important to God. He never spoke to her, never asked her opinion, and never incorporated her into his covenant with Abraham. Instead, he used her body to demonstrate his power. Ignoring her desire for children, he allowed her to suffer month after month, then perfected her humiliation by giving her a child when her exhausted, old body was no longer fully able to carry it. But she accepted the gift, grateful to experience the love of Isaac. It was worth all the suffering. But now, when Sarah fears Abraham's intentions, she can take no more and falls to the ground and dies (143–150).

## Sarah's Responsibilities

The poet Shin Shifra takes a further step away from the text when she uses the story of Abraham, Sarah, and Isaac in her poem "יצחק" (Isaac) to describe the violence that is practiced in modern Israel in defense of both God and country:

| No ram was caught in the thicket for me.<br>I bound<br>And I slaughtered.<br>God did not accept<br>He laughed. | לי לא נאחז איל בסבך.<br>עקדתי<br>ואשחט.<br>אלהים לא שעה<br>הוא צחק. |
|---|---|

This poem connects two biblical texts that both deal with violence against close family members. In Genesis 4:5, God accepts Abel's sacrifice but not Cain's, resulting in Cain's murder of Abel; in Genesis 18, Abraham binds and almost murders Isaac. Abraham and Cain, in Shifra's poem, become people who are prepared to commit murder because of God. For these two people, no ram will be at hand to save them. Moreover, Shifra allows Abraham and Sarah to merge so that both parents are held responsible. The laughter, which was originally Sarah's, now becomes God's evil laughter at humanity's willingness to do violence to each other and sacrifice each other to no avail.

This leads to the question of whether Sarah is partly to blame for Isaac's traumatic near-death experience. The poet Yehudit Kafri takes the question to its extreme in his poem "בראשית" (In the beginning). Should Sarah not have prevented Abraham from taking Isaac with him? Should she not have realized, even when father and son left without sacrificial animals, that there was danger ahead? Should she not have known by now that she could not trust God to preserve Isaac?

| | |
|---|---|
| And where was Sarai?<br>How could she depend<br>on a God so tyrannical<br>to protect at the last moment?<br>Why didn't she shout<br>even early on,<br>when he just hitched the donkey<br>and loaded the wood<br>(216–218) | ואיפו היתה שרי?<br>איך היא יכלה לסמך<br>על אל כל כך עריץ<br>שיגן ברגע האחרון<br>למה היא לא צעקה<br>עוד קדם,<br>כשרק רתם את החמור<br>והעמיס את העצים |

The poem makes a very strong case that Sarah should have protested, in the same way that Abraham had previously argued against God over God's plans to destroy Sodom and Gomorrah (Gen 18). If Sarah had protested, stood in the way, and prevented Abraham from taking away their longed for son, the son they had been waiting maybe more than seventy years for, then perhaps everyone could have escaped the utter fear and trembling of Genesis 22.

In a milder way, Halter also leaves some responsibility to Sarah. The difference lies in Halter's redemptive ending. Filled with dark forebodings, Sarah watches as Abraham takes Isaac in his arms and sets off for Mount Moriah. Sarah follows from a distance. She doubts her premonition—for how can it be true—but she continues anyway. When she sees Abraham with a drawn knife, she turns to God and cries out:

> "Yahweh, God of Abraham, listen to my voice. A mother's voice. You cannot demand my son's life, Isaac's life. Not you. Not the God of justice. [. . .] Who would obey a God who spreads death and kills the weak? [. . .] I've never seen you abandon a just man. You saved Lot. Is Isaac worth less than the just men of Sodom? [. . .] Don't reject my prayer, think of us, the women. Is it through us that your Covenant will sow the future, from generation to generation. I cry to you, Yahweh: keep your promise to me, and my hope will always be in you." (312–313)

Sarah then sees the ram stuck in the bush, calls out to Abraham who also sees it, and he releases Isaac, who runs into his mother's open arms (313).

In sharp contrast, Card completely chickens out. After having Abraham declare clearly to Sarah that he would never kill their son (315), Card ends his book with Sarah watching with love and faith in her heart as Abraham and Isaac set out for Mount Moriah (329). Card seems to find this open ending satisfying, but for me the last page of the book instead shows Card's total inability to relate to the precipitous depth of the Bible.

* * *

As I mentioned at the beginning of this chapter, there are aspects of the story of Sarah that are deadly. By this I mean that the Old Testament texts on involuntary childlessness can lead to much suffering if used carelessly in a theological context. It is important to understand that according to the Old Testament view, which was influenced by the lack of medical knowledge at the time, women are always guilty of infertility. Today we know that this is not the case. For this reason alone, these texts should be handled with care. The authors of the Bible lacked our knowledge of what leads to involuntary childlessness, and we should not embrace this ignorance and make theology out of it. At the same time, it is equally important to realize that the Bible itself does not hold God responsible for Sarah's inability to have children. Although Sarah claims this, her statement only reflects her personal opinion. It can be tempting in times of difficulty to claim that God is responsible for things that he has not caused at all.

What I do think a lot about, however, is God's at least seemingly one-sided communication. How can Sarah be part of Abraham's God-given vision if

God only talks to Abraham? How can Sarah trust that what Abraham claims that God is saying really comes from God? Is God speaking to both of them, but only Abraham is listening? This is of course a possible interpretation, but the text does not claim it. Overall, the story of Sarah and Abraham raises many questions about God's call and our (in)ability to hear God's voice. I have moved many times in my life, from Sweden to England, to Israel and back to England, to the US and then to Scotland, and most recently home to Sweden. I hope I have followed God's call in my life. What I do know is that my husband and I have deliberated every move since our wedding in Israel in 1998, sometimes because my husband got a job and sometimes because I got a job. We have prayed and discussed and prayed even more before each move. The story of Sarah scares me: How would I have reacted if my husband had suddenly informed me that God had called him to, say, Timbuktu, and asked me simply to pack my bags and go where God had called him (and by implication, me, even though I had not heard anything)? Maybe the story of Abraham and Sarah can convey the importance of actually talking to each other about God's call in our lives and not assuming that we all act according to the same plan and hear the same thing.

Moving on to Abraham. Let us return to the description of Abraham in Hebrews 11:8–12, where he is portrayed as a hero of faith (for vv. 17–19, see below). As in the case of Noah (chapter 1), the message of Hebrews is in line with the message of the Old Testament. Yes, Abraham shows excellent faith when he listens to God, leaves his homeland, and settles in a foreign land (vv. 8–10). Yes, Abraham shows outstanding faith when he begets Isaac (v. 11), even though he and Sarah are rather old. Moreover, Abraham's relationship with God in Genesis 18 is an extraordinary model as he dialogues with God in his attempt to save the inhabitants of Sodom (cf. chapter 1). At the same time, other texts in Genesis emphasize Abraham's unbelief. I would therefore like to add a few lines to the portrait of Abraham in Hebrews: "In unbelief, Abraham chose to jeopardize God's promise of a son by allowing Sarah to enter Pharaoh's harem. In unbelief, Abraham chose to beget Ishmael and not wait for God's promise of a son with Sarah to be fulfilled." Abraham becomes, for me, a man who combines both belief and unbelief. Abraham shows great faith in God's call to travel to foreign lands but considerably less faith in God's promise of children. This mixture of faith and unbelief is probably something that most of us recognize. We can be very confident in some contexts while doubting in others. This does not detract from our faith in the former area, but it leaves much to be desired in the latter.

So, without in any way disparaging or questioning Abraham's good qualities, I hold him deeply responsible for his views on what I call, for want of a better word, his macabre advocacy of an open marriage. I believe wholeheartedly that the very idea of subjecting one's spouse, on two occasions, to a period of time in another person's harem is reprehensible. I would go so far as to say that there may be times of persecution when forced infidelity is a necessary evil for survival, but that is not what the Bible talks about in Genesis 12 and 20. Yes, Abraham and his family suffer famine, but Abraham does not have to take Sarah to Egypt (or to Gerar). To draw a biblical parallel—as far as I know, none of Jacob's sons take their wives with them when they go to Egypt to try to buy grain from Joseph (see chapter 3). Nor am I entirely averse to what in wartime might be called "amorous infiltration" (think Mata Hari), that is, when spies seduce high-ranking people in the enemy camp in order to obtain classified information. So, with that in mind, the story of Sarah and Abraham raises the question of how we should relate to Abraham's unequivocal cowardice and his choice to prioritize his own good over the well-being of his fellow human beings. What would we have done in his place?

Sarah, of course, will not get off scot-free either. Like Abraham, she too is a fascinating combination of good and evil. I empathize with her longing for children and understand from the bottom of my heart her sadness and disappointment. At the same time, I refuse to trivialize her treatment of Hagar, which I find both cruel and undignified. Sarah insists that Hagar get pregnant with Abraham and then becomes upset when Hagar turns it against her. I feel sorry for Sarah, I really do, but that does not excuse her. Female solidarity is extremely difficult in a world where men have all the power, and it is easy for women to begrudge each other happiness because it is on men's terms and they themselves are dependent on their favor. If there is only one place near power (in this case Abraham's tent), then that obviously leads to envy and strife. What would Sarah do? The choice is perhaps obvious. If she has heard God's call, then she should trust God. What would Abraham do? Hearing God's call and his promise of an heir, he should have trusted God. What should Hagar do? Actually, nothing other than what she is doing. She hears God's call and obeys him. She returns to a situation that is far from ideal for her.

Last but not least, we must dare to speak of Abraham's faith when he shows himself willing to go to Mount Moriah to sacrifice Isaac. I trust that none of us would even entertain the idea that it would be God's will that we sacrifice our children, whether as burnt offerings or in other, less tangible ways. What is our responsibility, as fellow human beings, when we see people being sacrificed? It is basically the same question as in chapter 1, just with a slightly different angle. According to Hebrews 11:17–19, Abraham acts in faith when he brings Isaac as a sacrifice. Perhaps my challenge here is that Abraham believes too much and obeys too quickly. Do not misunderstand me: On the one hand, these texts point out the enormous faith required to do something that actively contradicts a previous God-given promise and every fiber of parental instinct. If God has told Abraham that he would have descendants through Isaac (v. 18), how can that same God now require Abraham to willingly risk the fulfilment of those words? On the other hand, the Abraham of Hebrews counts on God's power to raise from the dead (v. 19). Again, such faith shows Abraham's amazing trust in God, but to me such faith verges on challenging God and putting him to the test (cf. Luke 4:10–12). In the end, the portrait of Abraham in Hebrews 11:17–19 raises more questions than it solves.

Abraham's obedience and faith in Genesis 22 has implications for how we perceive Sarah. If Sarah discerns what Abraham is about to do when he and Isaac take the donkey and prepare to leave, then it is probably her human duty to try to prevent it. At the same time, to decide, as Abraham does, to kill his son without consulting the mother of said child, well, that is unacceptable. Do we really believe in a God who requires us to sacrifice what we hold most dear for no apparent benefit? Is our faith really strengthened by being forced to obey something that is ethically indefensible from every other point of view? Whatever the lesson God is trying to teach Abraham (and Sarah), however, the Israelites continue to believe that God wants human sacrifice. Two more fathers, Jephthah (Judg 11:39) and Saul (1 Sam 14:44), will prove willing to kill their children, and only one child, Jonathan, will survive (chapter 6).

CHAPTER THREE

# Joseph

## *Spoiled Brat or Traumatized Survivor?*

> Joseph is a fruitful bough, a fruitful bough by a spring; his branches run over the wall. The archers fiercely attacked him; they shot at him and pressed him hard. Yet his bow remained taut, and his arms were made agile by the hands of the Mighty One of Jacob, by the name of the Shepherd, the Rock of Israel, by the God of your father, who will help you, by the Almighty who will bless you with blessings of heaven above, blessings of the deep that lies beneath, blessings of the breasts and of the womb. The blessings of your father are stronger than the blessings of the eternal mountains, the bounties of the everlasting hills; may they be on the head of Joseph, on the brow of him who was set apart from his brothers. (Gen 49:22–26)

JOSEPH IS PROBABLY the most annoying person in the Bible. I have a younger brother myself, so I know that younger brothers can be difficult, but I have never been on the verge of selling him as a slave, in contrast to Madicken, Astrid Lindgren's fearless and kindhearted seven-year-old hero, who for a brief moment is willing to sell her younger sister Lisabet, only to regret it deeply afterwards.[1] Rather, I want to keep my sibling. Joseph's brothers, however, do not, and I must say that I understand them, at least in part. Who wants to hang out with such a self-righteous guy who also has the insensitivity to talk openly about his dreams of greatness and dominance? Who wants to be told to bow down to the ground before such an insufferable human being? He is also gifted, a high-flying careerist, rather vindictive, and definitely a looker. The Joseph story reminds me of an advert I once saw for a fancy car, with the caption "Do you not wish you had studied a bit harder?" The implication was clear: Doing well in school pays off in the long run.

Despite his brilliance, the motherless Joseph also gives a fragile impression. He is the victim of systematic bullying, and the situation is so serious that he almost dies. Home is not a safe haven for Joseph, given that his bullies are in his immediate home environment. Moreover, there seem to be no adults around him to come to his defense. Joseph is left alone and takes refuge in his pride and intelligence. He refuses to give up and is forced to realize that empathy has no place on the map when it comes to survival.

So, while Joseph is a bit of a handful, he is also one of the most fascinating and complex characters in the Bible. Together, we are going to take a closer look at this superintelligent, incredibly talented, yet lonely and rather broken person.

## Narratives

In order to deepen our dialogue with the story of Joseph found in Genesis 37–50, and to increase our understanding of Joseph as a character, we shall analyze in more detail a number of novels, poems, and songs.

**Anita Diamant** (b. 1951) is an American Jewish author. Her book *The Red Tent* retells and extends the material about Dinah found in Genesis 34 from the point of view of Dinah. In this way, it serves as a counterpoint to the Bible's own, male-centered perspective where Dinah is only the victim of men's actions.

*The Red Tent* (St Martin's, 1997).

**Britt G. Hallqvist** (1914–1997) was a Swedish hymn writer, poet, and translator, and Bertil Hallin (b. 1931) is a Church of Sweden musician and music teacher. Together they released two collections of children's songs, *Titta vad jag fann!* and *Det visste inte kejsarn om*, both of which were recorded on gramophone disc by Ulla Neumann.

"Josef Får En Ny Rock" (Josef Gets a New Coat), in the album *Titta vad jag fann!* (released in 1973).

**Angela Hunt** (b. 1957) is an American Christian author who has written more than a hundred books, many centered on biblical characters. Although they often retell the biblical stories from a female perspective, they also tend to embrace their inherently patriarchal outlook.

*Dreamer* (Steeple Hill, 2004).

**Yehudit Kafri** (b. 1935) is an Israeli Jewish writer (see Chapter 2). Her poem about Potiphar's wife explores how men can abuse their power over women by refusing to give women sexual satisfaction.

"אשת פוטיפר" (Potiphar's wife), in *Does David Still Play Before You? Israeli Poetry and the Bible*, ed. David C. Jacobson (Wayne State University Press, 1997), 171–172.

**Thomas Mann** (1875–1955) is considered one of the truly great German writers. He was awarded the Nobel Prize in Literature in 1929, and his best-known works include *Buddenbrooks: Verfall einer Familie* (*Buddenbrooks: The Decline of a Family*) and *Der Zauberberg* (*The Magic Mountain*). Mann's retelling is deeply influenced by Jewish stories about Joseph, preserved in, among others, Jubilees (second century BCE), Testaments of the Twelve Patriarchs (second century CE), and later material in the rabbinic Genesis Rabbah.

*Joseph and His Brothers*, trans. John E. Woods (Knopf, 2005). Originally published as *Joseph und seine Brüder* (S. Fischer, 1934–1943).

**Regina Rushing** is an American author who has so far only written this book, although its last page promises a sequel. The book is based on the brief description in Genesis 41:39–45 of Joseph's time as ruler of Egypt, but also includes flashbacks of Joseph's earlier experiences.

*Seal Of The Sand Dweller* (Dominia, 2018).

## An Insufferable Young Man

Joseph first appears in Genesis 30:24, the record of his birth. After that, we do not hear from him for six chapters, although theoretically, as a young teenager, he could have participated in the atrocities against the men of Shechem, which were led by Simeon and Levi with the help of "the other sons of Jacob": "And the other sons of Jacob came upon the slain, and plundered the city, because their sister had been defiled. They took their flocks and their herds, their donkeys, and whatever was in the city and in the field. All their wealth, all their little ones and their wives, all that was in the houses, they captured and made their prey" (Gen 34:27–29). We meet Joseph again when he is seventeen, and we immediately suspect that this young man is probably rather tiresome. Is he a snitch or a person with (a little too much) pathos for justice? "This is the story of the family of Jacob. Joseph, being seventeen years old, was shepherding the flock with his brothers; he was a helper to the sons of Bilhah and Zilpah, his father's wives; and Joseph brought a bad report of them to their father" (Gen 37:2). To make matters worse, he is also his father's favorite, which of course contributes to his brothers' envy and disgust. "Now Israel loved Joseph more than any other of his children, because he was the son of his old age; and he had made him a long robe with sleeves. But when his brothers saw that their father loved him more than all his brothers, they hated him, and could not speak peaceably to him" (Gen 37:3–4). In parallel, there is something sad about Joseph. He loses his mother, Rachel, before his seventeenth birthday but probably much earlier. It is difficult to know how big the age gap is between Joseph and Benjamin, his younger brother whose birth leads to the death of their mother Rachel. There is thus no warm and safe maternal figure to whom Joseph can turn, and there is no sign that his aunt, Leah, is looking after him in her sister's place. Rather, there is reason to suspect that the rivalry between the two sisters has led Leah to disregard Rachel's child.

His father, Jacob, is grieving for Rachel and is probably trying to ease the pain by spoiling Joseph. All this pampering, however, is unlikely to make Joseph feel any better. A mollycoddled child rarely feels good and usually wants to blend in with the crowd rather than be singled out and noticed by the adults around him. Joseph is caught in the middle, spoiled but neglected. He is lost, lonely, and unbearable.

Jacob unwittingly favors his eleventh son by giving him, according to the NRSV, "a long robe with sleeves." What has happened to Joseph's "multicoloured dreamcoat" that Andrew Lloyd Webber and Tim Rice write about and that appears in the Authorized King James Version ("a coat of many colours"; Gen 37:3)?[2] The word denoting Joseph's garment (כתנת פסים) occurs in only two places in the Old Testament: here in Genesis 37:3 and in 2 Samuel 13:19, where it describes King David's daughter Tamar's dress, which she tears after her half brother Amnon rapes her. There are vague indications that the Hebrew word may mean *multicolored* (the Greek translation has ποικίλον, meaning "many-sided" or "varied"), but it is difficult to judge. It is, however, beyond doubt that the garment is beautiful, as befits a princess's attire. Jacob, the shepherd, gives his son Joseph an outfit similar to that which the later King David gives his daughter. I imagine how Reuben, Simeon, Levi, Judah, Dan, Naphtali, Gad, Asher, Issachar, and Zebulun are forced to inherit each other's clothes, only suddenly to see that the next brother, Joseph, is given wonderful, brand-new, perhaps rainbow-colored (girl?) clothes. Quite extravagant, perhaps a little queer, but also quite ominous, as Tamar's fate is not to be envied.

*Excursus: Clothing in the Old Testament*

Joseph is concerned about his appearance: Not only does he have a beautiful body, he also seems to be a little obsessed with clothes. No fewer than six passages mention clothes that Joseph either wears himself (Gen 37:3; 41:14, 42) or gives to others (Gen 45:22). Joseph's clothes play an important role in his interaction with Potiphar's wife, where she grabs his clothes and uses them as "evidence" of Joseph's attempted rape (39:12–18). Finally, when Jacob sees his son's blood-soaked clothes, Jacob tears his own clothes in an expression of grief (Gen 37:31–34).

Clothing in the Bible often plays a symbolic function. A person's clothes say a lot about identity. Getting new clothes often means taking on a new and better role (see Zech 3). At the same time, when you lose clothes, things often go downhill. In Joseph's case, his garment is removed when he is sold into slavery, and his clothes are ripped off by Potiphar's wife just before he goes to prison. Meanwhile, he is given a much-needed new outfit when he is brought before Pharaoh and another when he becomes ruler of Egypt. The brothers are likewise given new garments as an indication of their new status in Egypt as Joseph's brothers.

Joseph and David are the biblical characters who gain the most clothes, and both climb the social ladder. While David gains clothes and weapons on his way toward the throne, Saul and his family lose the same. The exchanges of clothing symbolize the transfer of God's promises from Saul to David (cf. 1 Sam 15:27, where Saul tears Samuel's cloak). Initially, David is not ready to take Saul's place and thus rejects Saul's armor (1 Sam 17:38–39). After defeating Goliath, however, he has grown into his kingly role so that he can accept Jonathan's gift of clothing (1 Sam 18:4). Later still, David steals Saul's robe (1 Sam 24:5), symbolizing how David will steal Saul's throne. Only Saul's son Jonathan, willingly and seemingly without ulterior motive, gives not only his clothes but also his weapons to David. He thus gives up his kingship and symbolically abdicates in David's favor (see chapter 6).

Joseph is a dreamer who, at a young age, lacks rudimentary emotional intelligence. While it is possible to dream of power and honor, even if it is probably a bit much to see oneself as exalted and adored by one's family, including one's parents, it is absolutely not becoming to broadcast it. Even Jacob, who would probably otherwise lets Joseph get away with quite a bit, soon has enough: "But when he told it to his father and to his brothers, his father rebuked him, and said to him, 'What kind of dream is this that you have had? Shall we indeed come, I and your mother and your brothers, and bow to the ground before you?' So his brothers were jealous of him, but his father kept the matter in mind" (Gen 37:10–11). Jacob later sends Joseph to check on his brothers: "Go now, see if it is well with your brothers and with the flock; and bring word back to me" (Gen 37:14). It is not clear what Joseph is supposed to do. Why does Jacob think something is wrong? Is he sending Joseph to spy on his brothers? Is this the kind of occasion Genesis 37:2 has in mind when it says that Joseph reported all the evil the brothers had done to his father? At the same time, Jacob's action is deeply irresponsible. Is he blind to not see the hatred simmering beneath the surface of his older sons? Does he refuse to see, even though he knows of the massacre that his sons carried out on the men of Shechem (Gen 34:25–31), that Joseph is in mortal danger when he goes, alone and exposed, to meet his brothers? Jacob does not seem to understand that his favoritism toward Joseph hurts Joseph significantly more than it benefits him.

Once Joseph appears, the brothers start planning to commit new atrocities. They first lean toward murdering Joseph but eventually decide to throw him into an empty well and then sell him into slavery. They also take Joseph's hated robe, soak it in blood, and thus trick their father into believing that Joseph has been killed by wild animals. Joseph's megalomania does not excuse this behavior. It will never be right either to murder people or sell them into slavery, no matter how troublesome they may be. The brothers also hurt their father as their behavior leads to Jacob's lifelong grief. "Then Jacob tore his garments, and put sackcloth on his loins, and mourned for his son for many days. All his sons and all his daughters sought to comfort him; but he refused to be comforted, and said, 'No, I shall go down to Sheol to my son, mourning.' Thus his father bewailed him" (Gen 37:34–35). For the rest of their lives, Joseph's brothers are thus forced to live with the consequences of their offense in a very tangible way.

## The Little Tattletale

The question is whether Joseph is a snitch or a man with a strong sense of justice. The difference is that while the former reports so that the perpetrator will be brought to justice, the latter reports so that the victim will not be harmed. In some cultures, there is a blurred line between these two characteristics and a person who reports injustice can easily be seen as disloyal to the group and prevailing social structures. Personally, I tend to favor the other extreme: What is right is right and those who do not do what is right should be held accountable for their actions. I strongly dislike the social requirement to protect someone in cases where it is not deserving. So, having said that, I can easily identify with Joseph, who refuses to turn a blind eye to abuses and dangers.

The author who best emphasizes this aspect is Regina Rushing in her book *Seal Of The Sand Dweller*. Her Joseph, now an overseer in Egypt, has discovered that several of Pharaoh's closest men are skimming off the incoming treasure, stealing valuables from the storerooms and thus deceiving him. Joseph, scared and exposed despite his high position of power, debates with himself whether to remain silent about the situation or expose it: "His fears cornered him here in the darkness of such naked solitude. Temptation whispers. Keep quiet and manage the king's house. He'd kept quiet in the storerooms, and still someone tried to burn him alive. Yet there was some merit to staying quiet [. . .] And how long would that last before you are, once again, made a scapegoat for another man's lie? The king's watchmen mocked him with their flattery in spite of the king's favor. Or because of it" (194–195). Joseph continues to recall what happened the last time he tried to make men in power, on that occasion his father, aware of irregularities. His father, Jacob, had been his only defender, and Joseph had done everything, even spying on his brothers, to stay on his good side. In many ways, the young Joseph's behavior sheds light on his precarious situation between his father and brothers. In Rushing's hands, Joseph is not a tattletale but a person who wants justice. As a teenager, however, he had lacked both the wisdom and the maturity to do it well, and so everything had gone wrong: "How clever he'd once thought himself, bringing his father the news of warring wives and sons with an arrogance that only added to the rift in their camp. He gripped the side of his couch and licked at bitter tears. If he'd kept his mouth shut, they might have all been spared a few nights of contention in the camp, a few episodes of revenge. They might have loved him better if he had simply said nothing" (195–196). Joseph also remembers how he became Jacob's spy to try to keep his father's love:

> Yoseph neared the king's hall as a nuance of bitter memories wafted by him like the scent of old wounds. He could still see Asher's smirk. He could feel Gad's stinging smack on his chest, a hard shake of his

thin shoulders. Little tattler, they would call him when he reported their escapades to Father. Yes, he was certainly that. He was the little tattler in the camp, the weakling, a poor desperate boy, fearing the loss of his father's love and attention after his mother's death. He had no one else. They told him he had no one else and kept him from Leah to prove it. He blew out the wounding memory with a ragged exhale. There was greater sense in staying quiet on the matter of the king's coffer, but he knew he would not do it. (205)

## A Spoiled, Lonely Child

Many authors comment on Joseph's childhood more generally. Notably, Anita Diamant allows Dinah, her narrator, to emphasize Joseph's loneliness as a child. In a conversation with Dinah when they meet in Egypt many years later, Joseph tells her how he used to hate Benjamin for taking his mother away from him. Now he would do anything to see his younger brother again (351).

Others recognize Joseph's position in the family as both different and special. Does Joseph understand how exposed and unprotected Jacob's favoritism makes him? On one side, Britt G. Hallqvist and Bertil Hallin's children's song emphasizes how Joseph does not want to be noticed at all and would rather he had never been given the beautiful outfit:

| | |
|---|---|
| Joseph got a coat from Father, long and fine and expensive it was.<br>Look at Joseph, he has finery, said Reuben sourly and bitterly.<br>And the others agreed, including little Benjamin.<br>Look at Joseph, he is proud, because he has received a robe.<br>Joseph thought his coat was too long and wide and thick<br>He took it off at last and went out in the meadow.<br>Joseph was quite sad because of the coat he got from Father.<br>(My translation) | Josef fick en rock av far,<br>lång och fin och dyr den var.<br>Se på Josef han har fjäsk,<br>sade Ruben sur och besk.<br>Och de andra stämde in,<br>också lille Benjamin.<br>Se på Josef han är stolt,<br>för att han har fått en kolt.<br>Josef tyckte att hans rock,<br>var för lång och vid och tjock.<br>Han tog av sig den till slut,<br>och i hagen gick han ut.<br>Ganska ledsen Josef var,<br>för den rock han fått av far. |

On the other side, well represented by Thomas Mann, we find a Joseph who has not the faintest idea of how to deal with people. When Jacob's wives see Joseph dressed in his marvelous coat, having earlier belonged to his mother and now given to him by his father, their words of admiration are dripping with irony. Joseph, however, does not hear the undertones:

> It seems almost implausible, but Joseph did not sense the thickly spread bitterness and cunning in the women's words. His sense of fulfilment, his childlike but nonetheless reprehensibly blissful self-confidence left him deaf and unreceptive to any warnings. He took pleasure in the sweetness of their words, convinced he deserved nothing but sweetness and incapable of making the least effort to probe any deeper. That was the reprehensible part! An indifference to, an ignorance of other people's inner lives reveals a fully skewed relationship to reality and gives birth to delusion. [. . .] His blissful self-confidence was, despite all unambiguous signs to the contrary, a kind of self-pampering that told him everyone loved him more than they loved themselves and he therefore need not take them into consideration. (393)

Mann's Joseph is highly intelligent and knows a lot of facts. He can read and write, he can count, and he knows stories, myths, and the constellations of the heavens (15–29), but he lacks understanding and interest in his fellow human beings. At the same time, there is another side to Joseph that realizes the need to hide his intelligence. He lets his father win when they play games together (120). Reuben ponders the situation when he notices Joseph's strategy: "'Yes, that's how it's done,' Reuben thought to himself, his gaze turning farther inward than before. 'Such is the deceit of men who are blessed, that is their sort of deception. They must keep their lamp under a bushel to prevent its light from doing them harm, while others must lie about their own brightness just to stay even'" (402). Joseph, the gifted young man, glimpses, but not enough, how precarious his situation really is. He understands, but not fully, how he unconsciously influences those around him, making them both admire and loathe him, because they are jealous and because they feel inadequate.

## A Powerless Slave

Joseph is sold as a slave to "Potiphar, an officer of Pharaoh, the captain of the guard, an Egyptian" (Gen 37:36; 39:1). The Hebrew word used here can be translated as eunuch (*saris*; סריס), and this is how it is understood in the Septuagint (σπάδοντι). We will come back to the possible implications of this for our understanding of Joseph and the people around him.

The Bible now chooses to tell us clearly, twice, that "The Lord was with Joseph, and he became a successful man; he was in the house of his Egyptian master" (Gen 39:2–3). Although it is terrible to lose one's personal freedom and to be forced to become someone's property, it could have been even worse for Joseph. He does not end up in the fields and is not forced to do hard physical labor; there will be no dirty pyramid building for our handsome young man but rather administrative office work combined with valet duties indoors. "So Joseph found favor in his sight and attended him; he made him overseer of his house and put him in charge of all that he had" (Gen 39:4). Why, we may wonder, is Joseph being treated differently? The answer is probably to be found in verse 6, namely that Joseph was "handsome and good-looking." It would be such a shame to spoil this beauty with heavy manual labor. "So he left all that he had in Joseph's charge; and, with him there, he had no concern for anything but the food that he ate. Now Joseph was handsome and good-looking" (Gen 39:6). There is again something androgynous about Joseph. His handsome appearance and beautiful form are depicted in words that are often used in connection with women. The Bible uses exactly the same language in its portrayal of Joseph and Rachel. Unfortunately, the NRSV does not reflect this similarity, as it deems Rachel to be "graceful and beautiful" (Gen 29:17) while it denotes Joseph as "handsome and good-looking" (Gen 39:6). The language is thus adapted to fit the person's perceived gender rather than the original Hebrew. Elsewhere, the Bible uses similar expressions to describe Sarah (Gen 12:11), Absalom's daughter Tamar (2 Sam 14:27), and Vashti (Esth 1:11), who all have "a beautiful appearance," and Abigail (2 Sam 25:3), who has "a beautiful form."

Joseph's beauty, however, does not lead to anything good, but instead to even more jealousy and sadness. Joseph becomes the first, but unfortunately not the last, sexual assault victim in the Bible. Potiphar's wife takes advantage of her position as Joseph's superior and decides to have sex with the handsome young slave. Joseph does not want to cooperate and instead flees, (half) naked as he abandons his garments.

> She caught hold of his garment, saying, "Lie with me!" But he left his garment in her hand, and fled and ran outside. When she saw that he had left his garment in her hand and had fled outside, she called out to the members of her household and said to them, "See, my husband has brought among us a Hebrew to insult us! He came in to me to lie with me, and I cried out with a loud voice; and when he heard me raise my voice and cry out, he left his garment beside me, and fled outside." (Gen 39:12–15)

The scorned woman soon takes her revenge on Joseph, turning the story to her advantage and accusing Joseph of attempted rape. In her accusations, she emphasizes Joseph's status as an outsider by calling him "the Hebrew slave." This ethnic slur alludes to prejudices about how foreign men pose a sexual danger to women (39:17). The ethnic and social differences between the two means that everyone believes Potiphar's wife, and no one believes Joseph, the foreign slave.

This story has different dimensions. From the ancient Egyptian perspective, Joseph belongs to Potiphar and his wife, and if the wife feels like using her slave sexually, that would be perfectly fine. It can be seen as her right. It is also quite possible that Joseph's sexual favors are part of his "job description" and the main reason why he was bought in the first place: If Potiphar is a eunuch, he may have purchased Joseph to provide him and his wife with an heir. When Joseph fails in this elementary task, he no longer fulfils any function in the household. From this perspective, it is Joseph and not Potiphar's wife who does not know his place.

This attitude is of course unthinkable from a modern Western perspective where a no is a no. You cannot own another person, and every person has the right to their own body. From this modern perspective, the reason for Joseph's reluctance is irrelevant. It does not matter whether Joseph is acting out of respect for Potiphar, lack of desire for his wife, or general unwillingness to have sex.

A comparative reading with Genesis 16 and 21 gives us even more to think about (chapter 2). In several respects Joseph is comparable to Hagar. Both are slaves and thus find themselves in a subordinate position of dependence. Hagar is commanded to give Abraham a child, and she obeys, despite all that this entails. How would we readers have reacted if Hagar had refused, left Abraham's tent, and fled into the night? Would we have seen her as the heroine who managed to resist Abraham's invitation, or do the different gender perspectives of the texts influence our perception and understanding of the characters' similar behavior? Do the men become heroes while the women are either seen as servants who should know their subordinate place or as seductresses who should be given short shrift? Or does the Bible's built-in ethnic bias play a role? Do we intuitively root for the Israelites (Abraham and Joseph), while we do not feel the same inclination to show compassion toward the Egyptians (Hagar and Potiphar's wife)?

## The Irreproachable Hero Who Passes the Test with Flying Colors

The story of the encounter between Joseph and Potiphar's wife can be understood from many different perspectives. The story may be read as a step in Joseph's development curve. Joseph goes from being the spoiled dreamer, who does not know when to talk and when to shut up, to a man who is in full control of his life and does not let his emotions rule his actions. Joseph then becomes the man of action who does not allow himself to be led astray but stays on the right, narrow path, thus showing respect to both God and Potiphar. The woman, Potiphar's anonymous wife, is in turn reduced to a test that Joseph must pass. We are used to this version, where the man is the person who acts, if only to flee from danger. We are so used to it that we often and too quickly give Joseph the active role, whatever the situation.

Most books choose the traditional interpretation. First up is Mann, who devotes almost half of the third volume of Joseph und seine Brüder (Hereafter, *Joseph and His Brothers*) to the episode. His retelling is heavily influenced by early Jewish traditions in which Potiphar's wife is portrayed as a desperate woman who, blinded by love or lust for the beautiful Joseph, subjects Joseph to one more intricate seduction attempt after another over the course of three years. Mann describes in elaborate detail how this seductress gradually succumbs to her unbridled and unrestrained passion. At the same time, Mann shows some understanding of Potiphar's wife, as he insists that Potiphar was a eunuch, which, as stated above, the Hebrew word *saris* can mean. Potiphar's wife is thus stuck in a situation of forced celibacy. Mann is clearly saying that we should not judge Potiphar's wife too harshly as she suffers not only from a dead marriage but from having to endure Joseph's tempting presence, which was a joy to her but at the same time a great torment: "Then one must admit that the fate of 'Potiphar's wife' (popularly regarded as a shameless seductress and the honeyed bait of evil) was not an easy one and at least grant her the sympathy arising from the insight that the implements of such a testing carry their own punishment within them" (886). Joseph himself tries to change Potiphar's wife's mind, but at the same time he enjoys the role of educator, that is, he is trying to "cure" her of her infatuation by talking only about practical matters related to the running of the house: "It was a kind of cure—and young Joseph enjoyed playing the role of instructor. His intention was—or so he thought—to divert his mistress's mind from personal to practical matters, from his eyes to his cares, and in the process to cool, disenchant, and heal her, so that he might enjoy the honor, advantage, and fine pleasure of associating with her as the object of her favor, but without any danger of plunging into that pit with which overanxious Bes had threatened him" (899–900). Joseph, consciously or subconsciously, enjoys his power over Potiphar's wife while refusing to satisfy her desire. He acts like a god, bestowing his favor by his mere presence but without giving anything concrete in return. Joseph's behavior leads both Mann and the reader to feel a strong urge to shake Joseph out of sheer frustration. Joseph, unmoved by Potiphar's wife's attempts at seduction, plays with fire to prove that he can pass the test. For Joseph, it ultimately becomes a matter of pride: "Moreover there was some self-assured cockiness, the confidence that he could venture far into danger—and always return if need be; and, as the more praiseworthy reverse of all this, there was a will to demand the impossible of himself, a proud desire to take the hard knocks, to not spare himself, to push things to their limits in order to emerge from temptation all the more triumphant to be a virtuoso of virtue" (931).

A considerably more modern but also more sordid perspective is found in Angela Hunt's portrait of Potiphar's wife. Hunt describes a woman who spends months trying to ensnare Joseph. This is not a seduction in the heat of the moment but a well-planned action. Joseph, of course, manages to escape naked into the garden with his honor intact. Despite this biblical fidelity, Hunt's portrayal disturbs me more than it should. What she does with her biblical portrait is to highlight some of the difficulties embedded in the biblical text itself. Hunt, like Mann before her, chooses to portray Potiphar as a man who has been castrated during his time as a prisoner of war. Potiphar is thus not a man who should marry. According to Hunt, however, it does not seem to dawn on Potiphar to inform his future bride of this physical aspect. He is a respectable man who has been offered a wife by Pharaoh and chooses not to decline the honor. At no point in the book does Potiphar acknowledge his part in his wife's behavior. Already, at this early stage, Potiphar's wife has become a victim and not a perpetrator. In addition, Hunt chooses to make Potiphar's wife an eighteen-year-old virgin. It takes her quite some time to realize that something is amiss in her marriage and by then it is unfortunately already too late. She is forced to face the fact that she will remain childless and that Potiphar will never give her any attention. Only then does Potiphar's wife decide to seduce the attractive Joseph and thus kill two birds with one stone.

Things do not go according to plan because Potiphar's wife falls in love with Joseph. Joseph, in turn, is flattered by her attention but seems not to have grasped what else is going on in his owners' marriage. Moreover, Joseph describes Potiphar's wife as "an indulged, lustful, bloodless creature" (163) and later speaks of her "lust-laced infatuation" (165). This contrast between Potiphar's wife's perception of the situation and Joseph's view is odd. Potiphar's wife is by no means necessarily lustful, indulged, or infatuated; she is a young woman in a completely loveless marriage who, well, bungles the situation with very severe consequences for Joseph. What makes the whole thing even more patriarchally sordid is the implicit message that women, be they Potiphar's wife or, as earlier in the book, Joseph's non-biblical love interest Tuya, should not take any initiative at all in a relationship. They should just sit quietly and passively and wait to be wooed.

## A Victim of Sexual Assault

The alternative is to read the story as an attempted rape. Potiphar's wife then becomes the perpetrator, driving the plot forward as she subjects Joseph to sexual violence. In this version, Joseph is not in control: He is the foreign slave with no self-determination. He is also not the "manly man" who appreciates that women want him and sees Potiphar's wife's behavior as a confirmation of his masculinity. Rather, he is a victim of sexual exploitation. This Joseph does not manage to resist a temptation. The fact that he gets away unscathed is purely down to luck or natural circumstances. Joseph, as the physically stronger of the two, manages to escape the danger. This brings us back to David's daughter Tamar, who wears the same kind of clothing as Joseph when Amnon rapes her. A further similarity is that Potiphar's wife uses exactly the same words as Amnon later does (Gen 39:7; 2 Sam 13:11): "Come, lie with me." The idea that Tamar would fail some kind of test when she is unable to escape unscathed is horrific. The reason she cannot escape Amnon is entirely due to the fact that her older brother, being a man, is physically stronger than she is and not because she would have been in any way flattered by his attentions. Joseph and Tamar are both victims, and the fact that one manages to escape and the other does not reflects neither their morality nor their steadfastness.

Rushing's description of Potiphar's wife falls into this category. She emphasizes that rape is usually not about sex at all but about power. This is not a woman obsessed with Joseph's beauty but one who wants to make her husband jealous. Potiphar prefers discussing the administration of the house with Joseph rather than spending time with his wife. Potiphar knows Joseph is innocent, but his pride forces him to uphold his wife's version of events (104). Potiphar's wife wants her husband to see her, and she uses Joseph for this purpose. Joseph himself is not important except as a tool to achieve this goal. In the end, Potiphar's wife is forced to realize that her action toward Joseph had everything to do with her feelings for her husband: "She swallowed, willing away the longing that scorched her belly. She lowered her gaze. 'You made far more time for Yoseph than for your wife.' There. She'd spoken from her heart. That was the last of it. 'That was no reason to ruin the reputation of a good man.' His voice croaked in soft reprimand [. . .] She smacked his hand away. 'I wanted to hurt you'" (437). Rushing's focus, however, is not on the incident itself but on the consequences that it has for Joseph. He does "not only" end up in prison but is also seen as a rapist.

## The Power-Hungry Seducer

We can also challenge the biblical text and play with the idea that it does not give us all the information we need to understand the story as a whole. Could it be that Potiphar's wife loves Joseph, and he loves her back? Is the text about seduction, where emotions are involved? Alternatively, and partly in line with a traditional male perspective, could it be that Joseph, the man, is taking advantage of Potiphar's wife? Could it be that Joseph, well aware of his beautiful body, is toying with Potiphar's wife and at the same time showing his power over her (cf. Mann above)? Joseph, taking the moral high ground, denies her sexual fulfilment.

On the one hand, Kafri's poem "אשת פוטיפר" (Potiphar's wife) is a critique of Hunt's and her peers' view of Potiphar's wife. Kafri wonders what really happens between her and Joseph. What does he whisper to her, and what invitation is in his eyes?

| | |
|---|---|
| A woman doesn't just ask a man<br>to come and lie with her.<br>Something happened between them<br>but the Bible doesn't tell<br>Joseph did get thrown in the pit<br>but he managed<br>[. . .]<br>This dreamer of dreams<br>was more practical than all the politicians | אשה לא מבקשת סתם כך מאיש<br>לבוא לשכב עמה<br>משהו קרה ביניהם<br>אבל התנ"ך לא מספר<br>יוסף אמנם השלך לבור<br>אבל הוא הסתדר<br>[. . .]<br>חולם החלומות הזה<br>היה פרקטי יותר מכל הפוליטיקאים |

Kafri refuses to believe that any woman, biblical or modern, would have so little self-respect that she would just throw herself at a man without first having received an indication that her intimacy would be welcome. In this way, Kafri deconstructs the biblical portrait of Potiphar's wife as a vengeful woman who accuses the innocent Joseph. Rather, she is a victim of Joseph's ambitions on his climb to the top of society.

On the other hand, Diamant assumes that Joseph was the lover of Potiphar's wife. At the same time, she allows Joseph to become a victim: He is sexually exploited but not by Potiphar's wife but by Potiphar himself. Joseph's sister Dinah, Diamant's narrator, hears the whole sordid tale much later from a woman in Joseph's household who is not overly impressed by the master of the house. In her conversation with Dinah, the servant disdainfully recalls how the now powerful governor, whom she calls "an arrogant son of a bitch" (341), came to Egypt. He was skinny as a stick, beaten, raped, and forced to do the dirtiest of chores. This abuse continued even in Potiphar's house, where Potiphar, attracted by Joseph's good looks, sexually exploited him. According to this squalid story, Joseph eventually became Potiphar's wife's lover as well, until it all ended in tragedy when Potiphar discovered them together in bed and Joseph was thrown into prison (342).

Dinah slowly realizes that this Zaphenath-paneah of whom the servant woman speaks is none other than her younger brother Joseph, the sibling who was closest to her growing up (344). Yet when she later meets him, they are unable to rekindle their childhood closeness. The two siblings have suffered too many traumas to ever become friends again. Dinah finds Joseph's self-confidence repulsive and holds him, along with their other brothers, responsible for the murder of Shechem, whom Dinah loved (Gen 34:1–5, 21–31; at least according to Diamant, unlike most modern biblical interpreters and translations, who rather maintain that the textually ambivalent biblical text describes how Shechem has sex with Dinah against her will: "When Shechem son of Hamor the Hivite, prince of the region, saw her, he seized her and lay with her by force" [Gen 34:2–3]). Diamant thus gives Joseph a negative rather than a positive development curve. Life has turned Dinah's kind younger brother, who was her closest friend growing up, into a haughty and traumatized ruler.

These different retellings challenge us to look with new eyes at the well-known story of Joseph and Potiphar's wife. Next time we read the story, let us stop and problematize the usual interpretation of this so-called femme fatal. At the same time, it is important to let Joseph remain a victim and to maintain that the behavior of Potiphar's wife will never be okay. Instead, let Potiphar's wife join the company of King David, who also has a lot to answer for in terms of sexual offenses, as well as his son Amnon, who rapes his half sister Tamar, the owner of the other famous (and torn) garment, not to mention his other son Absalom, who deems it suitable to rape David's ten concubines on the palace roof in front of the whole city (2 Sam 16:22). The main thing is that we do not distinguish between them, insisting, on the one hand, that David is some kind of romantic seducer while also insisting, on the other hand, that Potiphar's wife is an abomination. At the same time, it is worth noting that Joseph escapes the situation unharmed not only because of his robust sexual ethics but also his physically superior strength.

## An Innocent Prisoner

Joseph ends up in prison, not only sexually assaulted but also wrongly accused. Things can hardly get worse for Joseph, who is now at the absolute bottom of society. First down the well, then down to Egypt, and now down into the dungeons. At the same time, this is the beginning of Joseph's journey to the pinnacle of power. God is with him and turns the favor of the jailer toward him. The jailer, like Potiphar, is able to delegate his duties to Joseph and take things easy (Gen 39:23). What a life for the warden and, I suppose, more pleasant even for Joseph than sitting in his cell twiddling his thumbs. At the same time, what is it that makes first Potiphar and then the jailer feel so safe with Joseph? Is it God's providence, or Joseph's pleasant appearance, or a fascinating mix of both factors? Joseph seems like an Israelite version of Carl Jonas Love Almqvist's Tintomara, to which everyone, both men and women alike, are drawn.[3] This impression is reinforced later in the story by Joseph's beautiful clothes, clean-shaven Egyptian style, and almost theatrical, but at the same time completely genuine, storms of emotions.

During his time in prison, Joseph develops emotional intelligence. He begins to care about other people and recognize when something is amiss. Joseph notices that Pharaoh's cupbearer and baker are distressed and shows interest in their welfare. "When Joseph came to them in the morning, he saw that they were troubled. So he asked Pharaoh's officers, who were with him in custody in his master's house, 'Why are your faces downcast today?'" (Gen 40:6–7). His emotional attention to others turns out to be the beginning of Joseph's slow and gradual ascent to power, which does not end until he reaches the pinnacle when he becomes Pharaoh's vizier. At the same time, it is a disheartening story, as Joseph is forced to experience how his hope—that had suddenly flared up when he correctly interpreted the dreams of the cupbearer and the baker—is being quenched again. The cupbearer, who had promised to bring Joseph's case before Pharaoh, simply forgets about him: "Within three days Pharaoh will lift up your head and restore you to your office; and you shall place Pharaoh's cup in his hand, just as you used to do when you were his cupbearer. [. . .] Yet the chief cupbearer did not remember Joseph, but forgot him" (Gen 40:14, 23). Two long years later, after Pharaoh's dreams of fat and skinny cows, the cupbearer finally remembers Joseph's ability to interpret dreams. After what must have been much-needed visits to a barbershop and a men's outfitter, Joseph finds himself before Pharaoh. "Then Pharaoh sent for Joseph, and he was hurriedly brought out of the dungeon. When he had shaved himself and changed his clothes, he came in before Pharaoh" (Gen 41:14).

Joseph, thirty years old, has learnt both diplomacy and humility and makes sure to mention that it is God and not himself who can interpret dreams. It is now that Joseph, the man with a flair for economic planning, comes up with the Bible's best—or worst, depending on your perspective—strategic plan.

> "Now therefore let Pharaoh select a man who is discerning and wise, and set him over the land of Egypt. Let Pharaoh proceed to appoint overseers over the land, and take one-fifth of the produce of the land of Egypt during the seven plenteous years. Let them gather all the food of these good years that are coming, and lay up grain under the authority of Pharaoh for food in the cities, and let them keep it. That food shall be a reserve for the land against the seven years of famine that are to befall the land of Egypt, so that the land may not perish through the famine." [. . .] And since the famine had spread over all the land, Joseph opened all the storehouses, and sold to the Egyptians, for the famine was severe in the land of Egypt. Moreover, all the world came to Joseph in Egypt to buy grain, because the famine became severe throughout the world. (Gen 41:33–36, 56–57)

Pharaoh is impressed and decides to make Joseph ruler of all Egypt. It all ends with the entire population of Egypt enslaved and Pharaoh making a lot of money:

> Joseph collected all the money to be found in the land of Egypt and in the land of Canaan, in exchange for the grain that they bought; and Joseph brought the money into Pharaoh's house. [. . .] So Joseph bought all the land of Egypt for Pharaoh. All the Egyptians sold their fields, because the famine was severe upon them; and the land became Pharaoh's. As for the people, he made slaves of them from one end of Egypt to the other. [. . .] They said, "You have saved our lives; may it please my lord, we will be slaves to Pharaoh." (Gen 47:14, 20–21, 25)

I have thought a lot about Joseph's economic plan for Egypt, where he manages to convince its inhabitants to first collect and hand over their own crop to Pharaoh and then pay dearly to get it back. On the one hand, it undoubtedly saves people's lives, both in Egypt and elsewhere (41:56). On the other hand, first demanding 20 percent of people's crop and then forcing them to pay to get it back is not a fair system of taxation. However, relying on people to save themselves is irresponsible—that is why many countries have a state pension scheme, among other things. But, forcing them to save because they, by implication, do not understand their own best interests is patronizing. Yet again, if Joseph had not kept the stocks under surveillance, chaos and unbridled looting would soon have broken out. Still, you do not have to enslave an entire population just for the sake of it (47:14–25). Oh, I do not know what to think!

## Joseph's Vulnerability and Faith

Joseph's life is characterized by his vulnerability. His mother dies before he reaches adulthood, he is bullied and abused by his brothers, he is enslaved with all the physical and psychological violence which that entails, and he is thrown into prison. These experiences can break the strongest person and will certainly leave scars in both body and soul. No one rises unharmed from such experiences in their past. God can heal the damage, but the scars will always remain.

Mann's portrayal of Joseph's reaction to his imprisonment in *Joseph and His Brothers* fits Mann's other portrayals of Joseph, although it has aspects that may not be entirely psychologically plausible. Mann's Joseph has by now lost his naive innocence:

> Not that he had remained stuck at the boyish stage of blind expectation, when he had believed that people surely loved him more than they loved themselves. What he had continued to believe, however, was that he had been granted power to convince the world and its people to turn their best and brightest face toward him—which, as one can see, was a trust more in himself than in the world. To be sure, in his view these two, self and world, were bound up with one another and in some sense were one and the same, so that the world was not simply the other, turned in on itself, but in fact his world, which thus could be molded into something good and amiable. [. . .] Such was the nature of Joseph's confidence—or, to call a spade a spade, his trust in God. (1064)

Hunt describes Joseph's time in prison in a similar but considerably more psychologically untenable way. In her attempt to depict Joseph's development curve, Hunt makes him a saint to whom it is almost impossible to relate. Joseph realizes that he has been too proud and has trusted too much in his own abilities, his beauty, his intelligence, and God's election. Therefore, to learn humility, Joseph takes on the role of becoming the other prisoners' slave. Yes, yes, Hunt's scenario is absolutely flawless and pious, but I cannot handle it. I do not believe it. Joseph has just lost everything he has worked for and has also been falsely accused of rape when he may actually have suffered sexual abuse. Hunt's Joseph becomes such an utterly impeccable person that he loses all human credibility. Instead, let him cry out his pain, let him doubt properly, let him stay in the abyss of despair at least for a little while. Then, and only then, can I begin to relate to Joseph in an honest way.

Hunt's retelling also becomes quite entertaining, probably unintentionally on her part, in chapter 27 when Joseph, after six years in an ancient Egyptian prison, is brought before Pharaoh, and Tuya sees him again:

> Yosef had been attractive when she last saw him, but the man who stood before her now looked like a god. The boy she had known as Yosef had vanished, replaced by a stranger in the prime of manhood. In the golden torchlight of her chamber, the prisoner's skin glowed over tightly defined muscles. He stood tall and impressive beside those who imagined themselves his guards, and rough black hair fell past his shoulders in a wild tangle. His face, cleanly shaved and sculpted with angular lines, shone with an aloof strength. (210)

What a load of rubbish! Does Hunt really think there are gyms in Pharaoh's dungeons? Does she think that six years in prison is good for the skin? Does she believe that Joseph enjoyed three meals a day of cooked food and his "five-a-day" during his imprisonment? In its total exaggeration, Hunt's book challenges us again to consider what Joseph really looks like when he finally is allowed to leave prison. He is likely to be frighteningly thin, covered in ingrained dirt, probably with infected wounds and deep scars from years of neglect and unhealthy and inadequate food. We may only wonder how he feels mentally and spiritually. What nightmares haunt him at night? It is a miracle that he is alive at all.

Instead, let's turn to Webber and Rice's 1982 musical *Joseph and the Amazing Technicolor Dreamcoat*. The song that best captures Joseph's vulnerability as he sits in his prison cell, abandoned and forgotten, is the song "Close Every Door." This song manages to emphasize Joseph's bleak exposure and at the same time his strong faith. The reference to Joseph's number ("Just give me a number / Instead of my name") may allude to a variety of situations where people, incarcerated in prisons, have been reduced to numbers and their bodies thrown away. Joseph is forgotten by the world and finds himself in hell on earth. At the same time, he refuses to give up. Despite the total darkness around him, he dares to trust that God has a future planned for him.

## A Man with Power

Joseph becomes vizier over all Egypt, wearing Pharaoh's signet ring, beautiful linen clothes, and a gold chain around his neck (41:41–42). He travels the country in a fancy chariot and marries Asenath, daughter of Potiphera, priest of On (41:43–45). When Joseph's ten older brothers appear in Egypt a few years later, starving and bowing before him (42:6), Joseph realizes that his teenage dreams have come true.

### The Fragility of Power

Pharaoh's appointment of Joseph as vizier is often seen as the pinnacle of Joseph's career. He is now at the top of society and can enjoy his power and wealth:

> So Pharaoh said to Joseph, "Since God has shown you all this, there is no one so discerning and wise as you. You shall be over my house, and all my people shall order themselves as you command; only with regard to the throne will I be greater than you." And Pharaoh said to Joseph, "See, I have set you over all the land of Egypt." Removing his signet ring from his hand, Pharaoh put it on Joseph's hand; he arrayed him in garments of fine linen, and put a gold chain around his neck. He had him ride in the chariot of his second-in-command; and they cried out in front of him, "Bow the knee!" Thus he set him over all the land of Egypt. Moreover, Pharaoh said to Joseph, "I am Pharaoh, and without your consent no one shall lift up hand or foot in all the land of Egypt." Pharaoh gave Joseph the name Zaphenath-paneah; and he

> gave him Asenath daughter of Potiphera, priest of On, as his wife. Thus Joseph gained authority over the land of Egypt. (Gen 41:39–45)

Or can he? This is where Rushing's book *Seal Of The Sand Dweller* really comes into its own. It highlights in a surprising yet totally credible way that this is probably not the case at all. Her retelling begins with Joseph, badly beaten after his years in prison, being brought to Pharaoh's court to interpret Pharaoh's dreams. Joseph's injured feet torment him constantly, and he tries to hide the scars of shackles and handcuffs with jewelry. The scars on his back from whipping, which all slaves are forced to endure, are more difficult to cover given Egypt's fashion ideal of being rather scantily clad: "The permanent scars on his arms were fairly easy to cover with bracelets and armbands, but there was nothing to be done for the marks on his back. Every slave received a portion of those though his were thankfully few in number. The rope scars at his ankles were covered with jeweled cuffs of electrum, lined with soft wool" (141). The spiritual scars are just as deep, but Joseph has learned to use his experiences to his advantage. He has a slave's ability to hide his feelings from others (only to let them come to the surface when no one is looking), to never bluster, and to always be polite despite public insults.

Pharaoh's spur-of-the-moment decision to elevate Joseph to the position of vizier is not looked upon favorably by the rest of the court but instead seen as an act of ridicule. How can a former slave and convicted rapist hold his own among Egypt's aristocracy? Who would even obey his edicts? The answer is obvious. Rushing describes how Joseph, slowly but surely, tries to implement his economic reforms, and how he is constantly opposed, threatened, humiliated, and ridiculed. Potiphar's wife poisons his life with her continued accusations, the courtiers make racist attacks, and the Egyptian clergy despise his faith in the God of Israel. The book's title alludes to Pharaoh's signet ring, which in Joseph's hands lacks authority, at least at first. Pharaoh himself is a weak monarch who is an easy target for Joseph's opponents. Pharaoh's decree that no one in all of Egypt should lift a hand or foot without Joseph's command shows the difference between words and deeds: Power must be accompanied by respect, otherwise you become a puppet of those who have the real power, or you perish quickly. In this situation, Joseph is forced to choose whether to take the easy way out and turn a blind eye to the corruption he sees around him or to be faithful to God's calling to save Egypt from famine. He chooses the narrow path but Rushing shows, again and again, the price Joseph pays in anguish, threats, and physical abuse when he chooses to do the right thing.

## A Forgiving Man

Less than ten years later, Joseph is given the opportunity to fulfil his dreams of revenge. He appears before his brothers, his former bullies, in all his splendor, wealth, and power while they stand there, poor, caps in hand, begging for bread. What a triumph! Yet, as anyone who has ever been bullied knows, it is not enough. The pain and insecurity remain in the soul, despite all the success. Joseph, standing before his brothers, cannot help but remember all the times they did not want him and all the times they hurt him.

The big question for me in Genesis 42–45 is whether Joseph is unrestrainedly indulging in his revenge fantasies or whether his actions have a more altruistic aspect in that he wants to ensure that his brothers have become better people. The text can be read both ways. Joseph begins by treating his brothers singularly harshly: He accuses them of being spies and throws them in prison without further ado (Gen 42:7–17). The brothers, although they do not recognize him, nonetheless discern that this is the punishment for what they themselves did to Joseph many years ago: "They said to one another, 'Alas, we are paying the penalty for what we did to our brother; we saw his anguish when he pleaded with us, but we would not listen. That is why this anguish has come upon us.' Then Reuben answered them, 'Did I not tell you not to wrong the boy? But you would not listen. So now there comes a reckoning for his blood'" (Gen 42:21–22). When Joseph hears the brothers talking, he turns around and cries (v. 24). What is it that moves and upsets him so? It may be that Joseph is moved by his brothers' realization of guilt, but it may also be that his brothers' words remind him of the anguish and despair he felt growing up and that culminated in his brothers' decision to sell him into slavery (rather than murder him). Joseph's crying does not necessarily mean that he has forgiven his brothers but that their presence is tearing open all the old wounds that have festered and never fully healed.

Together with King David, Joseph tops the list of the Bible's greatest weepers. I am convinced that their emotions are genuine. At the same time, both of them manage to use their favorable appearance and rich emotional register to charm the men and women around them (cf. chapters 6–7). What is interesting about Joseph, however, is that he cries much more when he is a successful adult than when he is a defenseless youth. It seems that Joseph does not dare to cry if he is vulnerable. He does not cry when he is thrown into the well, sold into slavery, falsely accused of rape, or cast into prison—then he hides his feelings under a tough skin. It is only in adulthood, perhaps when he finally begins to feel safe, surrounded by his new family—Asenath and their two children, Manasseh and Ephraim—that his hard shell begins to crack. Once the shell is broken, all his emotions come to the surface, and Joseph weeps most of the time. He sometimes tries to hide his tears, but mostly he cries in front of people. He weeps when he is emotionally affected: when he sees his brothers (Gen 42:24; 43:30; 45:2, 14–15), when he meets his father (46:29), and when his father dies (50:1, 3, 15–17).

Joseph later welcomes his brothers into his house where he shows them respect and hospitality. When Joseph sees his younger brother Benjamin (who has come with the brothers on their second trip to Egypt), his facade is in danger of cracking, and he rushes out to burst into tears in private: "With that, Joseph hurried out, because he was overcome with affection for his brother, and he was about to weep. So he went into a private room and wept there. Then he washed his face and came out; and controlling himself he said, 'Serve the meal'" (Gen 43:30–31). Joseph manages to keep a straight face in front of his brothers later when they eat together. His love for his younger brother shines through, however, as he gives him a larger portion of food. Joseph's testing of his brothers—or is it more likely an elaborate and sophisticated revenge?—is not over. After several additional twists and turns, Judah proves willing to atone for his crime when he offers to become a slave in Benjamin's place: "Now therefore, please let your servant remain as a slave to my lord in place of the boy; and let the boy go back with his brothers. For how can I go back to my father if the boy is not with me? I fear to see the suffering that would come upon my father'" (Gen 44:33–34). No longer able to keep his emotions under control, Joseph sends everyone but his brothers out of the room. He bursts into tears and reveals his true identity. Then there is even more crying and emotional outburst:

> Then Joseph said to his brothers, "Come closer to me." And they came closer. He said, "I am your brother Joseph, whom you sold into Egypt. And now do not be distressed, or angry with yourselves, because you sold me here; for God sent me before you to preserve life." [...]

> Then he fell upon his brother Benjamin's neck and wept, while Benjamin wept upon his neck. And he kissed all his brothers and wept upon them; and after that his brothers talked with him. (Gen 45:4–5, 14–15)

Ironically, he also gives each of the brothers a festive garment, and Benjamin receives five of them (Gen 45:22). None of these garments resemble the one given to Joseph by his father; these garments are more mundane. At the same time, the gift of clothing is a delicate reference to the trigger that caused the brothers to turn against Joseph, namely the clothing that Jacob gave to Joseph a decade or more ago.

Yet the story drags on, and Joseph needs to reaffirm that he is not planning revenge in chapter 50, a full nine chapters after his brothers' first visit to Egypt: "But Joseph said to them, 'Do not be afraid! Am I in the place of God? Even though you intended to do harm to me, God intended it for good, in order to preserve a numerous people, as he is doing today. So have no fear; I myself will provide for you and your little ones.' In this way he reassured them, speaking kindly to them" (Gen 50:19–21).

## Are the Brothers Really Asking for Forgiveness?

This dragged-out story raises questions. Why does it take so long for Joseph to (perhaps) manage to forgive his brothers, and why does he have to repeat his promise not to harm them? To answer our questions, let us take a closer look at the brothers' behavior. There are aspects of the text that suggest that Joseph's doubts about their honesty are not entirely unfounded. This doubt, in turn, makes it difficult for Joseph and his brothers to reach genuine reconciliation.

A first indication of the brothers' incomplete repentance is found already in Genesis 43. I have often wondered about poor Simon who has been imprisoned since 42:24. If the famine had not forced the brothers back to Egypt in 43:1, would Simon have stayed in his Egyptian prison for life? At the same time, Judah insists that they stayed for the sake of their father and younger brother Benjamin (43:10). So, although there is much to suggest that the brothers have matured and changed for the better, I am not entirely convinced that their deepest motivation is sincere regret or if it might be results-oriented pragmatism.

A second indication that makes me doubt the brothers' repentance occurs when Joseph accuses them of theft in chapter 44. Judah manages to evade his own responsibility in Joseph's "disappearance." He insists that Benjamin's brother "is dead" (Gen 44:20), and he avoids telling the truth by repeating Jacob's words that Joseph "surely has been torn to pieces; and I have never seen him since" (44:28). At the same time, as we saw above, despite the absence of a clear admission of guilt, Judah shows himself ready to atone for his crime when he offers to become a slave in Benjamin's place.

A final indication is found right at the end of the story (Gen 50:15–17): "Realizing that their father was dead, Joseph's brothers said, 'What if Joseph still bears a grudge against us and pays us back in full for all the wrong that we did to him?' So they approached Joseph, saying, 'Your father gave this instruction before he died, 'Say to Joseph: I beg you, forgive the crime of your brothers and the wrong they did in harming you.' Now therefore please forgive the crime of the servants of the God of your father.' Joseph wept when they spoke to him." These verses prompt the question of whether the brothers are telling the truth. There is no indication whatsoever in the chapters leading up to Jacob's death that Jacob had asked his older sons to say anything to Joseph. Moreover, Joseph himself was personally present during his father's last hours (Gen 49). So, there are many indications that the brothers are lying. If this is true, the brothers are engaging in some serious emotional blackmail. The brothers worry, perhaps rightly, that Joseph has not been able to forgive the almost unforgivable. If the brothers had been in Joseph's place, would they have been able to do so?

The brothers' behavior, in turn, influences our understanding of Joseph's actions. Is it possible that Joseph, deep in his heart, still struggles to forgive his brothers? Could it be that while his words testify to his willingness to forgive them, in reality he is only able to do so in his brothers' absence? Could it be that Joseph's involuntary reluctance seeps out in his meetings with the brothers, even though he tries to hide his true feelings (something we already know he finds difficult)? The brothers are clearly afraid that Joseph will take revenge (Gen 50:15), and perhaps their fears are justified, at least from their point of view. It is one thing to want to forgive and quite another to be able to do so when faced with your tormentors who are still lying. I am absolutely convinced that Joseph sees through the brothers' lies and attempts at emotional blackmail. As I said, there is nothing wrong with his brain cells. That Joseph is capable of acting as he does in the next few verses, where he again insists that his brothers need not fear and where he promises to care for them and their children, is a sign of his own emotional maturity rather than the brothers' repentance: "'So have no fear; I myself will provide for you and your little ones.' In this way he reassured them, speaking kindly to them" (Gen 50:21). This is not necessarily forgiveness, but it is a promise to refrain from vengeance. Joseph has done his part; he is able to be the adult in the conversation with his brothers and to reassure and encourage them. The scars, both mental and physical, are still there and will never leave him, but he has finally reached a kind of reconciliation with himself. Perhaps we cannot ask more of him? Perhaps it is enough that Joseph really wants to forgive his brothers, regardless of whether he succeeds in doing so in practice?

## Genuine Forgiveness

Most retellings give Joseph a positive development curve. When Joseph has finished testing his brothers and made sure they realize not only his power but also the debt they owe him, he shows himself to be righteous and magnanimous and forgives them. This is very clear in Mann's book *Joseph and His Brothers*. At the same time, Mann has made a small but very important adjustment to the biblical text: In his speech in Genesis 44:28, Judah mentions the eleventh son who "disappeared," whereas in Mann's novel, Judah confesses his and his brothers' crime: "Our eleventh, our father's lamb, the first son of the true wife—no animal mutilated him, but rather we, his brothers, sold him out into the world.' With these and no other words Judah ended his famous speech. He stood there, swaying on his feet, and his brothers were ashen pale, yet profoundly relieved that their secret was out" (1376). Judah's confession makes it easier for Joseph to reveal his identity and later to forgive his brothers. Mann's Joseph simply says who he is; without grand gestures but rather with an embarrassed laugh, Joseph shows his honest relief. At the same time, Mann's retelling highlights that something is lacking in the biblical narrative. The biblical text muddies the waters as, strictly speaking, the brothers never admit their crime and never ask for forgiveness. Mann's Joseph manages to do what the Bible's Joseph only might manage to do because of Judah's confession.

## Incomplete Forgiveness

With this biblical ambiguity in mind, it is easy to understand why Diamant pauses to reflect on Joseph's forgiveness not only of his brothers but also of his father, who had failed to protect him. In her retelling, Joseph comes to Dinah's house late one night and tells her that Jacob is on his way to Egypt. Dinah's husband bursts out asking whether Joseph really has any obligations to a father "who sent you to the long knives of men known for their ruthlessness" (361). It is implied that Jacob should have known better than to expose his son to this obvious danger. Joseph replies honestly that he does not want to see his father. He thought he had forgiven him, but the bitter truth is that he has not:

> The hurt of the past clung to him, caught in the folds of his long dark cloak. He flailed around like a drowning lamb. As he talked [. . .] I searched for the brother I remembered, the playfellow who listened to the words of women with respect and who once looked at me as his friend. But I saw nothing of that boy in the self-absorbed man before me, whose mood and voice seemed to change from moment to unhappy moment. "I am a weakling," said Joseph. "My anger has not abated and I have no pity in my heart for Jakob" [. . .] "If I do not go, he will haunt me forever." (362–363)

Diamant's Joseph is a mixture of the proud man with power who is used to people, including his sister, obeying his every command, and the little boy who is still afraid of the tormentors of his youth. He is not free of his past and notices that Dinah is not either. Joseph sits silent and tense throughout the journey to Jacob, and only his sons Manasseh and Ephraim manage to make him relax a bit (368). Joseph is still tense when he arrives at the camp of his father and brothers. Later, Joseph and Judah have a stilted conversation, where Judah shows both his anger and his defeat. Joseph himself keeps his distance.

As expected, Joseph's meeting with Jacob does not go overly well. Afterward, Joseph throws himself wordlessly to the ground in grief but eventually tells Dinah everything with both pity and disgust in his voice. Jacob is old and cranky but still ultimately manages to bless his grandchildren Manasseh and Ephraim. Jacob is filled with self-reproach but is so self-absorbed at the same time and sees no other side of the situation than his own. Joseph leaves the tent with his sons without Jacob noticing. Jacob is immersed in his own private grief for Rachel and never even mentions Dinah. She is dead to him (371–373).

* * *

Of all the characters in this book, Joseph is probably the one I can relate to the most. To avoid being misunderstood, I should add that I find it easier to identify with Joseph's more annoying aspects rather than his more admirable ones. I was bullied at school but not in any way near what happens to Joseph; I have always been ambitious, and I am not the most empathetic person in the world. My friends often accuse me of living in a rose-tinted world of my own, blissfully unaware of things around me. I am also extremely stubborn and usually trust that things will work out if you just grit your teeth enough. Last but not least, I cry regularly, always honestly, but sometimes with unexpectedly favorable consequences, like when my tears terrified the infamous (and feared) administrator of the department of biblical studies, causing her to treat me with kid gloves for five years.

So, much of the Joseph story is a direct lesson for me. First of all, the biblical story of Joseph challenges me to forgive my enemies. My whole being recoils when I hear such a message because I do not want at all to forgive those who hurt me. I hope that I do not harbor too many dreams of vengeance, but I fear that I would like to be seen in a better light than some of the bullies I unfortunately have had to deal with during my academic career. I realize, of course, that these feelings reveal flaws in myself, and it does not make it any easier to meet my gaze in the mirror. So, both Joseph's desire for revenge and his ability to forgive evoke many emotions that require honesty and self-awareness.

Joseph's story also makes us see what suffering can do to our lives. God can heal, but the scars do not go away. It is possible to get through incredibly horrible experiences with our souls intact, but suffering rarely makes us better people. Suffering does not always lead to compassion but may instead result in bitterness. Joseph's weeping shows that he chose, somewhere along the way, not to allow his suffering to solidify into harshness but that he allowed himself to feel, for better or worse.

The story of Joseph also shows that life does not always turn out the way we expect. Joseph is not in control of his destiny, and his life is very different from that of his brothers. His years as a slave are not of his choosing, and they leave a deep mark on his life. Joseph loses his homeland but gains a new culture: Joseph becomes an immigrant who marries an Egyptian woman and whose children grow up abroad with dual nationalities. At the same time, there are aspects of Joseph's life that exceed his wildest hopes. Joseph's fate and adventures help us realize our limitations. We can lay our plans with precision, but sometimes things just happen.

At the same time, the Joseph story also shows the opposite. Joseph could have become a mediocre slave, doing only what was expected of him. Instead, he chooses to excel. He becomes the top slave whose administrative talents bless everything from Potiphar's house, via the prison, to the entire land of Egypt. Joseph is an overachiever who embodies willpower and stubbornness, again for better or worse. The story of Joseph teaches us about the need for balance in our lives: the realization that we are not in control of everything and, at the same time, the importance of facing up to our problems. Joseph himself is far from an expert in this regard, but his life, in all its brokenness, testifies to the need.

Joseph's story also challenges our attitudes to living in a land characterized by the "Law of Jante," where nobody is to think they are special or better than the rest. How do we relate to people around us who are intellectually gifted? The prodigious Joseph, with his high activity level, his interest in problem solving, his perfectionism, his self-awareness, his independence, his sense of justice, and his sensitivity, is a classic example of giftedness. Do we force people like Joseph to hide their light under a bushel to avoid being bullied and isolated, or is there a place for the bright, energetic, and frankly, sometimes very trying Josephs in our society where everything is supposed to be so fair and equal? At the same time, how can we help this same Joseph to find empathy and humility in his relationship with God and his fellow human beings? Throwing him into a well, selling him into slavery, abusing him, slandering him, innocently accusing and punishing him, so that he learns his lesson, is clearly not the way forward.

Last but not least, the story of Joseph in Genesis 39, along with the (in many ways) parallel story of Dinah in Genesis 34, is an example of sexual exploitation. No matter how we problematize the story of Joseph and Potiphar's wife, the fact remains that the latter's actions are wrong, regardless of her family situation and feelings. She uses her power over Joseph and tries to force him, the socially inferior foreigner, to do her bidding. This behavior quickly recalls many modern situations where people in power take unfair advantage through a mixture of threats and promises: "If you do what I want, I have the power to favor you, but if you refuse, I have the power to harm you." The story of Joseph is an example of the latter and hopefully not a deterrent but instead a message we can take to heart. Yes, when we challenge unjust power structures, we may have to pay a very high price, but ultimately God remains on our side.

CHAPTER FOUR

# Ruth and Naomi

## *Best Friends or Awkward Collaborators?*

THE BOOK OF Ruth is primarily about human relationships. God is barely mentioned and his providence takes place mostly behind the scenes. God remains in the background. He cares but very gently and carefully. The scene belongs instead to a number of women who act and make decisions based on what seems most appropriate to them in their given situation. This story of migration, (lack of) integration, culture clashes, homesickness, and grief resonates with the experiences of many.

Although God never acts directly, his influence is nonetheless felt throughout the book of Ruth. God's presence is expressed most strongly in Ruth's well-known "confession of faith" where Ruth declares that Naomi's God is also her God (1:16). Ruth's statement forms the center of the book and sets the rest of the plot in motion. Ruth's "creed" is the hub around which everything revolves. Furthermore, both Naomi (1:8) and Boaz (2:12; 3:10) regularly wish God's blessing on Ruth, and God responds by allowing Ruth to be a blessing to others (4:12, 14). Taken as a whole, Ruth is a sermon on God's grace and providence.

## Narratives

To gain a deeper insight into this story, we will analyze how several poems and fictional novels have portrayed its characters.

**Tessa Afshar** is a Persian American author who has written many books about biblical characters. They all focus on female characters and have an explicitly Christian perspective. Unfortunately, at least this book, *In the Field of Grace*, is also unusually boring as it lacks surprises and plot twists. Ruth herself seems more like someone's ideal of the godly woman than a flesh-and-blood person: She is beautiful, slender, graceful, pious, selfless, self-sacrificing, and intelligent but at the same time polite, quiet and appealingly unsure of her own worth—you know what I mean. At the same time, it is worth reading as it brings out Naomi's grief and despair over the death of her sons in a poignant and authentic way.

*In the Field of Grace* (River North, 2014).

**Rabbi Rachel Barenblat** (b. 1975) is an American rabbi and poet. She has published several collections of poetry, including *70 Faces: Torah Poems* (2010), *Waiting to Unfold* (2013), and *Texts to the Holy: Poems* (2018). Her poetry is inspired by the Bible and classical rabbinic commentary (midrash [singular], midrashim [plural], that is, exegetical expositions explaining a biblical text).

"The Handmaid's Tale (Ruth)," https://velveteenrabbi.blogs.com/blog/2011/05/a-ruth-poem-for-shavuot.html, 2011.

"The One Who Turned Back," https://velveteenrabbi.blogs.com/blog/2012/05/a-poem-about-orpah.html, 2012.

**Samuel Bass** (1899–1949) was an Israeli newspaper editor, poet, and literary critic. He was born in Ukraine and immigrated in 1906 to Palestine, then part of the Ottoman Empire.

"ערפה" (Orpah), trans. Barry Dov Walfish, https://www.thetorah.com/article/the-defamation-of-orpah.

**Tamar Biala** (b. 1970) is an Israeli author and lecturer. Her most famous book, written together with Nehama Weingarten-Mintz, is *Dirshuni: Contemporary Women's Midrash*, the first book to contain modern midrashim written by women.

"מכתב של ערפה להוריה" (Orpah's Letter to Her Parents), trans. Barry Dov Walfish, https://www.thetorah.com/article/the-defamation-of-orpah.

**Eva Etzioni-Halevy** (b. 1955) is professor emerita of political sociology at Bar-Ilan University in Israel. In addition to several academic books, she has written three fiction novels about biblical women: Deborah, Hannah, and Ruth. Her book *The Garden of Ruth* is a considerably more interesting read than Afshar's *In the Field of Grace*, as Ruth is less kind and predictable while being endowed with a robust self-confidence and sense of humor. The reader meets a radiantly beautiful and fiery Ruth with both faults and flaws. Her great grandson David will later inherit her red hair and perhaps also many other character traits.

*Garden of Ruth* (Plume, 2007).

**Kathryn Hellerstein** (b. 1952) is an American professor of Yiddish and German, specializing in language and literature. Her research focuses on Yiddish female writers.

"Naomi: 'Call Me Bitter,'" in *Reading Ruth: Contemporary Women Reclaim a Sacred Story*, eds. Judith A. Kates and Gail Twersky Reimer (Ballantine Books, 1994).

**Abraham Huss** (1924–2015) was an Israeli poet and professor of meteorology.

"ערפה" (Orpah), trans. Barry Dov Walfish, https://www.thetorah.com/article/the-defamation-of-orpah.

**Anna Kamieńska** (1920–1986) was a Polish Catholic poet, writer, translator, and literary critic. Her poems reflect her Christian faith but also express Jewish thoughts. Many of her poems long for the Yiddish culture that was destroyed in Poland during the Holocaust. Kamieńska lived in Lublin during World War II, where she taught in secret village schools.

"Naomi," in *Modern Poems on the Bible: An Anthology*, ed. David Curzon (Jewish Publication Society of America, 1994), 326–327.

**Marge Piercy** (b. 1936) is an American Jewish peace and environmental activist and writer. Her poetry is influenced by her Jewish upbringing and feminist ideals.

"The Book of Ruth and Naomi," in *Modern Poems on the Bible: An Anthology*, ed. David Curzon (Jewish Publication Society of America, 1994), originally published in *Mars and Her Children* (Knopf, 1992).

**Erin Phillips** (b. 1990) is an American Christian author. Her young adult fantasy novel *A Bond of Briars* is closely based on the book of Ruth. The fantasy genre allows Phillips to retell the biblical story as a battle between good and evil, freedom and bondage, where nothing less than the future birth of the messiah is at stake.

*A Bond of Briars* (Ethereal Echo, 2023).

## Time in Moab

The book of Ruth begins in 1:1–5 by introducing readers to the main characters:

> In the days when the judges ruled, there was a famine in the land, and a certain man of Bethlehem in Judah went to live in the country of Moab, he and his wife and two sons. The name of the man was Elimelech and the name of his wife Naomi, and the names of his two sons were Mahlon and Chilion; they were Ephrathites from Bethlehem in Judah. They went into the country of Moab and remained there. But Elimelech, the husband of Naomi, died, and she was left with her two sons. These took Moabite wives; the name of one was Orpah and the name of the other Ruth. When they had lived there for about ten years, both Mahlon and Chilion also died, so that the woman was left without her two sons or her husband.

Naomi, her husband, and their two sons live in Moab for ten years, but it is unclear how old the sons, Mahlon and Chilion, are when they arrive and how old they are when they marry Ruth and Orpah. The most obvious way to read the text is to assume that the sons are of marriageable age when they arrive (v. 1) and marry soon afterward (v. 4). Say that they are in their twenties, give or take a few years. We may further speculate that Ruth and Orpah are a little younger, perhaps between fifteen and eighteen. This would mean that, ten years later, Ruth and Orpah are just under thirty when they become widows (v. 5). The main difficulty with this reading is that both women appear to be childless when they are widowed, which is not entirely plausible after such long marriages in an era without contraception. However, we may wish to consider the high infant mortality rate of the time and assume that Ruth and Orpah have given birth to several children who have not survived. They would then not only be widows but also mothers who have been forced to bury one or more children. The only thing we know for sure is that they are childless widows at the end of verse 5.

The alternative is to read in a time lapse between verses 2–3 and verse 4. Naomi's husband Elimelech dies relatively soon after their arrival in Moab (v. 3) before Mahlon and Chilion are fully grown. They only marry later, just before their untimely death. According to this scenario, Ruth should be around twenty in verse 5. She has not been married very long and therefore has had no time to get pregnant. This reading is later reinforced by 4:12 where Ruth is referred to as "a young woman" (*na'ara*).

***Excursus: Names in the Book of Ruth***

All the main characters in the book of Ruth have significant names. This is most evident in the case of Naomi, whose name means "the sweet one." Later, when life gets rough, she changes her name to "the bitter one." The other characters also have names whose meaning reflects their narrative role. Naomi's husband is called Elimelech, which means "my God is king," and their two sons are called Mahlon, which translates as "sickly," and Chilion, which translates as "end of the line." In other words, when we meet these two individuals, we understand that they will not live long and fruitful lives. The name Orpah is more difficult to translate. It may mean "stubborn" but also "cloud." The meaning of her name, as well as her role in the story, is thus ambivalent. The next of kin is not even given a name, but is called Mr. Anybody, which emphasizes his insignificance and also his function as Boaz's counterpart, whose name means "strength." At the same time, the name Ruth lacks a clear meaning, although scholars have suggested several different translations, for example, "friend." In my opinion, the unclear meaning of the name is part of a deliberate narrative strategy: Ruth's identity and role are gradually revealed over the course of the story.

Verse 5 is upsetting not only because Naomi has now lost both husband and children but also because of her total disregard for her daughters-in-law. The stark statement that "the woman was left without her two sons or her husband" may be understood in different ways. One possible reading is that Orpah and Ruth mean nothing to Naomi. They do not count as they are not part of her biological family. Another possibility is to understand it to reflect Naomi's emotional state. She is on the brink of personal disaster and no daughter-in-law in the world can replace her own children. The statement may finally also be interpreted as a reflection of Naomi's precarious economic situation: With no male family members to support her, she lacks the means to care for herself.

The biblical text goes on to explore the relationship between Naomi and her daughters-in-law. In verses 7–9, Naomi asks Orpah and Ruth to return to their respective parental homes:

> So she set out from the place where she had been living, she and her two daughters-in-law, and they went on their way to go back to the land of Judah. But Naomi said to her two daughters-in-law, "Go back each of you to your mother's house. May the Lord deal kindly with you, as you have dealt with the dead and with me. The Lord grant that you may find security, each of you in the house of your husband." Then she kissed them, and they wept aloud.

The biblical text does not explain the characters' behavior to the reader. Naomi wants to return to Bethlehem without her daughters-in-law, but it is unclear why.

However, despite Naomi's stated wish to travel alone, both Orpah and Ruth initially insist on accompanying her (v. 10). Again, the text provides no information about their motivation. Do they sense that Naomi really is not well and that her self-imposed solitude is destructive? Alternatively, do they themselves have nowhere to go? Naomi seems to assume that they still have parents who are alive but that in itself does not mean they are welcome back home. Besides, who wants to move back in with their parents as an adult? Perhaps it would be rather unpleasant to return home after living away from home for several years? Finally, what future awaits them there? A new marriage may not be the most likely outcome, especially if you are already thirty and still childless after almost ten years of marriage (our first scenario).

Yet Naomi insists that they should return to their homes. She expresses her gratitude for what Orpah and Ruth have done for her so far but declares that they have no future with her (1:11–13). While her own future, bitter and hopeless, lies in Judah, Orpah and Ruth's futures lie in Moab. The question is why Naomi is so convinced that Orpah and Ruth should stay in Moab. On the one hand, is she testing their determination by insisting that they should remain in their homeland? After all, she may want them to come with her, but she is afraid of becoming a burden to them and standing in the way of their happiness. She, of all people, knows how difficult it is to be the permanent foreigner somewhere, and she does not want Orpah and Ruth to experience the same thing. On the other hand, could it be that she is ashamed of them? Would she rather avoid returning to Bethlehem with these foreign women when, deep in her heart, she would have preferred her sons to marry women from Judah? Was Elimelech the driving force behind their journey to Moab ten years earlier, and did Naomi in fact disapprove of her sons embracing the new and foreign culture? Is it possible that Naomi is afraid that her daughters-in-law's presence in Bethlehem will cause her to be vilified and ostracized herself? Or is Naomi so overwhelmed by her grief that she is unable to see anyone else's perspective and would rather just be alone in her despair?

Orpah gives in, but again we never learn what prompts her decision. Her path leads home, and the Bible does not blame her for her decision to leave Naomi. The book of Ruth is remarkable in that it never places any burden on any character for any decision. The people in the book do the best they can in every situation, and that is always enough.

## Orpah's Choice

The Bible leaves Orpah by the wayside, and we will never know what happens next. This narrative silence has not stopped poets from speculating about Orpah's later life, however. In her poem "The One Who Turned Back," Rachel Barenblat ponders whether Orpah goes home to her parents, whether she remarries, whether she has children, or whether she remains unmarried, and her lot in life is to care for her aging parents. Barenblat further contrasts Ruth, who becomes King David's great grandmother, with Orpah's descendants, who may die fighting against Israel:

did you birth Goliath
and rend your garments
when you lost him too

did you live for centuries
destined for the sword
of one of David's men

The reference to Goliath may seem strange as he was a Philistine and not a Moabite. However, Barenblat refers to a Jewish interpretive tradition that identifies Orpah with Goliath's mother (B. Sotah 42b) and maintains that all four of her sons are killed by David. This interpretation, in turn, is based on a pun derived from 2 Sam 21:18 where the name Rafa (הרפה), often translated as "giants," in Hebrew shares three of four consonants with the name Orpah (ערפה). Orpah, who remains in Moab, becomes a symbol of Israel's enemies, while Ruth, who journeys to Bethlehem, represents Israel. Although the women in the Bible appear to be friends, their choices will shape the respective destinies of their descendants. Yet Barenblat also challenges the rabbinic tradition, as she tacitly questions the necessity of distinguishing between Ruth and Orpah's children. Do we have to relate to "us" and "them," or can we not all be one "we"? Must there be a boundary between Orpah the Moabite and Ruth the Israelite and their later children?

Other poets have reflected on Orpah's choice and explained it in positive terms. In his poem "Orpah," Abraham Huss describes how Orpah is not ready to move on. She is still mourning her husband Chilion, Naomi's son, and does not want to forget him:

| | |
|---|---|
| ...The man who lay between my breasts<br>Indeed left memories, longing and pain [...]<br>And thus, from me was taken the taste of meaning. You can go, leaning on the staff of forgetfulness. I part company with you in confused resignation,<br>And here in Moab, one day, all alone, I shall die, I—will not go. | ... האיש ששכב בין שדי<br>אכן הותיר זכרונות כמיהה וכאב [...]<br>ובכן—ממני נטלו את טעם המשמעות.<br>אתן יכולות ללכת נשענות על מטה<br>שכחה. ואני נפרדת מכן מתוך השלמה<br>נבוכה, ופה במואב, יום אחד, ערירית,<br>אמות, אני—לא אלך. |

In contrast, Samuel Bass chooses to portray Orpah's homesickness and her relief at being able to return to the land of her childhood without guilt. She is happy and grateful that Naomi does not force her to abandon her home and culture.

| | |
|---|---|
| While she embraces her mother-in-law, over her shoulder<br>she sees the mountains of her home-land, at the well of Zohar, the blue<br>misty veil that embraces the valley<br>wherein is nestled her mother's house,<br>the garden of her youth. [. . .]<br>Here is the land of her youth, where<br>her spring burst into bloom,<br>How could she strike roots in another? | בחבקה חמותה, מעברו של כתף<br>תחזה הררי מולדתה בעין-זהר, את<br>צעיף האדים הכחל העוטף הבקעה,<br>בה שוכן בית אמה, גן הנער.<br>פה אדמת גדולה, אביבה בה הנץ, [. . .]<br>איך תוכל ותכה שרשים באחרת. |

Bass goes on to describe how Orpah feels young again. Her husband's death has not killed her passion, and she can leave her grief and widowhood behind.

Similarly, in her poem "Orpah's Letter to Her Parents," Tamar Biala describes how Orpah sees and accepts that her future lies in Moab. She looks forward to how she and Ruth, as two sisters, will settle together in Moab. When she realizes that Ruth has chosen to go with Naomi, Orpah feels betrayed:

| | |
|---|---|
| Ruth and I will appear all of a sudden<br>in our town, I imagined, people will<br>wonder, have pity,<br>be suspicious, but we will keep faith<br>with each other,<br>because we will always be sisters, just<br>as we had promised in<br>the past, and we will always remember<br>Naomi. [. . .] | רות ואני נופיע לפתע<br>בעירנו, דמיינתי, אנשים יתהו,<br>ירחמו, יחשדו, אך אנו נשמור<br>אמונים זו לזו,<br>כי לעולם נהיה אחיות, כמו<br>שהבטחנו<br>בעבר, ולעולם נזכור את נעמי [. . .] |
| Two sets of footsteps I heard, soft,<br>getting farther away,<br>and I did not understand what was<br>happening.<br>I wanted to turn around, to cry out to<br>Ruth,<br>call out, clarify, understand | שני זוגות<br>צעדים שמעתי, חרישיים, מתרחקים<br>והולכים ולא הבנתי מה קורה.<br>בקשתי להסתובב אחורה, לצעוק<br>לרות,<br>לקרוא, לברר, להבין, |

All four poems invite us to ponder Orpah's fate and what prompts her to stay in Moab. Orpah and Ruth choose different paths in life, even though, as Biala emphasizes, they are like sisters. Their choices affect both themselves and the lives of their future children, but this does not mean that one path is better than the other or that either of them makes a wrong decision.

## Sadness and Hope

Ruth, as I said, chooses a different path forward and that path leads straight into the unknown. She is driven by love and loyalty to Naomi, perhaps spurred on by a sense of adventure or, alternatively, unhappiness in Moab, and who knows, perhaps even driven by fear of being left alone.

The two women who are traveling to Bethlehem together are marked by grief. And yet there is a difference in how they relate to this grief and how it affects their relationship with each other. The biblical text describes a certain lack of symmetry in their relationship. While Ruth constantly shows, both in words and actions, how much Naomi means to her, there is no similar response from Naomi. Could it be that Naomi is unable to see beyond herself and her grief at this point? Ruth's behavior, in contrast, perhaps because she is younger or because she is generally more of a glass-half-full person, shows that she still has hope. This hope is most evident in Ruth's famous words to her mother-in-law: "But Ruth said, 'Do not press me to leave you or to turn back from following you! Where you go, I will go; where you lodge, I will lodge; your people shall be my people, and your God my God. Where you die, I will die—there will I be buried. May the Lord do thus and so to me, and more as well, if even death parts me from you!'" (Ruth 1:16–17). Ruth's words can be understood in many different ways. What lies beneath the surface? Is Ruth's decision to accompany Naomi to Bethlehem a form of pure self-denial, or does her behavior reflect their mutual love? Moreover, how can we understand Naomi's lack of reaction to Ruth's selfless act? "When Naomi saw that she was determined to go with her, she said no more to her" (Ruth 1:18). Could it be that normally, that is, before life fell apart when Naomi's sons, Ruth's and Orpah's husbands died, Ruth and Naomi had a close friendship? At this point in the story, however, Naomi seems incapable of showing much concern for her future and her daughters-in-law. Instead, she is completely consumed by grief and hopelessness.

## Naomi's Grief

Naomi, Orpah, and Ruth are all women who grieve. There is, however, a difference between them: While Ruth and Orpah lose their husbands, Naomi loses her children. There is a saying that when you lose your parents you lose your past, when your partner dies you lose your present, but when your children die you lose your future. I have only experienced the first and the last. When my son Caspian died at the age of four weeks (sudden infant death syndrome), I could not take in that my parents had lost their first grandchild. I had likewise no interest in the fact that my sister-in-law, who lived in the same town as my husband and I at the time, had lost her nephew. You can barely cope with your own life, and everything revolves around your own grief. There is no room for other people's grief at a time like that.

At the same time, Ruth's faithfulness is so important in these kinds of situations. When life falls apart, your friends often end up in one of two groups. The larger group contains those who find it too hard to continue socializing. You do not know what to say to a person who has lost a child. You almost feel ashamed that your own children are still alive. It is much easier to keep your distance and avoid the person. The smaller group consists of those who are willing and ready to talk about what has happened. They are not always the people you would expect. When Caspian died, some of my friends came forward, took me out to tea, and came with me to the grave. Most importantly, they talked about Caspian, and they let me talk about him without feeling awkward. He was not just a child who died but a fellow human being we learned to know. Similarly, I see Ruth emerge as the one who is willing to talk about what has happened, while Orpah becomes the friend who, for various reasons, is unable to share Naomi's grief.

The person who describes Naomi's grief best is Tessa Afshar. After the death of her sons, Naomi lives a shadowy life where she has stopped engaging with what is happening around her. She is grateful that Ruth is with her, but she herself is not really functioning. When they arrive in Bethlehem and see Naomi's old home in a state of disrepair, Naomi leaves it to Ruth to tidy up. She never bothers to give their donkey water and has no motivation to eat. Naomi sinks deeper and deeper into depression. Her faith in God, previously so strong, is also suffering. She sees everything that has happened as God's fault, where God has deliberately sent all this misfortune upon her: "She said to them, 'Call me no longer Naomi, call me Mara, for the Almighty has dealt bitterly with me. I went away full, but the Lord has brought me back empty; why call me Naomi when the Lord has dealt harshly with me, and the Almighty has brought calamity upon me?'" (Ruth 1:20–21). When we read these lines, we must remember that they express Naomi's view of the situation. They are not an impartial account of God's action but reflect what Naomi is experiencing at that moment. At the same time, these are important lines precisely because they show that it is permissible to feel this way. The Bible does not judge Naomi for her despair but allows her to vent her doubts and anger without reproaching her.

## The Faithfulness of Ruth

Many poets and writers recognize Ruth's expressed affection and loyalty to Naomi and interpret Ruth's words as signs of a deep, intimate, and mutual relationship. They challenge us to look beyond Naomi's lack of commitment in verse 18 and to see her through Ruth's eyes. Ruth sees a woman who is worth loving, for whom it is worth leaving country, language, culture, and religion. Ruth sets off into the unknown just to be with Naomi. In her poem "The Book of Ruth and Naomi," Marge Piercy writes about how women of all times

> cherished Ruth, more friend than
> daughter. Daughters leave. Ruth
> brought even the baby she made
> with Boaz home as a gift. [. . .]
>
> I will be a Jew for you,
> for what is yours I will love
> as I love you, oh Naomi
> my mother, my sister, my heart.

Piercy's poem highlights not only Ruth's acts of self-sacrifice but also her willingness to give up her old identity, even though her new identity is certainly nothing to carry lightly. It may be a burden to voluntarily choose to become Jewish, with all the persecution and suffering associated with it. In Piercy's hands, Ruth's identification with Naomi's people becomes a sign of the ultimate love.

## One Mother-in-Law Too Many?

Other retellings challenge us to think more deeply about Ruth and Naomi's relationship. Is it really likely that Ruth would give up everything for her mother-in-law, especially given that up to this point in the story, Naomi has not shown Ruth much enthusiasm? Erin Phillips makes this interpretation very clear in her book *A Bond of Briars*. Her Ruth (Caitrin) feels compelled to go with her mother-in-law because she has promised her husband on his deathbed to look after his mother. Without this promise, she would have stayed in Moab (Cairlich). The antipathy is mutual, as Naomi (Meara) is ashamed that her son has married one of Moab's hated and feared *cairlins*, women with magical powers who live in union with a spirit. Naomi's disapproval becomes increasingly clear the closer they get to Bethlehem (Soarsa). Once there, Naomi lies in bed and wants to die but at the same time expects Ruth to take care of everything practical and make sure that they have food to eat. When Ruth comes home with vegetables, Naomi complains that they have no eggs or meat. The situation escalates and ends with Naomi throwing Ruth out of the house.

Even so, Phillips's story ends with reconciliation. Ruth realizes that she can, if not actually love Naomi, at least act as if she did.

> [Naomi] certainly doesn't deserve to have me save her. After all, she wouldn't even consider helping me in my most dire hour. In fact, she basically cursed me to die. [. . .] I didn't deserve for [Boaz] to save me, to love me, to die for me. My life is barely even my own anymore. [Boaz], my sgaoileadh, my redeemer, has paid for me to be free. Perhaps I can be [Naomi's] sgaoileadh. Perhaps I can give her what she doesn't deserve but I know she needs, what I have in my possession: the priceless gift of a love given freely. (337)

After this, the two women slowly but surely approach one another. It takes a while before they can apologize to each other for their feelings of ingratitude and anger at unmet expectations. Later, when Obed (Gildas) is born, Naomi is finally able to let go of her grief and accept that her husband and sons are dead. For Phillips's Naomi, the grandchild becomes a reason to start living again.

## The Journey to Bethlehem

After Ruth declares her closing line in Ruth 1:17 that only death can separate them, Naomi gives up trying to convince Ruth to stay in Moab and the two widows head west toward Bethlehem. How does Naomi experience this remigration? Is it something she both longs for and fears? Could it be that Naomi feels guilty about having left her homeland ten years ago because of the famine? Does she feel like a traitor who should have stayed and helped? At the same time, she surely knows in her heart that there was nothing she could have done to alleviate the suffering. Everyone was probably grateful that the family left Bethlehem, as their absence meant four fewer mouths to feed. When some leave, those who remain have a better chance of surviving on the limited available food rations.

The Bible describes the journey from Moab to Bethlehem as a relatively lighthearted affair. It takes only half a verse: "So the two of them went on until they came to Bethlehem." (Ruth 1:19a). If you look at a map, however, you see that there is quite a distance between Moab and Bethlehem. Depending on where exactly in Moab Naomi and Ruth lived at the start, their journey should take between four days and a week. Furthermore, the road in between is far from easy. You first have to head north and then walk around the upper part of the Dead Sea. It is a hot, dry, and barren desert landscape. The Dead Sea region is not exactly known for its fertility, so to speak. Although the Bible does not give us any details, it is hard to avoid the conclusion that the journey for the two single women would be no holiday.

Several retellings highlight the hardships of two women traveling to Bethlehem. Eva Etzioni-Halevy describes in detail how one of their donkeys dies, probably from a combination of age and lack of water. Then Ruth miscarries (see below). Weak from anemia and thirst, Ruth is close to death. In the end, the women are rescued by a wandering group of Midianites who provide them with water and a place to rest (195–197, 199–204). Similarly, Afshar emphasizes the dangers of the journey. Her Ruth and Naomi are considerably more cautious than Etzioni-Halevy's characters. Even before they set off, they realize that two women should not travel alone and therefore pay for a place in a small caravan. While traveling, they are attacked by robbers. Just as they are brought to face their impending death, they are saved by a lion that kills one of the men and drives the other away (55–59).

Comparing these two narratives, Etzioni-Halevy, like the biblical narrative, chooses to keep God in the background. Instead, she invents other things that could have happened but that lack foundation in the biblical text itself. In contrast, Afshar chooses, like C. S. Lewis, to have God act in leonine form. She thus invents a miracle that also has no firm basis in the biblical text. At the same time, both stories shed light on the dangers and hardships faced by vulnerable travelers. Traveling from Moab to Bethlehem is risky business that should not be undertaken lightly.

## We Sail Away; They Sail Home

When they arrive, Naomi comes home while Ruth goes away. What is remigration for the older woman is immigration for the younger. Naomi can pick up her language, her food, and her customs, while Ruth has to learn new things. Ruth immediately ends up in the background as everyone welcomes Naomi, while no one seems to care about Ruth.

Sometimes it also seems as if Naomi shares this somewhat unwelcoming attitude toward Ruth. Naomi's focus is always on her own tragedy, ignoring the fact that Ruth is also a widow in mourning and alone in a foreign land. In Ruth 1:19b–21, Naomi describes how she has lost everything: "When they came to Bethlehem, the whole town was stirred because of them; and the women said, 'Is this Naomi?' She said to them, 'Call me no longer Naomi, call me Mara, for the Almighty has dealt bitterly with me. I went away full, but the Lord has brought me back empty; why call me Naomi when the Lord has dealt harshly with me, and the Almighty has brought calamity upon me?'" The Hebrew word *full* here (*me'lea*) comes from the verb "to fill." Thus, it is not a question of Naomi and Elimelech traveling to Moab with good financial means, but that they left Bethlehem full in the sense of being complete, that is, a whole family. Similarly, the word *empty* does not mean that Naomi returns without money but that she lacks what she set out with, namely her husband and sons. Life is empty because the people who previously gave it meaning are no longer alive.

I do not know whom I feel sorrier for at this point. I feel so sorry for Ruth who seems to stand there mostly as an appendage without being mentioned. How does she feel when Naomi tells the women of Bethlehem that she has returned empty-handed despite having Ruth by her side? Moreover, Ruth is referred to as the "Moabite" throughout the book in order to emphasize her exclusion (see 1:22). Wherever she goes, she is the foreigner who does not rightly belong in Bethlehem (and, by implication, therefore should not be there). At the same time, I understand Naomi. When you are as full of grief as Naomi is, you just want to crawl in somewhere and hide. When you have lost a child, you usually cannot be bothered to care about other people's well-being. It can become a kind of tunnel vision where you are unable to empathize with your fellow human beings. So, Naomi is probably unable to understand that Ruth is also grieving.

## Outcast

In her poem "Naomi: 'Call Me Bitter,'" Kathryn Hellerstein challenges us to consider Naomi's feelings toward Ruth when they both arrive in Bethlehem.

> I'm not alone, there's Ruth
> but how can I without my husband, sons,
> be coming home? The women peer out from
> their market stalls, their courtyard gates,
> at Ruth concealed beside me in her foreign veil

Naomi feels lonely, even though Ruth is with her, and she feels ashamed, at least a little, about the fact that Ruth is a Moabite. Her daughter-in-law's very existence testifies to the painful truth that her own sons, partly raised abroad, abandoned their culture and married foreigners. Hellerstein's Ruth says nothing but hides, perhaps out of shyness and perhaps also because she feels unwelcome.

As a parent, you give up some control over your children's experiences when you choose to move abroad. It can be very difficult for parents to see their children integrate more than they are prepared to accept. Many children who have grown up abroad do not have the same feelings for their parents' home country as their parents do, and it can be difficult for parents to face this. My own daughters, who grew up in Scotland, have never been part of a Swedish Lucia procession and have never sung the traditional end-of-the-school-year hymn "Den blomstertid nu kommer." Completely inconsequential details, I know, but it was a choice that I made for them, and now I have to face the consequences.

The earlier stanzas of Hellerstein's poem are reminiscent of Vilhelm Moberg's four-novel-suite *Utvandrarserien* (*The Emigrants*; published from 1949–1959) about a group of people (including Karl Oskar, his wife Kristina and their children, his younger brother Robert, the farmhand Arvid, and the local sex worker Ulrika) who leave Sweden due to poverty and starvation and settle in Minnesota.[1] Hellerstein describes how Naomi's husband, like a biblical Karl Oskar, dreams of being able to give his family a better life beyond starvation and hardship:

> My husband, hungry for
> a better life, trudged at my side, our sons
> walked, dreaming of their suppers in Moab

At the same time, Naomi becomes a biblical Kristina from Duvemåla who does not want to leave her homeland at all. Like Kristina, Naomi agrees to Elimelech's proposal only because the alternative, namely that the children starve to death, is even worse. In Naomi's case, however, the irony is clear: Naomi's children die despite her migration, or perhaps even because they leave Bethlehem.

## Alienation and Reconciliation

One of the main themes of the book of Ruth is alienation. Naomi flees Bethlehem because of starvation and ends up as a refugee in Moab, where her two sons at least try to integrate. At the same time, Ruth is and remains a stranger throughout the book. She chooses to follow Naomi to Bethlehem in Judah where she, like her husband Mahlon earlier, marries a native person. Ruth, however, goes much further than her previous in-laws as she also makes the religion of Judah her own. She renounces her original Moabite faith and embraces Naomi's belief in the God of Israel. Despite this, she remains a stranger and experiences the suspicion and stigmatization that so many immigrants and converts endure.

In her poem "The Handmaid's Tale," Barenblat expresses the hope that this separation between Jews and non-Jews will one day come to an end:

> and the seed of salvation grows in me
> the outsider, the forbidden [. . .]

and as my belly swells I pray
that the day come speedily and soon
when we won't need to distinguish

Israel from Moab

In Barenblat's poem, Ruth and Boaz become symbols of peace and reconciliation, where no distinction is made between Israel and its enemies in neighboring countries. Boaz and Ruth's common child embodies the hope of unity where the walls between people are broken down.

## Ruth on Fields and Threshing Floors

Ruth, perhaps because she is younger, is not prepared to become a burden to Naomi and she refuses to give in to grief. She takes the initiative to manage their shared living expenses when, at the beginning of chapter 2, she asks to glean ears of corn. "When you reap the harvest of your land, you shall not reap to the very edges of your field, or gather the gleanings of your harvest; you shall leave them for the poor and for the alien: I am the Lord your God" (Lev 23:22). Even though the gleanings were intended for people like Ruth, that is, the poor and immigrants, I can almost hear the whispering behind her back: "Now she has come here and taken both jobs and food from those in need in Bethlehem. Are we now going to provide not only for our own poor but also for all these immigrants?"

Then our hero appears on the scene. We know from the start that he is our hero, because the Hebrew name Boaz means strength. Our story could not have signaled its intention more clearly. Boaz inquires about Ruth, learns that she has traveled from Moab with Naomi, and learns that she is rather industrious (2:6–7). He gives Ruth permission to pick as much grain as she wants from his fields, to quench her thirst with the others working in the field, and later to eat with them (v. 14). He also makes sure that she is not molested by the male harvesters: "Then Boaz said to Ruth, 'Now listen, my daughter, do not go to glean in another field or leave this one, but keep close to my young women. Keep your eyes on the field that is being reaped, and follow behind them. I have ordered the young men not to bother you. If you get thirsty, go to the vessels and drink from what the young men have drawn'" (2:8–9). It seems that Boaz knows quite a lot about Ruth. Has he listened to gossip or spent time finding out things for himself? It is through Boaz that we learn that Ruth has helped her mother-in-law quite a lot: "But Boaz answered her, 'All that you have done for your mother-in-law since the death of your husband has been fully told me, and how you left your father and mother and your native land and came to a people that you did not know before. May the Lord reward you for your deeds, and may you have a full reward from the Lord, the God of Israel, under whose wings you have come for refuge!'" (2:11–12). Boaz is almost over-the-top in his care for Ruth, and Ruth recognizes this and feels encouraged (v. 13). Although the text does not say why, we can easily read the reason into the text. Boaz seems generally quite interested in Ruth. If we read the text "backward," we know that Boaz is Naomi's relative, and Boaz himself can hardly be unaware of this. Most people tend to keep pretty good track of their relatives. Has Boaz already begun to see Ruth as a potential spouse because he is aware of his duty to his relative's family member? Alternatively, does Ruth's physical appearance in the cornfield lead Boaz to consider what his relationship with Naomi might mean for his personal life?

This leads to the question of the age difference between Ruth and Boaz. If we assume that Ruth and Mahlon were married for just under ten years (see the "Time in Moab" section), Ruth and Boaz may be the same age. On the one hand, Boaz seems to be unmarried. In any case, there is no mention of a wife, either deceased or living. Ruth, on the other hand, is a widow and perhaps just under thirty. With this in mind, Ruth may even be the older of the two. What points in the opposite direction, that is, that Ruth is a relatively young widow, is Boaz's persistent habit of calling her "my daughter" (2:8; 3:10). However, the word *daughter* in Hebrew is often used as a term of endearment and does not necessarily imply a great age difference. When God calls Jerusalem "daughter Zion" (often in Isa 40–55), it may be best translated as "dear Zion," that is, as a way for God to express his love for Jerusalem. More important in this context, however, is Boaz's comment that Ruth came to him rather than looking for "young men" (*bachurim*), neither rich nor poor (3:10). This verse has led to the image of an octogenarian Boaz and a very young Ruth. Even in this case, however, it is important to look at the exact Hebrew word used. The Hebrew *bachur* is almost always the masculine equivalent of "virgin" (*betula*) (Deut 32:25; 31:13), that is, a person who has never been married. So what Boaz is saying is that Ruth is open to the possibility of remarrying a widower. Taken together, all of this suggests that Boaz himself is not completely young and that he may have been married before. At the same time, he is by no means old or frail. Let us settle for around thirty.

When Ruth comes home, she tells Naomi about her day and that she worked in Boaz's field. Suddenly, Naomi blurts out that this Boaz is her own relative. Later in the same discussion, Naomi says that it was a good thing Ruth stuck to Boaz's field, otherwise she would probably have been sexually harassed: "Naomi said to Ruth, her daughter-in-law, 'It is better, my daughter, that you go out with his young women, otherwise you might be bothered in another field'" (Ruth 2:22). So far, I have been sympathetic to the slightly skewed relationship between Naomi and Ruth and to the fact that Naomi does not openly express either concern for or gratitude toward Ruth. Now, however, I become rather annoyed with Naomi. Could she not have told Ruth a little earlier to go to Boaz's field? It would have saved a lot of effort and certainly been safer for Ruth. Alternatively, does Naomi think that sexual harassment is only to be expected at harvest time, but it was good that Ruth did not have to face it this time? Is Naomi forgetting that Ruth was not born and raised in Bethlehem and that this is a foreign culture to her? Has she suppressed her own experiences as an immigrant in Moab, when she herself did not know all the customs and traditions, or does she think that Ruth ought to manage on her own? After all, it was Ruth's own decision to accompany her to Bethlehem.

Ruth stays with her mother-in-law until the harvest is over (2:23). Then Naomi thinks that change is overdue:

> Naomi her mother-in-law said to her, "My daughter, I need to seek some security for you, so that it may be well with you. Now here is our kinsman Boaz, with whose young women you have been working. See, he is winnowing barley tonight at the threshing-floor. Now wash and anoint yourself, and put on your best clothes and go down to the threshing-floor; but do not make yourself known to the man until he has finished eating and drinking. When he lies down, observe the place where he lies; then, go and uncover his feet and lie down; and he will tell you what to do." (Ruth 3:1–4)

The fact that Naomi thinks Ruth should have "some security" raises the question of Naomi's motivation. Should we interpret Naomi's words as a newfound expression of genuine concern and an attempt to draw near to Ruth again? Is Naomi slowly emerging from her grief, now when she is back home, and able to consider others' wellbeing? Alternatively, is Naomi's behavior here in line with her initial hesitation about Ruth's presence in Bethlehem that we saw earlier in chapter 1? Should we interpret Naomi's desire as a disguised hint that she wants Ruth out of the house? Naomi's possible desire to get rid of her daughter-in-law certainly does not mean that she dislikes Ruth; it may instead suggest that Ruth's presence is a constant reminder to Naomi of her dead son. Both interpretations are supported by the text. At the same time, there is something in the story that is jarring, at least to me as a woman in the twenty-first century, and that is the assumption that neither Ruth nor Naomi can live a full and satisfactory life without husband and children. According to Naomi, Ruth, who for her part has appeared quite happy with her and Naomi's life so far, must get a husband or she will not have "security." Even so, we should not underestimate the economic and social problems that single women face in patriarchal societies. Naomi's words can therefore just as easily be interpreted as expressions of genuine concern: It would actually be so much easier for both of them if Ruth had a husband to support them.

Naomi's words are followed by an ambivalent and rather suggestive invitation. Naomi proposes an intriguing plan so that Ruth may catch a husband for herself. It is unclear whether Ruth is Naomi's willing accomplice, a victim of Naomi's power hunger, a seductress (the biblical archetype of the "strange woman"), a vulnerable stranger who sees no choice but to obey, or a mixture of all of these. In this context, we should keep in mind that Ruth is not an eighteen-year-old virgin but a widow with several years of marriage behind her.

Naomi's role and motivation in this intricate plan is also somewhat ambiguous. Is she using Ruth to get an heir and a good home, or is this an expression of her genuine concern in that Naomi really wants to make sure that Ruth gets a good husband who can take care of them both? Even so, sending a lonely, vulnerable woman out to spend the night among drunken men on threshing floors will never, at least in my opinion, count as responsible behavior.

Regardless of who motivates whom, Ruth goes along with Naomi's plan: "She said to her, 'All that you tell me I will do.' So she went down to the threshing-floor and did just as her mother-in-law had instructed her" (Ruth 3:5–6). What happens next is expressed in metaphors and shrouded in euphemisms.

> When Boaz had eaten and drunk, and he was in a contented mood, he went to lie down at the end of the heap of grain. Then she came quietly and uncovered his feet, and lay down. At midnight the man was startled and turned over, and there, lying at his feet, was a woman! He said, "Who are you?" And she answered, "I am Ruth, your servant; spread your cloak over your servant, for you are next-of-kin." [...]
>
> "Lie down until the morning." So she lay at his feet until morning, but got up before one person could recognize another; for he said, "It must not be known that the woman came to the threshing-floor." (Ruth 3:7–9, 13b–14)

There is a lot that is left out of the story, and readers can read in what they want between the lines. I maintain that this textual silence is entirely deliberate on the part of the narrator. Overly explicit language is seldom fun.

Naomi is cool as a cucumber when Ruth slowly wanders home in the early hours of the morning and reports on the fate and adventures of the night. According to Naomi, things have gone according to plan: "She replied, 'Wait, my daughter, until you learn how the matter turns out, for the man will not rest, but will settle the matter today'" (Ruth 3:18).

## Seducing a Man

Most writers struggle to understand the interaction between Ruth and Naomi, and what Naomi's plan actually aims to accomplish. In several cases (e.g., Afshar, Etzioni-Halevy), the two women are portrayed as working together for a better future. Furthermore, Boaz is not portrayed as a victim but merely as someone who needs to be pushed a little to do the right thing. The exception is Phillips, who describes a not too sympathetic Naomi, who earlier insinuated that Ruth should "cultivate" Boaz (Callen) to give them both advantages. Ruth, however, responds that "'I am not some cow you can sell for money,' I spit at her. 'If I marry again, it'll be for love.'" (167). Naomi laughs derisively, and Ruth feels used. Naomi later returns to the same idea and tells Ruth slyly and insultingly that "'you know, [Ruth], [Boaz] is very wealthy. Wealthy enough to buy back our family fields. So if something... untoward had happened while you two were alone... well, perhaps his... fascination with you can be used for our advantage'" (204). Ruth becomes angry and hurt, and she challenges Naomi to speak plainly: Is this really about Boaz, or is it about

Naomi's disappointment when Ruth did not give her any grandchildren while her husband was alive, to which Naomi retaliates by asking Ruth rather nastily if she was even trying. The situation escalates into a proper quarrel with hurt feelings on both sides.

It all ends with Naomi trying to coerce Ruth into seducing Boaz when he is drunk. Naomi greedily intends to blackmail Boaz and thus force him to buy back Naomi's property for her. For Naomi, Ruth is just a tool to fulfil her own wishes. Naomi ends her speech to Ruth with an extra dose of emotional blackmail: "'You owe me at least this, [Moabite], after everything you've done'" (285). Ruth leaves uncomfortably, as she does not trust Naomi to be really on her side—perhaps she intends to reject Ruth if the plan backfires? Once at the threshing floor, she soon realizes that she is unable to carry out her mother-in-law's wishes, as she respects (and loves but has not admitted this to herself yet) Boaz too much to hurt him. Boaz is also stone-cold sober. It all ends with Ruth confessing the whole shameful plan to Boaz, while Boaz, in turn, confirms his love for Ruth (291–298). Back home again, Naomi is furious that her plan has failed and throws Ruth out again (310–313).

Phillips's retelling highlights those aspects of the biblical Naomi's behavior toward Ruth that create a sense of unease. It challenges the reader to consider whether Naomi is acting responsibly and lovingly toward Ruth or whether she is more interested in recovering Elimelech's property and providing Elimelech with an heir. The book of Ruth ends, as is well known, with the somewhat unsettling statement that "A son has been born to Naomi" (Ruth 4:17).

## Naomi and Sarah, Boaz and Abraham, Ruth and Hagar

The book of Ruth has three (or four—we will return to this shortly) main characters: two women, Ruth and Naomi, and a man, Boaz. The biblical story describes the relationships between them in different ways. Some aspects of the text imply that Ruth and Boaz are roughly the same age, while other aspects suggest a generational difference, with Boaz and Naomi being the same age while Ruth is a generation younger (see above).

Our understanding of the age difference between the three main characters affects our interpretation of the interaction between them. A scenario in which Boaz and Naomi are the same age while Ruth is considerably younger makes me think of the relationship between Sarah, Abraham, and Hagar. There is a similarity here in that Naomi, like Sarah, uses a younger woman to get a son. Naomi herself has long since rejected the idea of remarrying and conceiving more children (1:12). Like Sarah, Naomi sends out the younger woman to have sex with a man not of her choosing and, like Hagar, Ruth agrees (3:1–5). Later, Ruth, again like Hagar, becomes the one who bears the child for the older, barren woman. The Bible makes it clear that by the time Obed is born, a son has been "born to Naomi" (4:17). Margaret Atwood picks up on this idea in her famous book *The Handmaid's Tale*. In Atwood's alternative future, where most women are barren, younger women are used as surrogate mothers who after giving birth lose the right to care for their own children.

This situation, in which Boaz chooses Ruth over Naomi, causes us to consider Naomi's own feelings in this context. Does she, like Sarah, feel jealous that it is the younger woman who gets to carry the child? Furthermore, how does Naomi feel when Ruth marries Boaz, while she herself remains a widow? Anna Kamieńska's poem "Naomi" challenges us to speculate whether, somewhere deep in her soul, Naomi might have wanted to be the one to remarry:

> Naomi perhaps you thought
> I'm still not so old
> I still may give birth
> didn't he ask about me
> let my daughter-in-law go to him
> perhaps she'll remind him of the young Naomi
> Perhaps waiting in the dark you thought
> he himself will come

Naomi's own self-image (rather than self-awareness), as reflected in her words in 1:12, suggests that she does not see marriage as a possible future for herself, even though she is the widow of Elimelech and thus the one whom the relative actually ought to marry. Instead, Naomi sees herself as old and barren: "Turn back, my daughters, go your way, for I am too old to have a husband. Even if I thought there was hope for me, even if I should have a husband tonight and bear sons." At the same time, her words in 1:12 do not necessarily mean that she is satisfied with her lot in life. It is difficult to determine Naomi's age here, depending on how old we make her sons when they arrive in Moab. Naomi may be between forty and fifty when she returns to Bethlehem and would, at least biologically, be able to bear a son. Despite this, Naomi does not want to remarry and sends Ruth out instead. At the same time, Kamieńska's poem invites us to consider whether there is not at least a touch of jealousy here, and perhaps even a sense of disappointment in Naomi's breast as she watches her younger daughter-in-law get both husband and child while she herself remains a lonely and barren widow. In the end, Naomi has to make do with a grandchild rather than a child of her own. She may still be useful but only as a nanny. She will never be a wife or mother again. Naomi tries not to cry.

## The Kinsman Redeemer

Things start to fall into place. There is another man in the story, the so-called kinsman redeemer or "next-of-kin." He is a shadowy and anonymous figure, who seems to have both rights and obligations toward Naomi and her inheritance. Boaz mentions him to Ruth on the threshing-floor (3:12) in response to Ruth's prayer that Boaz will become her kinsman redeemer (3:9). The next day, the two men meet and discuss the matter (4:1–8). It is very unclear what this discussion is about, but the lack of clarity is probably due to our contemporary lack of knowledge regarding inheritance laws and property relations in ancient Israel rather than any desire on behalf of the narrator to obfuscate matters. I suspect that an ancient Israelite audience had a much better idea of what the two men were talking about than we do today. Anyway, it all ends with Boaz getting the right to inherit Naomi's husband's estate and marry Mahlon's widow Ruth. Again, we get the strong impression that Boaz is either unmarried or a childless widower: He can act alone without considering either a wife or children, unlike the other man, who seems to have to make allowances for his own heirs (v. 6).

### An Abominable Man

The Bible does not tell us much about the kinsman redeemer. He is closer to Naomi than Boaz is, but in the end he refuses to marry Ruth. The reasons for his behavior are shrouded in mystery. He seems to be interested in taking over Elimelech's estate but uninterested in marrying Mahlon's widow and unwilling to allow their first son to be counted as Elimelech's heir. It is clear that money rather than compassion underpins his behavior. I imagine him as someone who is happy to do his job but only if he benefits from it. He is willing to work outside normal working hours, but only if he receives the usual overtime pay and preferably also an overtime allowance. This does not make him a bad man in any way. At the same time, perhaps because of the way the story is constructed, we instinctively doubt his good will: the kinsman redeemer is Boaz's antithesis. We almost feel prompted to look for something dark and perhaps even slightly villainous in him.

Many writers have been fascinated by this obscure man who lives in the shadow of the other characters. Our two chosen novelists speculate on this elusive man. Etzioni-Halevy makes Mishael, as she calls him, a charming but ultimately rather repulsive man. After Mahlon's death, Mishael flirts with the exhausted and grieving Ruth, who has spent the last four years caring for her slowly dying husband. Ruth herself, starved of affection and sex, falls for the eloquent and handsome stranger from Bethlehem and eventually begins to hope that he will propose marriage (170–184). Her hopes are dashed, however, when he suddenly leaves for home. Ruth, alone and pregnant, chooses to accompany her mother-in-law Naomi to Bethlehem not only out of loyalty to Naomi but also because she is not quite satisfied with a future as a single parent in Moab (187–190). When she eventually arrives in Bethlehem, no longer pregnant after the miscarriage on the road, she still dreams of a life with Mishael, but it quickly becomes clear that he does not want her at all (219). She was just a superficial pastime (274–275). Then follows a little cockfight between Boaz and Mishael in which Boaz makes it clear to the latter that he should leave Ruth alone if life is dear to him (238–240). Ruth, for her part, realizes that Boaz is a far better man than Mishael in more ways than one.

Afshar again chooses a different path. She introduces the reader to our fourth character in the first half of the book, where she describes how Boaz has a maidservant, Mahalath, who has been hunted by her former owner, Jaala. When Naomi hears about this, she is very worried but chooses not to say anything (116). Later in the book, Jaala reappears as Naomi's closest relative and thus Ruth's potential kinsman redeemer. In Afshar's retelling, the man is basically not necessary. Boaz is prepared to marry Ruth and enter into a "normal" marriage where their common children become Boaz's heirs. It is instead Ruth, who is willing to do anything to make Naomi happy, who suggests that her first child should belong to Elimelech's, or rather Naomi's, family. Ruth's initiative complicates the situation, as Boaz must first outmaneuver the debtor before he can marry Ruth. Boaz manages the situation gallantly, of course, by playing on the kinsman redeemer's greed, and so all is well that ends well (208–213).

Both narratives demonstrate, each in its own way, that we do not really understand what is going on in chapter 4 of the book of Ruth. As I mentioned earlier, it is likely that our lack of understanding stems from our insufficient knowledge of the legal situation in ancient Israel that is presupposed in the book. We keep suspecting that something is going on behind the scenes, but we are unable to grasp it fully. The anonymous man arouses our curiosity and invites us to speculate about his relationship with Naomi, Ruth, and Boaz.

### Boaz: Redeemer and Savior

In a completely different way, made possible by the fantasy genre, Phillips chooses to make Boaz a savior figure. This reading is motivated by the Hebrew word *go'el* (cf. Lev 25:47–49; Deut 5:8), which is also used of God and then translated as "savior" (e.g., Pss 19:14; 78:35; Job 19:25). In Phillips's hands, Boaz becomes the real redeemer—and also a picture of Jesus's later salvation on the cross (cf. Gal 3:13; Eph 1:7; Heb 9:12)—when he shows himself willing to redeem Ruth from her destructive relationship with the spirit with whom she is bonded. Boaz is willing to give up his blood (i.e., his life) to set Ruth free. Phillips's retelling stands clearly in the biblical tradition that a blood sacrifice is required to redeem humanity from sin (Gen 12:3–7; Luke 22:20; Heb 9:22; 1 Pet 1:19, etc.). Boaz gives his blood, willingly and motivated by love, to save Ruth but survives because his sacrifice was based on selfless love.

## A Son of Naomi

After the financial investigation in Ruth 4:1–8, Boaz marries Ruth, and she quickly becomes pregnant. This is the last we hear of Ruth. The narrative perspective shifts back to Naomi. Although Ruth is indeed the one who gives birth to Obed, she is once again overshadowed, as all the women in Bethlehem relate to Obed as the son of Naomi (not Elimelech, as one would have assumed given what had previously unfolded in chapter 4):

> So Boaz took Ruth and she became his wife. When they came together, the Lord made her conceive, and she bore a son. Then the women said to Naomi, "Blessed be the Lord, who has not left you this day without

> next-of-kin; and may his name be renowned in Israel! He shall be to you a restorer of life and a nourisher of your old age; for your daughter-in-law who loves you, who is more to you than seven sons, has borne him." Then Naomi took the child and laid him in her bosom, and became his nurse. The women of the neighborhood gave him a name, saying, "A son has been born to Naomi." They named him Obed; he became the father of Jesse, the father of David. (Ruth 4:13–17)

So, all's well that ends well? I am not sure. As a reader, I'm a little saddened that there is so little focus on Ruth in the end and that it sometimes feels like she has been reduced to a secondary character in the book that bears her name. Ruth and Boaz become the two heroes that no one really gets to know. I often think of Snow White when I read the book of Ruth: Of course it is the good Snow White who gets the prince, but at the same time, it is the stepmother who fascinates and captures our attention. Now I do not mean that Ruth is boring or that Naomi is evil, but the book of Ruth makes demands of its reader. When I read the book, I make an effort to remember Ruth and to bring her out of the shadows. I actively want to put her in the center and see her for who she is: the woman who sets out on adventures in foreign lands, in foreign fields, on foreign threshing floors. She does not know she is going to win the prince, and I am not entirely sure that the prince and the child are her main driving force. She wants to get away, out, to something new, but at the same time, she acts with such generosity, honesty, and caring that it is easy to forget what she wants deep in her heart. I would love to give her the lead role in her own story.

* * *

The book of Ruth raises many questions about exclusion and xenophobia but also about community and belonging. Naomi and her husband choose to leave Bethlehem and head out into the unknown to save themselves and their children from starvation. In many ways, Naomi symbolizes the refugee fleeing their country to save their family and find a better life elsewhere. Once they arrive, they try to make the best of the situation. Just like today, the younger generation (Mahlon and Chilion) find it easier to integrate into the new society, while the older generation (Naomi) seems to have a much harder time. Eventually, the situation is reversed when Ruth decides to accompany Naomi to Bethlehem. She is not fleeing starvation and hardship; instead, she is driven by loyalty and love for Naomi. Ruth is not a refugee but rather an example of marriage migration.

The book of Ruth does not constitute an argument for or against different kinds of migration. Rather, it highlights the diversity of situations we can face ourselves, either as strangers in another country or in our encounter with people who have moved to our own. Ruth's experiences then become interesting precisely because she sometimes gets lost in her own story. Much of the focus is on Naomi, both as a refugee and as a representative of remigration. She, the woman from Bethlehem, is the indigenous Israelite and is the focus of the Bible. Reading the book from Ruth's perspective is more difficult. She is the outsider, the Moabite, whom Israel undeniably dislikes and whose origin is not something to be flaunted. Everyone in Bethlehem has heard the unsavory story of how the Moabites are descended from an incestuous relationship between Lot and one of his daughters (Gen 19:31–38). At the same time, Ruth is the real heroine of the book because, through her self-sacrificing actions and her love for both Naomi and God, she is the one who will become the ancestress of David's lineage and thus also of Jesus. If the book of Ruth teaches us anything, it is to judge a person not by her origins but by her actions.

Ruth is also an important book about grief. What happens to us when we grieve, and how do we relate to other mourners? The book of Ruth does not provide any ready-made answers, but it encourages us to think about Naomi's behavior toward Ruth and Orpah and their respective responses. To reiterate, there are no wrong answers in the book. Orpah chooses to do what she can in the situation and what is ultimately the best for her. Ruth, for her part, takes the harder path. She decides to swallow her own grief and instead reach out to Naomi, thus putting Naomi's welfare before her own. Naomi herself also chooses, at least initially, to allow herself to be consumed by her grief so that she no longer sees her fellow human beings. The most important thing to note in the story is that none of the characters are criticized for their choices. As readers, we can choose Ruth as our heroine, but not everyone is capable of being a Ruth, nor is it required. In the eyes of the Bible, there is no shame in being either an Orpah or a Naomi, and we should therefore not place that burden on our neighbors.

Ruth is, last but not least, a book about the presence and absence of God in our lives. God works in secret and is visible within the fabric of the book. At the same time, it is not always easy to understand when God works behind the scenes. Is it God's will that Naomi and her family go to Moab when people are starving to death in Bethlehem? Why do they travel, while others stay behind? To reconnect with Vilhelm Moberg's quartet *The Emigrants*, it is the brave who dare to break away and heed God's calling to find new life beyond society's restrictions and expectations. At the same time, it is equally important to emphasize that not all those who have the courage to emigrate are doing well. For every Ulrika of Västergöhl, the sex worker who finds vindication in America, there is an Arvid, the farm hand, who succumbs to defeat.

So, to what degree is God involved in the happenings in the book of Ruth? It may seem that God is not involved at all, as things are certainly not going well for Elimelech, Mahlon, or Chilion once they arrive in Moab. At least, that is what Naomi concludes. At the same time, the reader knows that Ruth must come to Bethlehem, because she must marry Boaz—otherwise King David will not be born and eventually neither will the messiah. If we read the text backward, as many readers have done throughout the ages, God's providence becomes clearer. Even though the circumstances seem less than ideal, God is still guiding, silently but steadily, making sure that Ruth is exactly where she needs to be to become David's great grandmother.

This uncertainty about God's role in the events of the book makes its message less evident than that of the Joseph story, where Joseph declares unequivocally that "even though you intended to do harm to me, God intended it for good, in order to preserve a numerous people, as he is doing today" (Gen 50:20). Perhaps the story of Ruth is closer to our own experiences? How many of us can exclaim with Joseph that we know for sure that our adversities are part of God's plan for us? I cannot. Rather, God has worked in my life in a much gentler way, never more than one step at a time, and without any great display. When I look back on my life, I can clearly see God leading me, for better or for worse, but I can usually only see his guidance in retrospect. Only a few times, and then in absolute crisis situations like the day my son Caspian died, have I truly experienced God's care in real time. That is why I recognize myself in the characters in the book of Ruth, who likewise resist drawing any overconfident conclusions. Like Joseph, they trust in God's grace and provision, only in a slightly humbler manner.

CHAPTER FIVE

# Saul

## *Sinful Culprit or Sinned-Against Hero?*

I HAVE ALWAYS had mixed feelings about Saul, the first king of Israel. On the one hand, he is such a tragic figure. He is rejected by God and lives the rest of his life knowing that he is not up to God's standard. He is not good enough and therefore must be replaced. I struggle to understand the magnitude of what that would mean and how it would feel. What if I were Saul? How would I live my life then? The message being preached from church pulpits around our world is diametrically opposed to the one Saul hears: You are fine just as you are; you are loved for who you are; there is no sin too great for God to forgive; God loves a returning sinner and so on. That message applies to us all but not to Saul. He is the exception, and exceptions scare me, because what if there are more exceptions, and what if I am one of them? I find it unsurprising that Saul ends his life in deep depression, and when I read that he chooses to fall on his sword, I mourn but am not surprised. What would Saul have to hope for? What future would he have had if he had survived the slaughter on Mount Gilboa? To live another few years in the knowledge of being rejected by God?

On the other hand, Saul is not always a nice person. After God rejects him, Saul commits one of the most heinous acts of violence in the Bible when he has the entire city of Nob (consisting of priests and their families and associated livestock) killed just because they might have helped David in his escape from Saul's murderous plans (1 Sam 22). It is, however, important to remember that this happens after God has rejected him. It is as if all his inhibitions have left him: What is the point of being good anyway, when one is rejected by God? We know that grace does not give a person license to kill but neither does judgment. Nonetheless, Saul seems to sin because he has already received the worst possible punishment. What could be worse than being cast out from

God's presence? Although Saul seeks God again and again, God answers him only with silence.

To fully understand Saul and God's relationship, we need to understand that God's communication is nearly always delivered to Saul via Samuel, Israel's judge and God's prophet. Samuel is God's representative and has the authority to speak in God's name. This raises the question of whether it is really God who displaces Saul or whether it is Samuel, God's mouthpiece. Samuel, in his role as prophet, controls God's communication with Israel to a large extent. Could it be that Samuel, disappointed with God's decision to give Israel a king, listens selectively to God and delivers God's message even more selectively? Maybe we should hold Samuel, rather than God, accountable for Saul's bitter fate?

The conflict reaches its climax when God, through Samuel, rejects Saul. Saul lives the rest of his life with the certainty that he will be replaced by a "man after God's own heart" and Saul, already insecure, sinks into despair, filled with doubts and suspicion. The identity of this chosen man is quickly and devastatingly revealed. Saul soon discerns that David, the beautiful musician, who he first thought would rescue him from the darkness of depression through his wonderful music, is none other than the man God has chosen to replace him.

Saul is a dead end. He is the first king of Israel but also the last of his line. He will always stand in David's shadow; he will always be the one God rejected. His heartbreaking fate leaves few of us untouched.

## Narratives

We will deepen our understanding of Saul, whose story is found in 1 Samuel 9–31, by studying a number of poems, books, and a theater play. It is interesting to observe the difference between Jewish and Christian interpretations of King Saul. Although there are of course several exceptions, Jewish interpreters show a considerably greater interest in and understanding of King Saul than Christians do. While many Jewish poets make Saul a tragic hero, he is rarely mentioned by Christian writers, who instead more often choose to ally themselves with David, Saul's successor. This can be explained not only by Christianity's clear identification of Jesus as the son of David but also by the often triumphal tone of much Christian interpretation.

**Yehuda Amichai** (1924–2000) was an Israeli poet and writer. He was born in Germany but emigrated to the then British Mandatory Palestine in 1935.

"King Saul and I," in *The Poetry of Yehuda Amichai*, ed. Robert Alter (Farrar, Straus and Giroux, 2015), 39–41.

**Karl Beck** (1817–1879) was a Jewish poet from Austria-Hungary.

*Saul: Tragödie in fünf Aufzügen* (E. Polz, 1840).

**Lord George Gordon Byron** (1788–1824) was an English poet active during the Romantic period.

"Saul," in *Hebrew Melodies* (Murray, 1815).

"Song of Saul Before His Last Battle," in *Hebrew Melodies* (Murray, 1815).

"Thou Whose Spell Can Raise the Dead," in *Hebrew Melodies* (Murray, 1815).

**Gustaf Fröding** (1860–1911) was a Swedish poet, best known for his collection *Stänk och flikar* (Bonniers, 1896). His collection *Nya dikter* (New poems) has a section entitled "Biblical Fantasies," which includes his poem about Saul and David.

"Saul och David," in *Nya dikter* (Bonniers, 1894).

**Amir Gilboa**, (1917–1984) was an Israeli poet. See chapter 2.

"Saul," in *Voices Within the Ark: The Modern Jewish Poets*, eds. Howard Schwartz and Anthony Rudolf, trans. Shirley Kaufman (Avon, 1980), originally published as *Shirim baboker baboker* (Hakibbutz hameuchad, 1953).

**Dan Pagis** (1930–1986) was an Israeli poet, lecturer, and Holocaust survivor. Born in Romania, he was held as a child in a concentration camp in Ukraine before escaping in 1944. He arrived in the then British Mandatory Palestine in 1946 and obtained a PhD from the Hebrew University of Jerusalem, where he later taught medieval Jewish literature.

"תפילת שאול האחרונה" (Saul's last prayer), in *Does David Still Play Before You? Israeli Poetry and the Bible*, ed. David C. Jacobson (Wayne State University Press, 1997), 232.

**Eric Shaw Quinn** (b. 1959) is an American writer, actor, and producer.
*The Prince's Psalm* (DSP Publications, 2016).

**Gladys Schmitt** (1909–1972) was an American author. She was a professor of English at Carnegie Mellon University from 1942 until her death. Her second novel, *David the King*, was an instant bestseller and has since sold more than 1 million copies.
*David the King* (Dial, 1946).

**Thomas Shapcott** (b. 1935) is an Australian poet and writer.
"Portrait of Saul," in *Begin with Walking* (University of Queensland Press, 1972).

**Shaul Tchernichovsky** (1875–1943) was a Russian-born, Hebrew-speaking poet and physician who immigrated to the then British Mandatory Palestine in 1931. He is considered one of the greatest Jewish poets ever. He often identified with King Saul, maybe because they shared the same name. He wrote another poem about Saul ("The King," published in 1926), which is not mentioned here.
"בעין־דור" (At Endor), https://benyehuda.org/read/6101, 1897.
"על חרבות בית־שן" (At the ruins of Beth-shan), https://benyehuda.org/read/6234, 1897.
"על הרי גלבוע" (On Mount Gilboa), https://benyehuda.org/read/4581, 1929.
"אנשי־חיל חבל" (The faithful fighters), https://benyehuda.org/read/6369, 1936.

## Saul Becomes King

Bible readers are introduced to Saul in 1 Samuel 9. We meet a handsome young man looking for his father's missing donkeys.

> There was a man of Benjamin whose name was Kish son of Abiel son of Zeror son of Becorath son of Aphiah, a Benjaminite, a man of wealth. He had a son whose name was Saul, a handsome young man. There was not a man among the people of Israel more handsome than he; he stood head and shoulders above everyone else. Now the

> donkeys of Kish, Saul's father, had strayed. So Kish said to his son Saul, "Take one of the boys with you; go and look for the donkeys." (1 Sam 9:1–3)

It is undoubtedly a rather comical beginning to the long and poignant story that will end in disaster on Mount Gilboa many chapters later in 1 Samuel 31. After a fruitless search far and wide, Saul is encouraged by his servant to ask for help from the prophet who lives in the neighborhood where they are, quite far away from home. At the same time, God tells the same prophet, who is none other than Samuel, that a young man will appear and that Samuel's task is to anoint him as prince over Israel (vv. 15–16).

Saul is certainly not very worldly. When he meets Samuel, he does not recognize him but asks him if he knows where the prophet is (vv. 18–19). Saul does not see himself as important but is honestly humble and surprised that Samuel invites him home and gives him the best seat and the best meat (vv. 22–24).

The next day, Samuel anoints Saul as prince of Israel. Samuel, known for failing to look beyond a person's outer appearance (see 1 Sam 16:7), chooses the handsome, stately Saul, who has never ruled a kingdom before. Interestingly, at this stage, Samuel anoints Saul prince (*nagid*; 1 Sam 10:1–2). This differs from Samuel's later mission in 1 Samuel 16:1, where he anoints David as king (*melech*). This difference can be interpreted as a sign that David is given a higher rank from the very beginning: While Saul is only appointed prince, David is anointed king. After Samuel's anointing, God's spirit falls on Saul (cf. 1 Sam 16:13, where God's spirit falls on David), and Saul becomes ecstatic (10:10–13).

The young man that we meet in these early chapters (9–12) is a modest and rather insecure person. For example, Saul chooses not to tell his uncle about his exaltation: "When his prophetic frenzy had ended, he went home. Saul's uncle said to him and to the boy, 'Where did you go?' And he replied, 'To seek the donkeys; and when we saw they were not to be found, we went to Samuel.' Saul's uncle said, 'Tell me what Samuel said to you.' Saul said to his uncle, 'He told us that the donkeys had been found.' But about the matter of the kingship, of which Samuel had spoken, he did not tell him anything" (1 Sam 10:13–16). When Samuel later asks him to appear before the people, the shy Saul prefers to hide away: "So they inquired again of the Lord, 'Did the man come here?' and the Lord said, 'See, he has hidden himself among the baggage'" (1 Sam 10:22). Despite his apparent insecurity, however, Saul soon proves to be a good military leader. He manages to rally the people and form an army and then defeats the Ammonites (1 Sam 11).

## Saul and Samuel

Throughout the first part of the story of Saul, Samuel is there at his side (1 Sam 9–15). Yet Samuel is seldom a supportive and benevolent mentor but more often a jealous and envious one. From the beginning, the relationship between Samuel, the savvy prophet and judge, and Saul, the country bumpkin who comes out of nowhere and is suddenly elevated to king, is relatively unequal. Samuel has the power, and Saul obeys him. After a while, though, the power balance shifts between them. Slowly, when the inexperienced and young Saul turns out to be a military genius who manages to keep the Philistines at bay, and when he slowly but surely begins wishing to make his own decisions and not always submit to Samuel, their relationship becomes untenable. Samuel wants a puppet so that he can lead Israel himself, but Saul has his own ideas about how the kingdom should be run.

At the same time, the portrait of Samuel has mitigating aspects. I sometimes think about Samuel's childhood. Being given away to the temple at Shiloh by his mother, Hannah, at the age of three and then brought up by the priest Eli, a man who, by all accounts, does not seem to be an expert in child-rearing, cannot have been easy. Eli's own sons are not well-behaved, to say the least (1 Sam 2:12–17), and his emotional intelligence leaves much to be desired when he accuses the distraught and praying Hannah of being drunk (1 Sam 1:13–14). Thus, given Samuel's upbringing, it is perhaps understandable that the adult Samuel is not a completely harmonious person. Perhaps there is a fear, deep in his soul, of once again being rejected and abandoned that affects his relationship with God and his fellow human beings.

It is therefore not difficult to empathize with Samuel's own disappointment when God chooses to listen to Israel's request and give them a king. Samuel, in his role as judge, probably thinks that the time of the judges, when God raised up individual leaders in crisis situations (see Judg 3–16), was an ideal way of governing a people. Now he is forced to face the disappointing truth that not only does Israel prefer a king but also that God agrees with them. To rub salt further in the wound, God has the nerve to ask him to choose this very king. What a humiliation. Not only is Samuel himself rejected as a leader, but he is also given the task of choosing his own successor.

Shortly afterward, Samuel engages in a piece of light sedition: While asking the Israelites to obey the king he has just appointed for them, he also takes the opportunity to proclaim that this is not God's ultimate plan. It is implied that it would have been better if they had obeyed God directly (with Samuel as judge, of course):

> Samuel summoned the people to the Lord at Mizpah and said to them, "Thus says the Lord, the God of Israel, 'I brought up Israel out of Egypt, and I rescued you from the hand of the Egyptians and from the hand of all the kingdoms that were oppressing you.' But today you have rejected your God, who saves you from all your calamities and your distresses; and you have said, 'No! but set a king over us.' Now therefore present yourselves before the Lord by your tribes and by your clans." (1 Sam 10:17–19)

Samuel's bitterness toward God (and Saul) is most evident in 1 Samuel 12, where Samuel exclaims how he has served Israel well since his youth (vv. 2–4). This is accompanied by a mild dose of power abuse when Samuel, with God's help, calls down thunder and rain so that the people understand what a great sin they have committed in asking for a king (vv. 16–20).

The relationship between Samuel and Saul, which started out rather benignly in 1 Samuel 10, soon takes on all the characteristics of a power struggle. Almost immediately after Samuel has made Saul king, he gives Saul many instructions to do both this and that (1 Sam 10:3–9). First Samuel 10:8 is of utmost importance for understanding what has already started to go wrong: "And you shall go down to Gilgal ahead of me; then I will come down to you to present burnt-offerings and offer sacrifices of well-being. For seven days you shall wait, until I come to you and show you what you shall do.'" This command, which Samuel seems to give Saul at the very beginning of his reign, becomes a growing problem. It becomes a sign of Samuel's manipulative relationship with Saul (and their respective relationships with God). Saul has just received authority to rule from both God and Samuel, but the first thing Samuel does is to rein him in. The command to wait seven days "until I come and tell you what to do" does not respect a monarch's sovereign authority.

The chronological sequence of 1 Samuel 9–15 is extremely difficult to piece together. It takes until 1 Samuel 13:8 before we readers learn what happens to Samuel's earlier command. In general, it is unclear how many years pass in these chapters. At the beginning of chapter 9, Saul seems to be a very young man, but by chapter 13 we know that he has a son, Jonathan, who is old enough to lead a battalion in battle against the Philistines. Thus at least fifteen or maybe even twenty years could have passed in the meantime.

At the same time, other aspects suggest that only one week has gone by. Samuel asked Saul to wait seven days in 10:8, and this wait ends only in 13:8–14. To solve the obvious chronological problem, many biblical scholars choose to either move 10:8 a few decades forward in time to a later period during Saul's reign or move 13:8–14 back to the period immediately after Saul was anointed king. I choose the former option for narrative reasons, which leads to Saul having matured in his role as king by this time. Samuel, in contrast, still seems to be angry about the situation, perhaps because he in the meantime has been forced to realize that the idea of having a king did not immediately fail but instead led to a number of victories against Israel's enemies (cf. 11:12–15). The alternative is that God chooses to reject Saul as king after only seven days, which is theoretically possible but less likely.

> He waited for seven days, the time appointed by Samuel; but Samuel did not come to Gilgal, and the people began to slip away from Saul. So Saul said, "Bring the burnt-offering here to me, and the offerings of well-being." And he offered the burnt-offering. As soon as he had finished offering the burnt-offering, Samuel arrived; and Saul went out to meet him and salute him. Samuel said, "What have you done?" Saul replied, "When I saw that the people were slipping away from me, and that you did not come within the days appointed, and that the Philistines were mustering at Michmash, I said, 'Now the Philistines will come down upon me at Gilgal, and I have not entreated the favor of the Lord'; so I forced myself, and offered the burnt-offering." Samuel said to Saul, "You have done foolishly; you have not kept the commandment of the Lord your God, which he commanded you. The Lord would have established your kingdom over Israel for ever, but now your kingdom will not continue; the Lord has sought out a man after his own heart; and the Lord has appointed

> him to be ruler over his people, because you have not kept what the Lord commanded you." And Samuel left and went on his way from Gilgal. (1 Sam 13:8–15)

This episode has all the signs of a power struggle. I can imagine how Samuel is crouching behind a bush with the timer in his hand, just waiting to see if Saul will obey him or dare to make his own decision. Then, when Saul feels pressured to act, Samuel suddenly appears like a jack-in-the-box, insisting that God has rejected Saul. To me, this feels like an overreaction on Samuel's (God's?) part. If we compare for a moment with the later King David, David takes the initiative all the time, including offering burnt offerings (see 2 Sam 24:18–25), without anyone caring. Moreover, is Saul's sin, if it is a sin at all, really serious enough to justify the decision to take the kingdom away from him and give it to someone else? Most readers would probably say no.

After this episode, things begin quickly to unravel. A little later (depending, as discussed above, on how we understand the chronology of 1 Sam 9–15), a battle takes place between the Israelites and the Amalekites. Samuel decides to interfere in Saul's warfare and tells Saul that God has commanded him to annihilate the Amalekites: "Now go and attack Amalek, and utterly destroy all that they have; do not spare them, but kill both man and woman, child and infant, ox and sheep, camel and donkey" (1 Sam 15:3). Saul has a different opinion and decides to pardon King Agag (no doubt for diplomatic reasons) and to sacrifice the animals to God. This displeases Samuel greatly and he resorts to violence, both verbal and physical:

> "Why then did you not obey the voice of the Lord? Why did you swoop down on the spoil, and do what was evil in the sight of the Lord?" Saul said to Samuel, "I have obeyed the voice of the Lord, I have gone on the mission on which the Lord sent me, I have brought Agag the king of Amalek, and I have utterly destroyed the Amalekites. But from the spoil the people took sheep and cattle, the best of the things devoted to destruction, to sacrifice to the Lord your God in Gilgal." And Samuel said,
>
> "Has the Lord as great delight in burnt-offerings and sacrifices,
> as in obedience to the voice of the Lord?
> Surely, to obey is better than sacrifice,

> and to heed than the fat of rams.
> For rebellion is no less a sin than divination,
> and stubbornness is like iniquity and idolatry.
> Because you have rejected the word of the Lord,
> he has also rejected you from being king."
>
> *Saul said to Samuel, "I have sinned; for I have transgressed the commandment of the Lord and your words,* because I feared the people and obeyed their voice. Now therefore, I pray, pardon my sin, and return with me, so that I may worship the Lord." Samuel said to Saul, "I will not return with you; for you have rejected the word of the Lord, and the Lord has rejected you from being king over Israel." As Samuel turned to go away, Saul caught hold of the hem of his robe, and it tore. And Samuel said to him, "*The Lord has torn the kingdom of Israel from you this very day, and has given it to a neighbor of yours, who is better than you.* Moreover, the Glory of Israel will not recant or change his mind; for he is not a mortal, that he should change his mind." *Then Saul said, "I have sinned*; yet honor me now before the elders of my people and before Israel, and return with me, *so that I may worship the Lord your God."* So Samuel turned back after Saul; *and Saul worshipped the Lord.* (1 Sam 15:19–31; emphasis mine)

Saul shows mercy to the wrong person and makes a wrong decision regarding the sheep. At the same time, he asks for forgiveness twice (vv. 25, 30). Even so, this episode marks the end of Saul's kingdom. God decides to give the throne to someone else (vv. 23, 28). Samuel himself is despondent and goes home: "Then Samuel went to Ramah; and Saul went up to his house in Gibeah of Saul. Samuel did not see Saul again until the day of his death, but Samuel grieved over Saul. And the Lord was sorry that he had made Saul king over Israel" (1 Sam 15:34–35). Samuel does not seem to mourn for too long, though, because in the very next chapter he goes to Bethlehem to anoint David as king. In fairness, Samuel's behavior here is comparable to high treason. Imagine if the archbishop of Uppsala (the archdiocese of Sweden) were to travel to some other town and anoint some unknown man as king. What do you think the reigning Swedish monarch King Carl XVI Gustav would say about that? Yes, the archbishop has God on their side in our hypothetical case but that does not make their actions any less illegal in the eyes of the world.

## The Tragic and Unjustly Treated Monarch of Poets

While the biblical narrative in 1 Samuel 15 seems to side with Samuel against Saul, most poets and writers side with Saul and uphold Saul's right to show compassion to King Agag. In their eyes, Saul's compassion is a positive quality contrasted with Samuel's murderous fanaticism.

In Karl Beck's 1840 tragedy *Saul: Tragödie in fünf Aufzügen* (Saul: A tragedy in five acts), for example, Saul serves as a symbol of the compassionate king. Saul exclaims early in act 1 that he refuses to kill prisoners of war, women, or children, no matter what Samuel says. Beck's Saul thus goes considerably further than the Saul of the Bible who, after all, seems prepared to kill everyone except the sheep and the foreign monarch. Eric Shaw Quinn's novel *The Prince's Psalm,* written more than 160 years later, reflects the same view. This retelling allows Jonathan to express his annoyance at how Samuel influences Saul and leads him to commit what are, at least in Jonathan's eyes, war crimes:

> "Punish the Amalekites for what they did to the children of Israel when they waylaid them as they came from Egypt," Samuel railed, pounding the table and his breast. He preached in a frenzy of conviction, as he so often did when he conveyed the word of God to King Saul and his elite commanders.
>
> "Lord, give me patience," Jonathan said, rising to leave. [. . .]
>
> Jonathan stood at his father's side during the ceremony. He harbored doubts. He was following his father into an ill-advised campaign at the behest of a priest he did not trust, on behalf of a God of whom he was, at best, uncertain. Samuel's insistence on the brutality of their tactics, killing the women, children, and livestock of the Amalekites as they razed their villages, was as abhorrent to the prince as the necessity of righting an old slight that had happened in the time of Moses. (136)

Both narratives thus problematize the relationship between not only Samuel and Saul but also between Samuel and God. Both sow the seeds of suspicion that it is Samuel rather than God who is advocating the annihilation of Israel's enemies. This, in turn, leads to Saul being reevaluated and shown in a better light. Saul is better, rather than worse, for choosing to obey his conscience and not Samuel. These retellings pave the way for other readers to take a stand for or against Saul. They make us wonder if it is really God speaking here or rather Samuel's jealousy and bitterness. Is it God or Samuel who has displaced Saul?

## Saul and David (with Jonathan in the Middle)

There is something deeply sad about 1 Samuel 16–31. Saul knows that he is rejected by God, and this knowledge is very likely the reason why he sinks deeper and deeper into the darkness of depression. The cure for his illness—but also the death blow—is David. David appears at court and manages to ease Saul's suffering with his music. At first, Saul loves David: "And David came to Saul, and entered his service. Saul *loved him greatly*, and he became his armor. Saul sent to Jesse, saying, 'Let David remain in my service, for he has found favor in my sight'" (1 Sam 16:21–22; emphasis mine). The Hebrew of verse 21 has the verb *ahab*, that is, "to love," the same verb that will later be used with Jonathan as the subject in 18:4 and with Michal as the subject in 18:20. Saul's love, however, soon turns to jealousy and hatred as he begins to understand that David is none other than the "man after God's own heart" appointed to succeed him to the throne. Although God, through Samuel, has told Saul that his line will never be established, it is quite another thing to see your replacement standing before you in all his youth, beauty, and talent. I suffer almost physically with Saul in his agony. Moreover, Saul is forced to face the fact that his two children, Jonathan and Michal, have sided with this upstart. Saul now lets his bitterness get the better of him, and he tries to kill David in all sorts of ways, only to realize once again that David escapes because Michal and then Jonathan choose to save him. To be betrayed by one's own children is a cruel fate (see chapters 6 and 7).

At the same time, there is still love in Saul's heart for David, this fascinating figure who constantly eludes him but at the same time professes his loyalty to him and refuses to face him in open battle. The situation reaches its climax in 1 Samuel 24, where David has Saul at his mercy but chooses to cut off only a flap of his cloak. Saul's heart breaks and he tells David that he accepts his own bitter destiny. He knows that David will be the next king of Israel:

> He said to David, "You are more righteous than I; for you have repaid me good, whereas I have repaid you evil. Today you have explained how you have dealt well with me, in that you did not kill me when the Lord put me into your hands. For who has ever found an enemy, and sent the enemy safely away? So may the Lord reward you with good for what you have done to me this day. Now I know that you shall surely be king, and that the kingdom of Israel shall be established in your hand. Swear to me therefore by the Lord that you will not cut off my descendants after me, and that you will not wipe out my name from my father's house." So David swore this to Saul. Then Saul went home; but David and his men went up to the stronghold. (1 Sam 24:17–23)

Despite this acceptance, however, Saul continues to pursue David, eventually forcing him to leave Israel and settle in the land of the Philistines until Saul's death (1 Sam 27:29–30).

While Saul loves David, he does not seem to think too highly of his biological son and heir, Jonathan. At times, David is portrayed as the son Saul wished he had. Jonathan is both a disappointment and a threat. Jonathan is also a "man after God's own heart." In 1 Samuel 14:6, Jonathan expresses his trust in God, and in the next verse Jonathan's companion urges him to "do what your heart leads you to do. Behold, I am with you according to your heart" (my translation). Saul seems to perceive Jonathan as an additional danger to himself. At the same time, Saul wants Jonathan to be the one to take over and become king after him at some point in the future. We will take a closer look at this wounded relationship in chapter 6. For now, it should be said that this dysfunctional situation cannot be entirely blamed on Saul. Jonathan's behavior in 1 Samuel 13–14, where he engages in spontaneous and reckless military activities without his father's consent, indicates a certain lack of respect. At the same time, it does not justify Saul's lack of concern for his son. Jonathan's total devotion and loyalty to David will not make things better either but rather adds to Saul's unease (1 Sam 19:2; 20:30–34). On the one hand, Saul is jealous of his son for his close relationship with David. On the other hand, he is furious with him for refusing to realize or even care that David will steal his future throne.

## Jealousy and Longing

Saul's relationship with David is complex and filled with jealousy and longing (1 Sam 16:21; 18:2). Is David the son Saul secretly dreams of having, and does Saul want David to look up to him as a father figure? This dimension emerges, for example, in Gustaf Fröding's poem "Saul och David," where Fröding's Saul exclaims in the penultimate verse:

| Then the curse from Saul receded again,<br>and he began to weep bitterly<br>and said, "David, are you there, my son!<br>Reach here a basin, say, your father weeps,<br>now I want to wash and get out of the house<br>and down among the people, from whom I kept myself apart!"<br>(My translation) | Då vek förbannelsen från Saul åter<br>och han begynte gråta bitterliga<br>och sade: "David, är du där, min son!<br>Räck hit ett bäcken, si, din fader gråter,<br>nu vill jag två mig och ur huset stiga<br>och ned bland folket, som jag höll mig från!" |
|---|---|

Alternatively, are there shades of desire in Saul's feelings when he sees David's beautiful figure? In his poem "Portrait of Saul," Thomas W. Shapcott does a good job of articulating Saul's conflicted feelings toward David and how Saul envies his son's easy relationship with David:

> Yes, but to remember them for their love
> is to remember them for their youth: Laughter,
> not a covert whispering; the noise clatter
> of playing field and bodies so alike they move
> in a teamwork; do not suppose that what they give
> each other is theirs to hold or withhold. Bitter
> and old I watch how they embrace each other
> free with the one gift I no longer have.

Saul wishes he could take Jonathan's place in David's heart and at David's side, but Saul realizes that he is too old and no match for a man of David's own age. Saul has enough self-awareness to see that his wish would only destroy something beautiful and turn it into something ugly.

The same ideas can be found in Gladys Schmitt's novel *David the King*. Saul longs for David's love and is jealous of his relationship with Jonathan. He watches with both indulgence and malice as Jonathan lays down his life at David's feet. Saul cruelly and self-deprecatingly comments on how they all—Saul, Jonathan, and even Michal—love David, and how Jonathan makes a public spectacle of himself in his unseemly infatuation:

> A cunning smile twitched his mouth. When he looked up again, his lively glance was for Jonathan. "So you have taken a friend?" he said. "So you have taken unto yourself a beautiful Judahite? And does this friend also fancy a madman's garland made of weeds and grass? No, now, if three of us divide his heart, each will have only an insignificant piece of it. That is, unless he has a mighty heart."
>
> "My lord!" said Jonathan, flushing to the roots of his hair. (94)

Schmitt's Saul continues to explore his need for David. One evening, after David has sung a song for him, Saul confronts him: Was the song really written for him, or was it rather meant for Jonathan? David blushes and cannot come up with a convincing lie. In the end, Saul admits how much he longs for David's attention, especially now after having experienced God's rejection at Gilgal (1 Sam 15): "'Lie to me, David,' [Saul's eyes] said. 'I have been to Gilgal, and I am exceedingly weary. Love whom you will, but love me also. Love me enough to tell me a kindly lie'" (100). In the end, Saul bitterly describes how David has intruded "into the bed of Michal, and into the tabernacle of the soul of Jonathan" (165–166). The pain is there, and so is the cruelty of unrequited love.

## Saul and the Woman of Endor

After 1 Samuel 15, Saul is left to fend for himself. He is rejected by God and gradually sinks into a deeper depression, tormented by an evil spirit (1 Sam 16:14). Even though Saul continues to reign for several more years (again, it is uncertain how much time passes in 1 Sam 16–31), from now on things go downhill faster and faster. Saul commits worse and worse crimes. The worst atrocity occurs in 1 Samuel 22, when he has all the inhabitants in Nob killed. Saul becomes lonelier and lonelier and more and more desperate.

Saul's biggest problem is God's silence. He wants to communicate with God, but God does not respond (see, e.g., 1 Sam 14:37). Saul's desperation reaches its peak on the eve of the fateful battle of Mount Gilboa (and what will be Saul's last battle). In vain he asks God for advice for tomorrow's confrontation with the Philistines, only again to be faced with God's silence: "When Saul saw the army of the Philistines, he was afraid, and his heart trembled greatly. When Saul inquired of the Lord, the Lord did not answer him, not by dreams, nor by Urim, nor by prophets" (1 Sam 28:5–6). Saul sees no other way out than to resort to unorthodox means and visit the necromancer in Endor, despite his own earlier efforts to exterminate such people because they do not belong to the official cult of the God of Israel. Saul asks the woman to summon Samuel from the dead. Perhaps Samuel can help Saul connect with God in this hour of need? The woman manages to contact Samuel, but he is furious when he appears, and rather than helping Saul, he proclaims not only Saul's imminent death but also that of his sons:

> Then Samuel said to Saul, "Why have you disturbed me by bringing me up?" Saul answered, "I am in great distress, for the Philistines are warring against me, and God has turned away from me and answers me no more, either by prophets or by dreams; so I have summoned you to tell me what I should do." Samuel said, "Why then do you ask me, since the Lord has turned from you and become your enemy? The Lord has done to you just as he spoke by me; for the Lord has torn the kingdom out of your hand, and given it to your neighbor David. Because you did not obey the voice of the Lord, and did not carry out his fierce wrath against Amalek, therefore the Lord has done this thing to you today. Moreover, the Lord will give Israel along with you into the hands of the Philistines; and tomorrow you and your sons shall be with me; the Lord will also give the army of Israel into the hands of the Philistines." (1 Sam 28:15–19)

Samuel brings up old grievances in the form of Saul's failure to kill King Agag in 1 Samuel 15. Saul falls devastated to the ground, and the woman, who now incidentally becomes my secret heroine, starts slaughtering the fatted calf and baking bread, so that Saul at least will get some food. What a power woman: After first having to conjure up an angry prophet, she now manages to slaughter a calf, bake bread, and cook boeuf bourguignon (or some similar stew) in the middle of the night.

After his last supper, Saul sets off to his death. When he realizes that the battle is lost and he himself is wounded, he chooses to fall on his sword. Whether this is an act of cowardice or courage is unclear and depends very much on the reader's own standpoint. Saul fears that if he is captured alive, he will have to suffer a horrible and humiliating death (31:4: "so that these uncircumcised may not come and thrust me through, and make sport of me"). He therefore asks his armor-bearer to give him the coup de grâce. Only when the armorer refuses does Saul commit suicide. There is another version of Saul's death in 2 Samuel 1:8–10 where Saul asks an Amalekite standing nearby (who does not seem to be involved in the fighting between the Philistines and the Israelites) to kill him, which he does. I think most people in the same situation would consider a similar course of action and few people would blame them for their decision. Saul's body is mutilated after his death and hung, along with the bodies of his sons, on the city wall of Beth-shan: "They cut off his head, stripped off his armor, and sent messengers throughout the land of the Philistines to carry the good news to the houses of their idols and to the people. They put his armor in the temple of Astarte; and they fastened his body to the wall of Beth-shan" (1 Sam 31:9–10). Eventually his body is laid to rest under a tamarisk in Jabesh (1 Sam 31:13) until David later reburies Saul's and Jonathan's remains in Saul's hometown: "He brought up from there the bones of Saul and the bones of his son Jonathan; and they gathered the bones of those who had been impaled. They buried the bones of Saul and of his son Jonathan in the land of Benjamin in Zela, in the tomb of his father Kish" (2 Sam 21:13–14a).

## A Dark and Stormy Night

Saul's visit to Endor has inspired many poets, in part because of its macabre nature and its rich cast of characters. Even Lord George Gordon Byron chose to render the biblical story into a poem, "Thou Whose Spell Can Raise the Dead." His narrator, Samuel, describes the end of Saul's house in pompous terms:

"Ere the coming day is done,
Such shalt thou be, such thy son.
Fare thee well, but for a day,
Then we mix our mouldering clay.
Thou, thy race, lie pale and low,
Pierced by shafts of many a bow;
And the falchion by thy side
To thy heart thy hand shall guide:
Crownless, breathless, headless fall,
Son and sire, the house of Saul!"

In the poem Samuel describes in detail how Saul falls, mortally wounded by arrows on Mount Gilboa and how then, "Crownless, breathless, headless fall, / Son and sire, the house of Saul!" The Samuel of the poem elaborates on the biblical Samuel's prediction in 1 Samuel 28:19 and amplifies the Bible's already tragic account. At the same time, Byron's poetic language leads to increased sympathy for Saul, and we suffer with this soon to be headless man (cf. 1 Sam 31:9).

Later poets have also been fascinated by Saul's visit to Endor. In his poem "At Endor," the Hebrew poet Shaul Tchernichovsky paints a poignant picture of the stoic yet despairing king who rides in the dark of night, defenseless and powerless ("without bow and spear"), in a last, desperate attempt to get God to speak to him. In the poem, the external circumstances—a smoking cauldron, snakelike smoke—reflect Saul's spiritual state. At the same time, the Saul of the poem remembers a brighter childhood, before God called him from his life "behind the cattle" and "behind the sheep" (a clear reference to 1 Sam 11:5) and made him king. Saul receives a glimpse of the life he never got to experience, where the young shepherd rests peacefully, where cattle dance in the meadows, and where the bell of the flock rings happily. Grief for all his dreams that were never allowed to materialize burns in his throat. When Samuel then asks why Saul had him summoned from the pits of death, Tchernichovsky's Saul answers with a counterquestion: Why did Samuel or God take him away from the simple life with the animals and make him king? Saul expresses how his happiness was consumed in all the wars he had to fight and how his family was destroyed:

| Why, Lord, did you anoint me king over your people?<br>Why did you take me from behind the flock?<br>(My translation) | מדוע, הה, מלך על עמך משחתני,<br>מדוע מאחרי הצאן לקחתני? |
|---|---|

The poem ends with Saul returning to the camp before the morning watch is over, his face dark and his eyes glimmering (with tears?), fearless but filled with sadness. He knows that his path leads only forward to battle and death.

In this way, Tchernichovsky problematizes God's decision to reject Saul. While the biblical text is on the side of God and Samuel, it also manages to evoke our sympathy for Saul. Tchernichovsky makes us, the readers, doubt the justice of God's action. Furthermore, Saul becomes in many ways a symbol of the Jewish people. Tchernichovsky, like so many other Jewish writers both before and after him, chooses to question God's election of Israel. Why did God have to choose Saul for a fabled life, when all he wanted was to live an insignificant life in harmony with nature? Saul wanted the small life rather than to feel the mighty wings of history.

Saul's questions to Samuel in Tchernichovsky's poems, in turn, lead us to doubt whether God was right to drag Saul into a life he did not want. By choosing Saul, God coerced him into constant warfare where he is forced to kill again and again. The same wrestling with God's call recurs in much Jewish interpretation of the Jonah story (see chapter 8). How can we relate to God's call if it is perceived as threatening instead of life-giving? Does God really want what is best for Saul? Does he really have plans for welfare and not for harm when he calls Saul to be Israel's king? Does he really want to give Saul a future with hope (cf. Jer 29:11–13)? Or is Saul just a stepping stone in God's much larger plans, where the individual and the person Saul has lost his importance?

## The Death of Saul

Saul, mortally wounded, prefers to commit suicide rather than wait for his enemies to come and "pierce him" (*odkaroni*). The Hebrew word used here is an unusual word that otherwise only occurs in Isaiah 13:15 and Jeremiah 37:10 and 51:4. It is what happens to people who are captured and to men who fall in battle. It can mean both being impaled with swords and spears and being raped. The latter is a perfectly reasonable translation as rape is a known weapon of warfare and an effective way to humiliate your enemies.

Many, mainly Israeli, poets have written about Saul's death and speculated about Saul's last thoughts before he chooses to fall on his sword (and thus pierce himself). His sons have died two verses earlier (v. 2). Is Saul aware of this? Does he know that all is lost whether he himself survives or not? He and his line have no future and everything Samuel said earlier is now coming true before his eyes.

Tchernichovsky's 1897 poem "על הרי גלבוע" (On Mount Gilboa) describes in three consecutive verses how Saul is gradually forced to accept that three of his sons have died. Saul first asks where Jonathan is and is told that he has fallen. Yet Saul fights on as he still has two sons fighting with him left alive. In the next verse, he learns that Malchishua has also died. Yet again, Saul chooses to continue fighting in desperate hope. In the next one, Saul hears of the death of Abinadab and realizes that all is over. He rhetorically exclaims, "If Israel is a sheep, shall we all be slaughtered like lambs?" (הכבש ישראל, אם נשחט כרחלים). Tchernichovsky ends his poem with the herald blowing the horn and proclaiming that Mount Gilboa is covered in blood (תקע תקיעה גדולה תקע ותקע / וישמעו העברים: דם דם על גלבע). Tchernichovsky continues to ask the herald to call in all directions and exclaim that the land is angry and the earth shaking. Yet we must never give up the struggle but rise up anew and take the place of the fallen.

Tchernichovsky paraphrases the biblical story, which implicitly criticizes Saul for committing suicide. Saul's choice of death represents how he lets despair triumph over hope. In contrast, Tchernichovsky paints Saul as a hero who refuses to give up. Tchernichovsky's poem gives a poignant impression of how Saul hopes, to the end, that at least one of his sons will survive the battle. He insists on fighting on until the bitter end, when he is left alone on the battlefield. His kingdom is shattered, his sons are dead, and he has no future. At the same time, there are nuances of Romantic nationalism in Tchernichovsky's poem that creates unease today, almost a hundred years later. Today we know what the last century has cost in human lives in the struggle between the modern state of Israel and its contemporary enemies.

A few years earlier, Tchernichovsky wrote the poem "על חרבות בית-שן" (At the ruins of Beth-shan). He conjures up the image of Saul's shadow (or ghost) wandering from Mount Hermon in the north to the Dead Sea in the south, stopping at the desolate ruins of Beth-shan. It was here that the Philistines desecrated and mutilated the bodies of Saul and his sons and impaled them on the city walls. All is silent and desolate, and his only company is a lone bat fluttering about.

| At night, at night, hither and thither<br>wanders King Saul's shadow<br>between the abandoned ruins of Beth-shan,<br>and his eyes are looking for his sword.<br>(My translation) | בליל בליל אנה ואן<br>יתהלך צל שאול המלך<br>בין עיי משואות בית-שן,<br>ועיניו מבקשות השלח. |
|---|---|

Tchernichovsky's image of Saul as a restless ghost depicts a man who is not satisfied with either God or his life. He searches for his weapons, and once he finds his sword, he calls his army together to take revenge. Yet it is unclear on whom and for what Saul wants retribution. Does he want to strike back at God who allowed him and his house to perish in this military slaughter, or does it go deeper than that? Does Saul want to retaliate because God chose first to call him king and then to abandon him? Or does Saul want to avenge all that he and his future descendants will suffer because of God's election? The poem alludes not only to the biblical text but also to millennia of persecution and more recent pogroms in Tchernichovsky's native Russia, and the question of God's silence hangs in the air: What does God do when his people suffer and die? At the same time, the real message of the poem is not revenge but reconciliation. The poem ends enigmatically with God crying out to Saul, "his anointed," to cease his thoughts of retribution. God has forgiven all bloodshed, and he has chosen to "avenge with mercy" (סלחתי, כי בחסד אנקם). There is a higher calling than insisting on an eye for an eye and a tooth for a tooth.

Years later, in his 1936 poem "The faithful fighters" (אנשי־חיל חבל), Tchernichovsky returns to Saul's death. Now he finally lets Saul and his sons rest in peace. The faithful soldiers of the poem's title are the men of Jabesh in Gilead who take down the bodies from the walls of Beth-shan and bury them under a terebinth (1 Sam 31:11–13). This poem lacks much of the pomp that characterizes Tchernichovsky's earlier poems about Saul. The focus is instead on the dead. Tchernichovsky's description of the men carrying the corpses echoes Numbers 13, where the Israelites once bore the gift of vines from fertile

Canaan. There are also allusions to Exodus 13:19, where Moses carries Joseph's bones to Canaan. The corpses become a gift, and their journey becomes a matter of honor and vindication. At the same time, there is something deeply ironic in Tchernichovsky's description, since so much blood is spilled. The question that keeps lurking beneath the surface of the poem is whether it was really worth it. Is Saul right to choose to sacrifice the lives of his sons and his soldiers in the fight against the Philistines? Are we right to demand that our children risk their lives in our fight for independence? For the biblical Saul, the question is whether ancient Israel would be devoured by the Philistines; for Tchernichovsky, the question is whether modern Israel has a right to exist, a question that in 1936 was still in the balance.

A more recent Jewish writer, Dan Pagis, who survived the Holocaust, also chooses to reflect on Saul's death in his poem "תפילת שאול האחרונה" (Saul's last prayer). Pagis's poem is considerably more bitter in tone than those written by Tchernichovsky:

| | |
|---|---|
| My God, like cattle at the ploughing<br>among all Your stones I was strong.<br>In the yoke of Your thunder I was silent.<br>But my silence became my foe.<br>I'm tired. And You the mantle of royalty<br>remove from my shoulders, and in the<br>innocence of Your furrows You bury<br>the purple of Your slaughtered army.<br>(My translation) | אלהי, כבקר בחריש<br>בין כל אבנים הייתי איתן.<br>בעל רעמיך הייתי מחריש.<br>ותהי שתיקתי לי לשטן.<br>יגע אני. ואתם את מעיל המלכות<br>מסיר מכתפי, ובתם רגביך טומן<br>ארגמן צבאך משחוט |

As I interpret it, this achingly beautiful poem speaks of Saul's life with God. The first lines allude to Saul's earlier life, when he was content with his lot and helped his father with the farming. He was strong then, but afterward everything went wrong. At that point, he should have protested and chosen to stay, but he obeyed God's command to become king and this obedience was the beginning of his pain. The later verses speak of the battle on Mount Gilboa where Israel's blood runs purple into the ground (see David's lament in 2 Sam 1). Saul does not storm against God, but he still holds him responsible for his bitter fate. Saul is done with being king and wants nothing more than to rest in the peace of God.

Gilboa also chooses to reflect on Saul's death. In his 1953 poem "Saul," he allows a modern spectator to visit the world of the Bible. The narrator describes how he looks away, not wanting to see Saul's corpse hanging on the city wall of Beth-shan. Earlier, the spectator has seen how Saul's armorer refused to give Saul the coup de grâce (1 Sam 31:4) and wondered what he himself would have done in the servant's place. The narrator also compares himself to the men of Jabesh in Gilead and faces his own lack of courage. He would not have been brave enough to take Saul's body down from the wall. Instead, he is more like Saul's cowardly armorer who did not dare to lay hands on the king.

| | |
|---|---|
| Then, when your boy refused to hand<br>you the sword as you had commanded<br>I stood mute, speechless<br>and my blood flowed from [my] heart | אז, במאן נערך להגיש לך החרב<br>לפני שצוית<br>עמדתי אלם, נטול הדבר<br>ודמי זב מלב |
| I really don't know to say what I in<br>his place<br>had I been your boy<br>And you are the King<br>And you are His Majesty the King<br>with your command. | אני באמת אינני יודע לאמר מה אני<br>במקומו<br>אם נערך הייתי<br>ואתה המלך<br>ואתה כבוד המלך במצותך |

The poem raises questions about our courage when confronted with the suffering and death of others. With the Holocaust lying like a muted undertone throughout the poem, Gilboa asks himself how he can bear to listen to all the Jews who have died throughout history. The poem also contains a shade of survivor's guilt: Why am I alive when you did not get to choose? Saul becomes a symbol for all those who died during the Holocaust; they did not die heroically in battle but were unjustly brutalized and dehumanized. In Gilboa's poem, Saul is not a hero but a victim of injustice. What would we have done, had we been in the place of the armor-bearer? Stand up for Saul or turn our faces away? Kill to save someone from humiliation or not? In many ways, as viewers we are victims ourselves, unable to save our loved one from terrible torment because the risk is too great for us. In the end, we are forced to ask ourselves whether Saul's passive resistance, which was all he was able to determine for himself, was an expression of desperate courage rather than godless hopelessness.

Yehuda Amichai likewise likens Saul to a modern man. In his poem "King Saul and I," Amichai compares an anonymous man to King Saul. The poem itself is in many ways a paraphrase of the biblical story of Saul's calling (1 Sam 9:1–10; 10:17–27; 11), something which can be seen in the references to donkeys and oxen and in the mention of Saul's height. At the beginning of the poem, the contemporary person—who may or may not be Amichai himself—appears to be far inferior to Saul. Saul, for his part, is described, in stark contrast with the biblical image of him, as strong, future-oriented, courageous, and always knowing how to do the right thing. At the same time, Amichai insinuates that Saul's heroic status is merely a chimera. Toward the end of this enigmatic poem (in part 4), the two characters, Saul and the narrator, become more equal. The latter depicts himself hanging his clothes on a chair, while someone (Saul? God?) hangs his kingdom on a wall, a clear allusion to Saul's corpse hanging, abandoned and mutilated, on the walls of Beth-shan. It is not clear who is hanging whose kingdom. The most likely interpretation is that God hangs Saul's kingdom to express his (i.e., God's) wrath. Saul's kingdom, which began so promisingly, will in the end be nothing more than chaff blowing in the wind (see Isa 17:13).

| | |
|---|---|
| I hung my clothes on a chair<br>For tomorrow.<br>He hung his kingdom<br>In a frame of golden wrath<br>On the sky's wall. [. . .]<br>He is a dead king.<br>I am a tired man. | תליתי את בגדי על כסא<br>בשביל מחר<br>הוא תלה את מלוכתו<br>במסגרת זעם זהב<br>בקיר השמים [. . .]<br>הוא מלך מת<br>אני אדם עיף |

The poem can be summarized as saying that it is better to live like a cowardly wretch than to be dead. Even the strongest person lacks the power to decide his own death. Overall, Amichai describes a modern Israel where the biblical characters live very much in people's minds and influence their actions. They are regarded with reverence and serve as role models, but there is also a longing to break free from them. Amichai is not sure he shares the values of the biblical tradition, but he finds it hard to completely shake off their influence. Saul is his older brother, whose clothes Amichai inherits, and there is no escaping Saul and his ilk. Amichai's retelling thus makes us question the values of the Bible. As above, should we embrace the values advocated by 1 Samuel, or would we do better to question at least those that favor violence?

Other, especially older, retellings choose to glorify the heroism of the Israelites as they fight against the vastly superior Philistine forces. To return to Byron, his "Song of Saul Before His Last Battle" expresses in Romantic terms the bravery of the Israelites and Saul's conviction that it was indeed worth it:

> Warriors and chiefs! should the shaft or sword
> Pierce me in leading the host of the Lord,
> Heed not the corse, though a king's, in your path
> Bury your steel in the bosoms of Gath!
>
> Thou who art bearing my buckler and bow,
> Should the soldiers of Saul look away from the foe,
> Stretch me that moment in blood at thy feet!
> Mine be the doom which they dared not to meet.
>
> Farewell to others, but never we part,
> Heir to my royalty, son of my heart:
> Bright is the diadem, boundless the sway,
> Or kingly the death, which awaits us to-day!

I am personally convinced that the reality of the battle was considerably harsher but maybe a little heroism does not hurt sometimes? Or should we rather listen to Gilboa and Amichai who tell us that, yes, it does hurt? I opt to end on this ambivalent note.

* * *

The biblical story of King Saul raises many questions about God's justice. There is something fundamentally unjustified in God's rejection of Saul and his later choice of David. Yes, I know that David is a man after God's heart. At the same time, we should never forget that this verse which appears in 1 Samuel 13:13–14 does not mention David by name but leaves the identity of the person open. It is only in retrospect that we readers identify this person with David. Yes, I also know that Saul disobeys God, chooses not to wait for Samuel, and actively decides against cutting King Agag into pieces, but he undeniably apologizes. Besides, a brief comparison between Saul's and David's transgressions makes the former pale in significance. So, I think Saul draws the short straw, and I do not understand why God chooses to reject him for such comparatively petty sins.

Furthermore, the story of Saul challenges us to think about God's call. The difficulty, as I see it, is that Samuel's choice of Saul in 1 Samuel 9–10 does not seem to be in line with what Saul is capable of doing. He is not raised to be a king, and he is not given the opportunity to go to some kind of "prince school" to learn how to rule. Rather, he is thrown into a task that he is not ready to take on and without being given any time to prepare for it. I also wonder about Saul's own desires. Does he really want to be Israel's military leader and lead the people into battle? Does he want to fight at all, or would he prefer to live in the country and look after the cows? In my imagination, I see him as an attractive candidate for the television reality show *Farmer Wants a Wife*. Joking aside, how do we handle God's call when we receive it, and how do we recognize it for what it is? I think we should be careful not to fall into the clutches of some Samuel-like person who does not stop and listen but just carries on with their own agenda. Does Saul have any choice at all? In an alternative narrative, would he be able to discuss the matter with God and perhaps even have the opportunity to choose a different path?

Saul's situation reminds me of a very minor event in my life on a Friday afternoon in Jerusalem many years ago. It is not nearly as profound as Saul's dilemma, but it has stayed in my memory. I have just written my final exam in Hebrew after two months of intensive study and am looking forward to three weeks off. On my way home from the bus stop, I bump into a woman from my congregation, and I happily begin to chat about my upcoming holiday. She stares at me and says that it must be God's will that we met. She knows an ill woman who needs someone to take care of her for exactly three weeks. An icy hand grabs my heart. Later that evening I am invited to dinner, and I confess, in tears and with a really bad conscience, to Karen, my "adopted mum," that I do not want to take care of this ill woman at all. I would much rather enjoy my time off by going to the beach. Karen looks at me, rather confused (and even a little amused), and asks a simple question: Has God spoken to me about this ill woman? I reply that, no, I have not heard anything at all. "Very well,"

Karen replies calmly, "God does not call anyone by proxy, and we recognize God's call in our lives when we hear a response in our hearts."

The texts about Saul are filled with violence, suffering, and death. Samuel's command for Saul to kill women and children appear to a contemporary audience as incitement to commit war crimes. Yes, soldiers can kill soldiers in battle, but it is not acceptable to kill civilians. If you do, you will be brought to justice and rightly so. Saul's decision to spare King Agag and the sheep is therefore often seen as a mitigating feature of Saul rather than a sin. In any case, most readers shudder, and so do I, when Samuel, like a wild-eyed fanatic, cuts the Amalekite king to pieces. How can we relate to a God who seems to prefer Samuel's behavior to Saul's? I have no easy answers to that question, but it is quite clear to me that the matter should not be put to one side but instead be grappled with continually. No, I will not side with Samuel and, no, if God, through a prophet, commands me to chop children into little pieces, I will blankly refuse and assume that the prophet does not speak the word of God.

This quickly becomes a question of biblical interpretation. Do I have the right to criticize a biblical text because it seems to advocate behavior that I find unacceptable? Again as in chapter 1, I maintain that a responsible reading of the Bible is one that wrestles with the message of the text rather than excuses it. It is also important in this discussion to recognize that Saul's behavior is not much better than Samuel's. We should thus be careful not to fall into the trap of treating Saul as some kind of pacifist. Saul's decision to spare King Agag is probably not motivated by a conviction to prevent bloodshed but rather represents a diplomatic consideration. With all that said, we must somehow find ways to condemn events in biblical stories and at the same time be able to continue to relate to those same biblical texts as the word of God.

The biblical story of Saul's death on Mount Gilboa also raises difficult questions about suicide, mercy killing, and heroism. Are there situations where suicide or assisted suicide is justified? The Bible itself is extremely ambiguous. On the one hand, Saul's young armor-bearer can be seen as a representative of those who insist that suicide is always wrong, no matter what the future holds. It does not matter if the future threatens tremendous suffering—one must persevere because it is God's plan. On the other hand, the story is constructed in such a way that we cannot help but feel sorry for Saul. He has lost everything, and his imminent death is a fact. Is it then not rather courageous to take matters into your own hands instead of letting your enemies humiliate you further? What responsibility do we have to ourselves if the choice is torture, exploitation, and ultimately, a shameful death? At the same time, not all situations are comparable to Saul's situation on Mount Gilboa. Would it have been better if Saul had called off the battle before it had begun, suffered defeat, and thereby saved lives, even if this meant that the survivors ended up as slaves in the Philistine cities? There are echoes of Masada in this choice: Were the people of Masada right to choose mass suicide over slavery, or should they have allowed themselves to be captured alive?[1]

Last but not least, the biblical story talks about envy. How do we behave when we realize that someone is so much better than we are? What happens when we have been the best in class or at work for as long as we can remember, and then, all of a sudden, a bright young person, clearly blessed by God, steps into the limelight and steals everyone's attention and love. At first, you may fall for their charm yourself and even enjoy their presence. However, eventually, when all your friends, and even your own children, take the upstart's side against you, well, then it really hurts. Slowly but surely, you see your own influence diminishing and how all those who used to listen to you have now started to listen to the newcomer. When you finally come face to face with the realization that this new person will usurp your place and task on earth and slowly but surely replace you and your family, then it is almost impossible not to get bitter and not to fight. The story of Saul and David, with Jonathan and Michal in between (see chapters 6 and 7), is not only a tear-jerking soap opera but also a full-fledged tragedy. Can we really blame Saul for his behavior toward David? How would we ourselves have acted had we been in his place? I challenge everyone to scrutinize their own motives. Honestly, with your hand on your heart, would you have laid down your arms, admitted defeat, and handed over the crown to David, or would you have taken up the sword and fought for your job, your family, and your very right to exist?

CHAPTER SIX

# Jonathan

## *Naive Pushover or Self-Sacrificing Paragon?*

THE BIBLE TELLS us that everyone loves David. This love is described throughout with the same verb, *ahab*. In this and the next chapter, we will take a closer look at two of Saul's children, Jonathan and Michal, and their relationships with David. Both love David and both are almost torn apart by the divided loyalties required of them in their balancing act between David and Saul. Moreover, both will choose David's side in the conflict, and both will end up on the losing side. Michal will be forced to remarry Palti to please her father and then be forced to leave the same man to satisfy David's hunger for power. Jonathan will not only risk his life when he stands up for David against his father but will ultimately lose it on Mount Gilboa when his death makes David's accession possible.

Jonathan, the elder of the siblings, is often seen as one of the most admirable figures in the Bible. His daring but undoubtedly courageous actions at the battle of Michmash (1 Sam 13–14) and his equally honorable death at the battle of Gilboa (1 Sam 31) give him almost a hero's halo. Jonathan's integrity, his unequivocal loyalty to David, and above all his humility, likewise make him something of a figurehead. For the same reasons, however, he is also a bit of an enigma, as we readers do not always understand what motivates him. What is behind his noble and self-sacrificing behavior? What makes Jonathan prioritize David's good in everything he does and willingly give up his crown for him?

### Narratives

Jonathan is given considerable space in the Bible as he is a key figure in the story of David's rise to power. He is mentioned in 1 Samuel 13–14, 18–20, 23, 31, and in 2 Samuel 1. We will explore these texts about Jonathan and his relationships with God and his fellow human beings through several novels, a short story, a poem and a drama.

**Rachel Bluwstein** (1890–1931) was a Hebrew-speaking poet who immigrated to Palestine, then part of the Ottoman Empire, in 1909. In many ways she identifies with Jonathan in her loneliness and longing for someone to love, as well as with Michal in her desire to have a child. Rachel died of tuberculosis at the early age of forty, and much of her life was characterized by illness, poverty, and hard physical labor.

"Jonathan," in *Flowers of Perhaps: Selected Poems of Ra'hel* (Menard, 1994), originally published in מנגד (Across from; Davar, 1930).

**Mats Berggren** (b. 1957) is a Swedish writer of young adult fiction. His short novel *Rami och Jonatan* (hereafter, *Rami and Jonathan*) alludes strongly to the biblical story of David and Jonathan in its depiction of the budding love between the teenager Jonathan and the unaccompanied refugee boy Rami.

*Rami och Jonatan* (Opal, 2019).

**Tomas Boström** (b. 1953) is a Swedish clergyman, author, hymn writer, and musician. He has, among other things, interpreted Leonard Cohen's songs for a Swedish audience.

"Den åttonde sången" (The eighth song), in *Och Gud skapade människan*, ed. Magnus Sundell (Libris, 2014), 70–83.

**Geraldine Brooks** (b. 1955) is an Australian Jewish author and winner of the prestigious Pulitzer Prize. Brooks's book attempts to portray the real David behind the legend. David appears with both all his charisma and all his flaws, violence, and political ruthlessness.

*The Secret Chord* (Viking, 2015).

**Joseph Heller** (1923–1999) was an American Jewish novelist. His book *God Knows* is a fascinating and at the same time rather irreverent retelling of the biblical David story. Like Brooks (and also Heym), Heller seeks to reveal the real David, who bears little resemblance to the pious psalmist so beloved of Jewish and Christian tradition. This book is anachronistic, often vulgar, but often also deeply moving and with serious undertones. David, like Job, argues with God and questions the connection between sin and punishment.

*God Knows* (Knopf, 1984).

**Stefan Heym** (1913–2001; pseudonym of Helmut Flieg/Fliegel) was a German Jewish author. In *The King David Report*, Heym's narrator, Ethan ben Hoshaja, is commissioned by Solomon to write the official version of King David's life and reign (i.e., the one found in 1–2 Sam). Ethan interviews many of the story's key figures, and in doing so he manages to uncover a considerable amount of inappropriate material that he shares with the readers but that ultimately does not make it into the biblical version. As a whole, Heym's book highlights how history is written by the victors and how other, less popular truths are silenced.

*The King David Report* (Kindler, 1972).

**David H. Lawrence** (1885–1930) was a British writer, poet, and artist who is probably best known for his novel *Lady Chatterley's Lover*. He wrote a play dedicated to David's early life in which Jonathan plays a prominent role and in which his vulnerable position between David and Saul comes to the fore. There are many indications that Lawrence looked up to and even identified with David, the man whose name he himself bore.

*David: A Play in Sixteen Scenes* (Knopf, 1926).

**Astrid Lindgren** (1907–2002) was a Swedish author who predominantly wrote children's books. She is most famous for her books about Pippi Longstocking. One of her best loved novels is *The Brothers Lionheart*, with its focus on brotherhood, courage, fear, love, and death. Unlike the other books in this chapter, this is not a biblical retelling at all. The fact that one of the book's main characters happens to be called Jonathan may be a coincidence, although I personally do not think so. Lindgren, well-versed in the Bible, shows several times in her writing that she is conversant with the David story. The clearest proof is in chapter 11 of *Mästerdetektiven Blomkvist lever farligt* (*Bill Bergson Lives Dangerously*), where the character Anders thinks about how David cut off a piece of Saul's cloak.

*The Brothers Lionheart*, trans. Joan Tate (Oxford University Press, 1975), originally published as *Bröderna Lejonhjärta* (Rabén & Sjögren, 1973).

**Moshe Shamir** (1921–2004) was an Israeli journalist and author. His novel (translated into English as *The Hittite Must Die*) uses Uriah, Bathsheba's husband, as its narrator. It depicts Uriah's time with David, from the time he joins David during his time on the run (1 Sam 24–26) until David orders his death (2 Sam 11).

*The Hittite Must Die*, trans. Margaret Benaya (East and West Library, 1978), originally published as כבשת הרש: סיפור אוריה החיתי (Davar, 1956).

**Grete Weil** (1906–1999) was a German Jewish writer. After the Nazis came to power in Germany, she immigrated to Amsterdam (1935). In 1941, her husband was arrested and killed shortly afterward in the Mauthausen concentration camp. Weil lived in hiding and managed to survive the Holocaust. She returned to Germany in 1947 and made a living as a writer. In Weil's novel *Der Brautpreis* (*The Bride Price*), which won the Geschwister-Scholl Prize, the two narrators, Michal and Grete, explore their shared experiences of war and persecution. They are both victims trying not only to understand those who hurt them but also to reach a state of forgiveness and reconciliation.

*The Bride Price: A Novel*, trans. John Barrett (Godine, 1991), originally published as *Der Brautpreis* (Nagel & Kimche, 1988).

## Jonathan and David

If love can be measured in time spent together, it is beyond doubt that Jonathan is the person closest to David. They first meet in 1 Samuel 18:1–4, a beautiful text describing two people whose souls are bound together: "When David had finished speaking to Saul, the soul of Jonathan was bound to the soul of David, and Jonathan loved him as his own soul. Saul took him that day and would not let him return to his father's house. Then Jonathan made a covenant with David, because he loved him as his own soul. Jonathan stripped himself of the robe that he was wearing, and gave it to David, and his armor, and even his sword and his bow and his belt." At the same time, the biblical text reflects a certain lack of symmetry in their relationship. It is always Jonathan who takes the initiative, talks, and acts. David is involved—it is difficult for one soul to be attached to another soul unless both are in on it—but his involvement is expressed through extreme displays of emotion rather than concrete actions. When they part at the end of chapter 20, both cry but David cries more:

> As soon as the boy had gone, David rose from beside the stone heap and prostrated himself with his face to the ground. He bowed three times, and they kissed each other, and wept with each other; David wept the more. Then Jonathan said to David, "Go in peace, since both of us have sworn in the name of the Lord, saying, 'The Lord shall be between me and you, and between my descendants and your descendants, for ever.'" He got up and left; and Jonathan went into the city. (1 Sam 20:41–4)

David and Jonathan meet once more in the Judaean wilderness (1 Sam 23:14–18). It is deeply ironic that Saul spends years searching for David in vain, while Jonathan simply walks straight into David's secret camp. At the same time, we should not underestimate Jonathan's courage and total trust in David in this context. He chooses to appear alone and unprotected among David's four hundred–strong crowd of men prone to violence. Jonathan, as King Saul's eldest son and the country's crown prince, would have been every enemy's dream hostage. It is natural to conclude that David and Jonathan are in constant communication with each other. It is also not inconceivable to assume that Jonathan acts as David's spy: Jonathan keeps David updated on Saul's position, which in turn enables David to stay away. When they meet here, however, Jonathan's role is to support and cheer David up rather than to provide military intelligence: "He said to him, 'Do not be afraid; for the hand of my father Saul shall not find you; you shall be king over Israel, and I shall be second to you; my father Saul also knows that this is so'" (1 Sam 23:17). It is only after Jonathan's death in 1 Samuel 31 that David puts into words the importance of Jonathan in his life. David's lament (2 Sam 1:19–27) is dedicated to "the beauty of Israel," "the majesty of Israel," "the gazelle of Israel" (the Hebrew expression *hatsvi Israel* has many shifting nuances) which seems to denote none other than Jonathan: "I am distressed for you, my brother Jonathan; greatly beloved were you to me; your love to me was wonderful, passing the love of women" (2 Sam 1:26). When we compare David's relationship with Jonathan with his other human relationships, the biblical texts show unequivocally that Jonathan is the most important person in his life. David does not express himself in a similar way regarding anyone else, including his parents, siblings, wives, or children. David's son Absalom comes in second place (2 Sam 18:33).

## Jonathan and Saul

The books 1–2 Samuel are filled with stories of conflict between fathers and sons. While most readers are familiar with Absalom's rebellion against David (2 Sam 15–18), the conflict between Saul and Jonathan is a less prominent but possibly even more tragic situation. According to Saul, his son is both a disappointment and a threat. First Samuel 13–14 describes an impulsive young man who trusts in God and follows his heart but does not always listen to his father. "Jonathan said to the young man who carried his armor, 'Come, let us go over to the garrison of these uncircumcised; it may be that the Lord will act for us; for nothing can hinder the Lord from saving by many or by few.' His armor-bearer said to him, 'Do all that your mind inclines to. I am with you; as your mind is, so is mine'" (1 Sam 14:6–7). Later in the same story, Jonathan eats a bit of honey, unaware that his father has forbidden his men to eat until the battle is over. Jonathan does not hesitate to criticize his father's, in his opinion unwise, oath before his own men:

> But Jonathan had not heard his father charge the troops with the oath; so he extended the staff that was in his hand, and dipped the tip of it in the honeycomb, and put his hand to his mouth; and his eyes brightened. Then one of the soldiers said, "Your father strictly charged the troops with an oath, saying, 'Cursed be anyone who eats food this day.' And so the troops are faint." Then Jonathan said, "My father has troubled the land; see how my eyes have brightened because I tasted a little of this honey. How much better if today the troops had eaten freely of the spoil taken from their enemies; for now the slaughter among the Philistines has not been great." (1 Sam 14:27–30)

We see here already the beginning of a broken relationship between father and son. The conflict between them reaches a first climax when Saul discovers that Jonathan has broken his oath. This act does not, at least in my opinion, excuse

Saul's willingness to kill his son: "Saul said, 'God do so to me and more also; you shall surely die, Jonathan!' Then the people said to Saul, 'Shall Jonathan die, who has accomplished this great victory in Israel? Perish the thought! As the Lord lives, not one hair of his head shall fall to the ground; for he has worked with God today.' So the people ransomed Jonathan, and he did not die" (1 Sam 14:44–45). Jonathan escapes with his life, but the bond between father and son has become a festering wound. What family relationship survives intact when it turns out that a parent is willing to sacrifice their child (see chapter 2)?

When David appears, the relationship between father and son deteriorates further. Jonathan's love for David is not well received by Saul, for obvious reasons. Saul soon realizes that David is a threat to himself, his throne, and his dynasty. According to Saul, Jonathan is a blue-eyed romantic who does not understand his own best interests. Does this starstruck crown prince not see that David is about to usurp royal power at his expense? At the same time, Saul understands his son because he, too, once fell for David's charms (chapter 5): "And David came to Saul, and entered his service. Saul loved him greatly, and he became his armor-bearer" (1 Sam 16:21). Saul tries to make Jonathan understand that he should stand united with his father against David instead of fraternizing with the enemy. However, Jonathan is as stubborn as a mule in his love for David: "Saul spoke to his son Jonathan and to all his servants about killing David. But Saul's son Jonathan took great delight in David. Jonathan told David, 'My father Saul is trying to kill you; therefore be on guard tomorrow morning; stay in a secret place and hide yourself. I will go out and stand beside my father in the field where you are, and I will speak to my father about you; if I learn anything I will tell you'" (1 Sam 19:1–3). It all comes to a second climax in 1 Samuel 20:30–34 when Saul realizes that he has completely lost his son's loyalty. He insults Jonathan in front of his commander Abner. Then, when Jonathan still refuses to obey his father, everything spirals out of control, and Saul throws his spear at his son with the clear intention of impaling him:

> Then Saul's anger was kindled against Jonathan. He said to him, "You son of a perverse, rebellious woman! Do I not know that you have chosen the son of Jesse to your own shame, and to the shame of

> your mother's nakedness? For as long as the son of Jesse lives upon the earth, neither you nor your kingdom shall be established. Now send and bring him to me, for he shall surely die." Then Jonathan answered his father Saul, "Why should he be put to death? What has he done?" But Saul threw his spear at him to strike him; so Jonathan knew that it was the decision of his father to put David to death. Jonathan rose from the table in fierce anger and ate no food on the second day of the month, for he was grieved for David, and because his father had disgraced him.

This is a very interesting passage from the point of view of conflict management. Despite his father's deeply inappropriate words and subsequent murder attempt, Jonathan chooses to leave the situation rather than escalate it. Moreover, Jonathan's behavior is quite remarkable when you consider how biblical men usually care about their honor and glory. Jonathan here does not seem to care about his father's coarse insult; instead, his anger is entirely focused on his father's behavior toward David. Although Saul has just tried to pierce him, Jonathan, as always, is most concerned about David's well-being: "He was grieved for David [. . .] because his father had disgraced him."

Although his heart and loyalty belong to David, in the end, when it really counts, Jonathan chooses to stand by his father in the battle against the Philistines on Mount Gilboa and to die with him: "Now the Philistines fought against Israel; and the men of Israel fled before the Philistines, and many fell on Mount Gilboa. The Philistines overtook Saul and his sons; and the Philistines killed Jonathan and Abinadab and Malchishua, the sons of Saul" (1 Sam 31:1–2). David mourns Jonathan's death in his lament: "How the mighty have fallen in the midst of the battle! Jonathan lies slain upon your high places" (2 Sam 1:25). David describes how Jonathan lies "slain." Here few translations do justice to the nuance of the Hebrew word *halal*. This relatively uncommon word means "pierced," which probably refers to Jonathan being killed by archers' arrows. This is fitting given Jonathan's own fondness for the bow as a weapon (e.g., 1 Sam 20:20–22). It is not the same verb as that used for Saul in 1 Samuel 31:4 (cf. chapter 5). Rather, the verb *halal* denoting Jonathan's death is found, although in a passive form, in Isaiah 53:5 to describe the suffering servant. Here the NIV reflects the Hebrew text the best as it translates how the servant was "pierced for our transgressions." We will return to this word choice below.

## Jonathan's Tragic Life

The story of Jonathan is steeped in tragedy. Although Jonathan ostensibly is an entirely positive character—faithful, courageous, resourceful, loving, loyal—if one looks a bit closer, there is something deeply tragic about this man whose life was cut far too short. Given that his only son is just five years old at the time of his father's death (2 Sam 4:4), it is likely that Jonathan dies before he is thirty. A nuanced reading of the biblical material about Jonathan leaves the reader with an acute sense of sadness about a life that never quite fulfils its potential or rather a life lived and poured out for others. Jonathan yields his throne to David and his life to Saul; he walks the narrow path, never shying away from difficulties. He always prioritizes others before himself.

Several creative retellings bring out these sentiments. Jonathan's personal tragedy is most vividly expressed in Rachel Bluwstein's poem "Jonathan":

| | |
|---|---|
| Through the veil of distances, the sweet<br>face of a youth in splendid dress;<br>a constant heart in need: in the success<br>of battle and in retreat. | מבעד לדוק מרחקים—צלם ענוג,<br>נער רך בתלבושת הדר;<br>לב אמונים, לא נטש רע בצר.<br>ובקרב אחור לא נסוג. |
| Jonathan, must you die? How sad the path<br>that each must follow in this world of<br>strife,<br>paying with his life<br>for even a little taste of honey in the<br>mouth. | ועליך למות יונתן?. . . מה עגום<br>נתיב אדם בעולם הזועם!<br>על כולנו במחיר החיים לשלם<br>את מעט הדבש הטעום. |

Rachel's poem brings out the bittersweet moments in Jonathan's life. Early modern Hebrew is very similar to biblical Hebrew and borrows many expressions from biblical imagery. Here, Rachel reuses many biblical formulations, as she describes Jonathan's loyalty, youth, and clothing. The Hebrew phrase for loyalty ties in with the reference to Jonathan's heart in his armorer's speech (1 Sam 14:7). It is Jonathan's heart that guides his actions, and it is a courageous, honest, and loyal heart. In the same way, the phrase denoting his clothes recalls the way Jonathan gives David his clothes and weapons (1 Sam 18:4). Without regard for his own prospects, Jonathan gives David everything in one magnanimous act of love and self-denial.

The last line of Rachel's poem focuses on Jonathan's personal tragedy. Through a beautiful play on words, the poem highlights Jonathan's longing for a "little bit of tasty honey" (*me'at hadvash hata'um*). Jonathan's longing is linked to his near-death experience when his father is ready to sacrifice him for his offense of eating a little honey. At the same time, the honey becomes a symbol of Jonathan's, in many respects, forfeited life. All Jonathan wanted was to taste a little bit of honey (1 Sam 14:27–30), but the one time he tasted it, his life was threatened (1 Sam 14:43–45). All he wanted was to share a little love with David (1 Sam 18:1–4), but that desire only led to conflict (1 Sam 19:1; 20:30–34) and eventually cost him his life on Mount Gilboa (1 Sam 31). Rachel's poem conjures up a poignant image of a tragic hero who dies prematurely because of his inner goodness and innocence. This image remains in our minds and in turn affects our understanding of the biblical text. We meet a Jonathan whose fate makes us mourn what might have been had life been different.

## Giving Your Absolute All

There is sometimes something almost exaggerated in Jonathan's behavior. He is a person who goes all in. There is no middle ground for him. We see this mainly in Jonathan's actions toward David. The total self-giving nuance of Jonathan's love for David comes to the forefront in 1 Samuel 18:1–4, where Jonathan, with no thought for his own well-being, gives David his all. We talked in chapter 3 about clothes and how Joseph loses clothes when he loses his standing in society and how he gathers clothes when he is regaining his power and authority. Jonathan, along with his father Saul, is one of the great "losers of clothes" in the Bible, but the difference between the two is that Jonathan gives them to David completely voluntarily. The whole image of Jonathan undressing before David and giving him his clothes and weapons is one of the most beautiful but also most vulnerable declarations of love in the Bible. The clothes and weapons symbolize his kingship and authority. Jonathan gives away both his heart and his throne in one single, spontaneous act.

Jonathan's self-sacrificing love is presented in a down-to-earth manner in Mats Berggren's novel for young adults, *Rami and Jonathan*. The biblical action is relocated to a soccer pitch outside Stockholm where the soccer coach's cherished son Jonathan gives his soccer clothes to the lonely but extremely skillful refugee boy Rami (7–8; his name has the same vowels as David). Jonathan understands early on that Rami will threaten his own place on the soccer team, but he nevertheless chooses to insist that his father bet on Rami.

> "I think we should sign that guy who scores all their goals," he suddenly heard himself say. [. . .]
>
> Dad looked at Jonathan in the rearview mirror.
>
> "Are you serious? You understand that there will be competition for your places in the attack?"
>
> "I don't care."
>
> In that moment he realized that it was true. (20, my translation)

The story continues but deviates at the last second from the biblical story when Rami dies. It is Jonathan who lives on and continues to play soccer.

Tomas Boström gives the same impression in his short story "Den åttonde sången" (hereafter, "The eighth song"), in which Jonathan is perfectly happy to give David everything and maybe a little more:

> With the same blind generosity, he also gave David everything else he himself owned. He gave David the finest shoes. Jewelry, watches, gadgets—he saw them all as reasonable interest on a lifelong friendship. He gave away the clothes he had on his body and dreamed of exchanging them for David's tattered t-shirt, worn jeans, and torn trainers. [. . .]
>
> More and more, David also grew into the family's innermost core. He became part of it. He was given benefits that Jonathan would never otherwise have had to share with anyone else. Jonathan was not asked but was happy to share anyway. Jonathan was otherwise the obvious heir in the family. But nothing was really obvious anymore. Jonathan felt no threat in this, quite the opposite. That one day he would probably have to give up inheritance and empire for David's sake did not worry him for a moment. Jonathan was perfectly happy with a little nearness, a little breath, a little David scent every now and then. And a little blues, of course. (76–77, my translation)

Similarly, Geraldine Brooks's narrator, Michal, describes how Saul suddenly notices what is going on. Jonathan has essentially abdicated in David's favor:

> I saw [Saul] look at Yonatan, saw him suddenly recognize what had been apparent to everyone else for many months. Yonatan was deferring to David as if David were the prince. David, in turn, was treating my brother as a beloved lieutenant. My father finally saw his throne—his house—at risk. And he saw that Yonatan didn't care. That Yonatan had willingly surrendered his birth-right to this upstart. He saw truly, for once, despite the madness that so often distorted his sight. My brother had laid his life at David's feet; his every action proclaimed this. (131)

Finally, we find the same vulnerable and self-sacrificial love in Schmitt's novel *David the King*. David, Schmitt's narrator, describes how Jonathan shares his innermost thoughts, feelings, and painful experiences with David, and how David wants to but is unable to show the same openness in return: "Not in renown, not in concealing robes of legends, had the King's son come to him, but naked and vulnerable, saying, 'Behold me as I am and love me as such, for I would not deceive you with appearances.' [. . .] He longed to hear his own voice matching shame for shame, but a full minute passed, and he did not open his lips. He sighed, knowing that confession was a virtue beyond his power" (68). Taken together, these narratives show a remarkably complex Jonathan, a mixture of a totally devoted, not to say almost dangerously self-disclosing and self-denying, person and a Christ figure (see below) who gives David his absolute all without a thought for his own good.

## Jonathan, a Trauma Victim

As Isaac (Gen 22) and Jephthah's daughter (Judg 11:30–40) have previously experienced, Jonathan is also forced to realize that his father is prepared to sacrifice him to satisfy God. In Jonathan's case, as in the case of Jephthah's daughter, it is all so incredibly unnecessary. God has commanded neither Jephthah nor Saul to sacrifice their children; instead, the two men have voluntarily taken their oaths. God is innocent, and I honestly wonder if Saul and Jephthah could have got out of their completely self-inflicted situations if they had only discussed the matter with God. I do not mean to be ironic, but I just get so angry that they do not even try. We are talking about the lives of their children here!

Schmitt describes very poignantly how a very young Jonathan is afraid of dying, and how he later experiences guilt at having survived at someone else's expense. Schmitt understands the verb "to ransom" (*padah*), used in 1 Samuel 14:45 (and in other ritual contexts), as a sign that another man dies in Jonathan's place. The Bible itself does not tell us how exactly Jonathan is ransomed, which forces readers to consider what is actually happening: "Then the people said to Saul, 'Shall Jonathan die, who has accomplished this great victory in Israel? Perish the thought! As the Lord lives, not one hair of his head shall fall to the ground; for he has worked with God today.' So the people ransomed Jonathan, and he did not die." Joseph Heller, in his novel *God Knows*, describes a much more bitter Jonathan who years later dwells on his father's behavior, and how he really could have seen himself as being forced to sacrifice his son. David echoes the same question later in the book when he asks himself: "What is it with these fathers who want to destroy their children? Whence comes this royal and noble willingness to spill the blood of their own offspring? Saul and Jonathan. [. . .] Abraham and Isaac [. . .] Jephthah and his daughter" (125). Both narratives force us to question whether Jonathan comes out of this episode unscathed, or whether, like Isaac before him, he lives the rest of his life in the shadow of this trauma. How does this experience affect Jonathan, and what are the implications for his subsequent behavior toward his father and David? Does Jonathan feel he is living on borrowed time? Does he struggle with survivor's guilt? Does he feel he does not deserve to be king? Alternatively, does the experience of someone giving their life for him become the very reason for his own self-sacrificing behavior toward David? Is he laying down his life for David to atone for a past debt?

## Jonathan's Moral Dilemma

Jonathan's relationship with his father, already broken in 1 Samuel 13–14, deteriorates catastrophically when David appears on the scene. At first, Saul sees David as the son he wished he had (1 Sam 24:16; 26:17). Soon, however, Saul discerns that David is an even greater threat to him than his biological son ever was, and love turns to hatred and fear. At the center of this conflict is Jonathan. He loves his father—children do, often no matter what their parents put them through—and he loves David. Jonathan finds himself in the middle of the conflict between the current and future ruler, and he must constantly, although unwillingly, choose sides.

Jonathan's inner conflict is highlighted by D. H. Lawrence's drama *David*. Throughout the play, Jonathan explores his feelings for Saul. In scene 5, Jonathan confesses to David that "sometimes I think the Lord takes from me the flame I have. I love my father. And my father lifts the short spear at me, in wild anger, because, he says, the fire has left him, and I am undutiful." Jonathan also wonders whether his father is really rejected by God, and if so, why? Jonathan, being a very empathetic man, puts himself in his father's shoes and realizes that he, like his father, would have had qualms about killing the defenseless King Agag (1 Sam 15:9). This realization in turn causes Jonathan to question whether God's rejection of Saul as king can be justified: Why would God demand of Saul something that any decent person (i.e., Jonathan himself) would hesitate to do? Jonathan gains a new understanding of his father's plight and is moved to compassion toward him. At the same time in this difficult situation, Jonathan finds comfort and joy in his relationship with David. The readers who know that David will take the throne, that Saul and Jonathan will die, and that David will emerge victorious from the conflict, naturally see both the irony and the tragedy in Jonathan's thoughts.

Jonathan's internal struggle, when his father forces him to choose between him and David, culminates in Jonathan's outburst in scene 8, where he describes how he is almost torn apart in his struggle to be loyal to both David and Saul: "The Lord sees fit to split me between King and King-to-be, and already I am torn asunder as between two wild horses straining opposite ways. Yet my blood is my father's. And my soul is David's. And the right hand and the left hand are strangers on me." The reader gets the same impression in Tomas Boström's short story "The eighth song." Toward the end of the story, Boström describes a completely exhausted Jonathan, whose time and energy are entirely spent mediating between them:

> In the midst of this stood an increasingly more powerless and exhausted Jonathan. His whole inner being was at risk of being torn apart between these two giants. He became the secret of one of them and the uncovering of the other. He became a spy, an ally, and a collaborator, all in one person. All or nothing, but gradually less

> himself. He took both their parts, but never considered himself. Love denied him the option of choosing sides, yet he did so all the time. Love also denied him the possibility to be something other than a shadow. True or false did not matter anymore; he was always someone else's pawn. (82, my translation)

The pain that the strife between David and Saul causes Jonathan is documented in the biblical text. Yet Lawrence's play and Boström's short story bring an immediacy to the biblical text that is almost unbearable. Most readers of the Bible are aware of David's pain as David, with customary expressiveness and pathos, describes it in his lament in 2 Samuel 1:26. Lawrence's and Boström's respective retellings shift the perspective from David to Jonathan, the humbler man who appears in the background. In addition, Lawrence and Boström emphasize the emotional burden that Jonathan is forced to bear in his devastating middle position. This focus is different from that of most biblical scholars, who instead tend to stress the political aspects of Jonathan's divided loyalties to David and his father and the broken trust between father and son. It takes strength and energy to stand not only between king and king-to-be but also between two people you love. Jonathan's explicit anguish, which Lawrence likens to being torn between two wild horses, and Jonathan's fatigue and sense of despair, which Boström highlights, help the reader of the biblical text to understand the whole of Jonathan's tragedy.

## Love, Not War

The biblical Jonathan is a man who both loves and fights. First Samuel 13–14 paints a picture of an impulsive person who willingly draws his sword and recklessly enters into military skirmishes that he should perhaps have stayed out of. Yet other aspects destabilize this impression. More than one reader of 1 Samuel 17 has wondered about Jonathan's absence in the Valley of Elah where David defeats Goliath. Why does the hero of Michal not pick up the thrown gauntlet and fight Goliath? Is he somewhere else, has his father forbidden him to fight, or has he suddenly become a coward? Furthermore, once Jonathan appears after the battle (in 1 Sam 18:4), how can that same battle hero apropos lay his future crown at David's feet in humble adoration? What has happened? Jonathan is as erratic and volatile as ever, but his spontaneity here has a distinctly pacifist flavor.

First Samuel 20:40 goes on to describe how Jonathan goes unprotected to David to say goodbye. The situation is politically risky, much is at stake, but Jonathan nevertheless chooses to give his servant his weapons to show how much he trusts David: "Jonathan gave his weapons to the boy and said to him, 'Go and carry them to the city.'" Heller captures this scene well in his novel *God Knows*. His narrator, David, describes a powerful Jonathan who chooses not to use violence but instead voluntarily relinquishes his power:

> I had no weapon. My death had been sanctioned. He could again be a hero. He wore his short sword in a scabbard and a knife in his girdle. He was older than I and much the larger and stronger, and I knew he could have seized me by the hair in his grip and stabbed or slashed me or run me through, as he desired. And I also knew by the look of him that if I had asked him for his sword and his knife, he would have lain both in my hand without question. (219)

In a very different way, Moshe Shamir highlights Jonathan's surprising and remarkable willingness to opt out of any desire for honor and give David the throne instead. In his retelling of 1 Samuel 23:15–18, Uriah eavesdrops on David and Jonathan's conversation about Saul's continued attempt to kill David. Their conversation reveals their deep trust in each other, their mutual love for Saul, and their sadness at the whole situation. Before Jonathan gets up to leave David's hiding place, he quietly tells David that he knows David will be the next king of Israel, to which David responds:

> "If I were the son of Saul," said David, his shadow of a smile relieving the gloom for the first time. "If I were Jonathan, I too, like my father, would hate the man who steals the crown from his rightful successor."
>
> "I will be second to you." Jonathan's face lightened in a smile that was equally faint. "My father knows that as well." (125)

Jonathan abdicates in favor of David, and he does so quietly and unassumingly. He knows his behavior is unusual, to say the least, but he trusts that it is the right path.

The most interesting and surprising interpretation is, in my opinion, found in Grete Weil's book *Der Brautpreis* (*The Bride Price*). This beautiful and thought-provoking book emphasizes, among other things, Jonathan's remarkable behavior in 1 Samuel 17–23. Her description of the battle of Elah is intriguing, in that she has Jonathan—rather than David—kill Goliath. Afterward, however, Jonathan magnanimously chooses to let David take the credit for the deed (31–33). Later, in a conversation with his sister Michal, Jonathan expresses his conviction that David will be the next king of Israel. Michal objects:

> "You dare not say that, you are the heir to the throne."
>
> A gesture of rejection. A smile. "I have seen it. It will be so."
>
> "And you?"
>
> "I will be long dead by then, or a priest, a scribe, or quite simply the brother of the queen." Then he continues quickly: "At that moment I thought only of the two of you, that the way was now clear for you to become man and wife. Father has promised a daughter to the one who vanquished the giant." He embraces me, closes his eyes, and sleeps. (22–23)

The ease with which Jonathan accepts that David, rather than himself, will be king after Saul ties in with what he had previously said to Michal: "'I am tired, Michal. War is a foreign condition for me. I like to look on, observe, deliberate. Then I feel that I am alive. In war I am dead.' My tall brother, who does not want to be a hero. Who is Israel's good, Israel's true soul" (21). Weil's pacifist Jonathan is reminiscent of the Jonathan painted by Stefan Heym in his book *The King David Report*. Here Michal expresses surprise that Jonathan does not aspire to be king. Jonathan's response shows not only David's suitability but also that he himself lacks what it takes to be king: "To rule, you must see one purpose only: power. You must love one person only: yourself. Even your God must be your exclusive God, who justifies your every crime and covers it by his holy name" (67). Heym's Jonathan knows who David is but loves him anyway. Jonathan, with great self-awareness, also knows that he himself does not want to become a person of power. Power corrupts, and Jonathan prefers to remain uncorrupted.

Weil's and Heym's novels undermine the dominant male ideal of the Bible while highlighting and illuminating other, more subversive aspects that are also found in the biblical texts. Weil's pacifist Jonathan, who stands in dialogue with the image of Jonathan as a war hero in 1 Samuel 13–14, criticizes both the patriarchal violence that pervades many of the biblical narratives and the traditional image of David as the successful hero. Similarly, in Heym's retelling, Jonathan draws our attention to David's hunger for power and encourages us to see it as a character flaw. Both novels make Jonathan a hero despite his military success. Their distinctly nonhegemonic Jonathan, who voluntarily relinquishes power, becomes a different kind of hero; one who is brave enough to say no to violence. This portrait of Jonathan in turn invites a reading of Jonathan's death on Mount Gilboa as a sacrificial act to bring peace to Israel. Jonathan's death enables David to take the throne without bloodshed.

## Jonathan, a Christ Figure

Lindgren's *The Brothers Lionheart* is certainly not a retelling of 1 Samuel. For me, however, having lived with the story of Jonathan for so long, it is difficult to read certain chapters of *The Brothers Lionheart* without thinking of the biblical Jonathan. I am hooked from the first line of Lindgren's book: "Now I'm going to tell you about my brother. My brother, Jonathan Lionheart, is the person I want to tell you about" (1). At the beginning of the book, Lindgren describes how Jonathan, thirteen years old, runs into the burning block of flats where he lives with his mother and younger brother Karl, grabs his bedridden brother on the back, throws himself out of the window and dies. A totally spontaneous, noble, and loving act that costs him his life but saves that of his brother. At the end of the book, Lindgren turns the situation around. Jonathan, paralyzed by dragon fire, asks Karl to take him on his back and jump off the cliff into the abyss. Karl is initially afraid but eventually dares, and the two brothers are united in death and new life.

In Lindgren's hands, Jonathan becomes a savior figure. He dies to save his brother, even though he knows that Karl is dying of tuberculosis. This is exactly what the biblical Jonathan does for David: He saves him time and time again to give him a future at the cost of his own life. If we choose to read 1 Samuel in dialogue with the New Testament, Jonathan easily becomes a Christ figure or a predecessor of John the Baptist (see the typology of the church fathers, where Old Testament figures were understood to foreshadow New Testament figures). Yet the picture has an unexpected twist. It is not, as in the New Testament, the son of Jesse who acts as savior; it is rather David who is offered salvation at Jonathan's expense.

In a completely different way, Weil emphasizes how the death of the biblical Jonathan resembles the death of Jesus. Her depiction of 1 Samuel 31:8–13 has strong Christian associations. The last image of Jonathan, nailed to the walls of Beth-shan with his arms outstretched, is strongly reminiscent of the crucified Jesus: "This image tormented me without respite, I could not push it away for a moment. Jonathan with his arms stretched wide apart, one who could endure, he must have suffered horrible pain and I suffered with him, without considering that he no longer felt anything" (65). There are strong echoes here of the prophecy of the suffering servant in Isaiah 53:5: "But he was wounded for our transgressions, crushed for our iniquities; upon him was the punishment that made us whole, and by his bruises we are healed." As mentioned above, the verb *pierced* (*ḥalal*) that David uses when describing Jonathan's death in his lament (2 Sam 1:25) is the same Hebrew verb root as found in Isaiah 53:5 (*meḥulal*). Weil reinforces the link by calling Jonathan a "Dulder," which is German for "a man who endures pain" (cf. Isa 53:3: "a man of suffering"). When we read both texts together, the impression of Jonathan's death as a sacrifice is emphasized. Jonathan dies to enable David's accession to the throne.

* * *

All the retellings we have looked at highlight the tragic aspects of Jonathan's life. Jonathan is a man who does not experience much happiness in life. His relationship with his father is painful, to say the least, as he is forced to face the fact that Saul is prepared to have him killed for a mere oversight. Yes, Saul swore an oath to God, which is an important ritual act that should not be ignored. Even so, other biblical stories show that it is possible to reason with God. Moreover, Saul's soldiers find an alternative solution that seems to work just as well. The situation goes from bad to worse when David appears, and Jonathan finds himself at the center of the conflict. Jonathan is forced to become a pawn in David and Saul's power struggle. His way out—putting David first in his life while continuing to stand by his father—becomes the only option that his love for them both allows. Openly allying himself with David, and thus openly rebelling against his father, is not an option for him.

Much of 1 Samuel speaks of interpersonal relationships, personal tragedies, and political power struggles. There are few heroes in this book and even fewer role models, but Jonathan is by far the closest to a heroic ideal. At the same time, can we really learn anything from Jonathan? Is he a good role model or a bad one? Is God calling us to deny ourselves as much as Jonathan does, or are we all entitled to a little honey in our lives? I have heard several sermons that present Jonathan as the ideal friend who does everything for David. Something in that theology and message rings false. A fellow human being who is prepared to sacrifice everything for you is of course invaluable, and we can all use and appreciate a Jonathan by our side. At the same time, I would not wish Jonathan's tragic fate on anyone, and I also do not believe that his sacrificial giving of his life ought to be a representative example of friendship. True friendship is characterized by sharing. Having said that, I do not want to underestimate David's role. It is possible to see David and Jonathan's relationship as completely mutual, but it is also possible (unfortunately) to see David as the lightweight who is not as invested as Jonathan. The biblical text is ambivalent, and David is hard to get to know. In contrast, Jonathan reads like an open book because of his impulsive and warm personality.

So, rather than being used as an example, Jonathan should in my view be treated as a rarity. His behavior in 1 Samuel is remarkable and intimately linked to David's road to power. Without Jonathan's help, David could never have become king of Israel. Neither biblical nor contemporary men have a habit of giving up their place in life for other men. What Jonathan, the crown prince, does, when he renounces his own claims to the throne of Israel and offers to take second place to David (1 Sam 23:17), is quite extraordinary. It need not be something we should necessarily aspire to in our human relationships—though of course it is not wrong to do so either.

The biblical portrait of Jonathan has another dimension that is rarely noted, and that is its christological aspects. There are many parallels between Jonathan's actions and those of Jesus that allow for a christological reading. First, Jonathan, motivated by love, makes a covenant with David. This act can be read in conjunction with the story of the Last Supper (Matt 26:27–28) where Jesus institutes the new covenant through his blood. Jonathan's covenant with David and his death on Mount Gilboa, which paves the way for David's kingdom, serve as models for Jesus's death on the cross and the coming kingdom of heaven. Further, though from a very different perspective, the image of the dying gazelle in David's lament (2 Sam 1:19) lying pierced on Mount Gilboa connects to the image of the pierced servant (Isa 53:5) who dies for us. There is something so self-sacrificing in the image of Jonathan's death that it is appropriate to read these two texts together. Second, Jonathan lays bare his body and soul to David (1 Sam 18:4) in a manner reminiscent not only of Jesus taking off his cloak and washing his disciples' feet (John 13:1–5) but also of the woman anointing Jesus with her tears and wiping his feet with her hair (Luke 7:36–50; John 12:1–8). Third, Jonathan allows David to take his place as Saul's son and heir, giving up his privileged position in favor of David. Read together with 2 Corinthians 8:9, Jonathan, like Christ, steps away from his riches to enable David to take the throne. Fourth, Jonathan's recurring role as intercessor, seen primarily in 1 Samuel 19:4, has parallels in Romans 8:33–34 and Hebrews 7:24–25, which state that Jesus prays for us. Jonathan's intercession before Saul serves as a model for Jesus's intercession for us. Fifth and finally, Jonathan's assurance in the wilderness of Ziph (1 Sam 23:14–18) can serve as a model of the Holy Spirit (John 14:26) sent to sustain us, as well as a picture of God's steadfastness and encouragement (Rom 15:4–5).

At the same time, Jonathan can be read as a type for John the Baptist. He is the older cousin who rejoices with Jesse's son and accepts that he himself must decrease so that David/Jesus can increase (John 3:28–30), and who ultimately dies to prepare the way for the ministry of David/Jesus. In this role, Jonathan embodies Jesus's words in John 15:13 that there is no greater love than the one who gives his life for his friend.

CHAPTER SEVEN

# Michal

## *Hapless Pawn or Resolute Royalty?*

POOR, POOR MICHAL. Her life must be so extremely difficult. At the same time, I admire her. There is something indomitable about her that I look up to. Despite all the sorrows of life, I imagine Michal, tall and beautiful like her father, facing her destiny, queenly and with a straight back. Yes, she is a pawn in the men's world, but despite that, she will not be subdued. In my fantasy world, she is the late Bronze Age equivalent of the medieval English queen Eleanor of Aquitaine. In 2 Samuel 6:20–23, like Eleanor (played by Katharine Hepburn in the film *The Lion in Winter*), Michal storms against her husband David (analogous to Henry II).

It is worth considering the material in 1–2 Samuel through the lens of Michal. She appears sporadically in 1 Samuel 18–19, 25, and in 2 Samuel 3 and 6. She then disappears from the story, and her death is never recorded. We know, because 2 Samuel 6:23 tells us so, that she is in no danger of dying in childbirth, the most common cause of death for women at a young age in biblical times. It is therefore quite possible that Michal, who is probably a few years younger than David, will survive him and see the beginning of Solomon's reign. She accordingly becomes our best witness, the only person to live through the whole turbulent period of Saul's and David's reigns and to be personally acquainted with all the characters. She is Saul's daughter, Jonathan's sister, and David's wife. She has seen kings and generals come and go, kingdoms rise and fall, rebellions flare up and be quenched. It is a sad and bitter life but rich in content. For her, the saying "may you live in interesting times" becomes a curse indeed.

At the same time, Michal's perspective becomes a healthy corrective lens against an overly romantic view of David. Michal, the daughter of the former king—whose dynasty God has rejected—looks at events from her doubly inferior point of view. She, the woman from the defeated dynasty, is forced to endure the humiliation of continuing to live at King David's court as the rejected wife from the rejected house of Saul. In the biblical text, she is consistently referred to as "Saul's daughter." Thus, from the Bible's point of view, Michal is first and foremost a princess of Saul's defeated lineage. Saul commits suicide to avoid humiliation, Jonathan dies the loyal death of a hero in battle and as a result escapes with both honor and love intact, but Michal—poor, poor Michal, the last of Saul's children—survives and is forced to watch, powerless and disgraced, as David, her own husband, destroys her family step by step.

## Narratives

I shall reuse several of the books mentioned in the previous two chapters on Saul and Jonathan but also add some more here.

**Yochi Brandes** (b. 1959) is an Israeli author whose book *The Secret Book of Kings* retells the biblical story of David from the perspective of the losers, that is, the House of Saul. She often uses the character of Michal as her narrator, who according to her outlives David and thus can look back on his entire rise to power and his later reign.

*The Secret Book of Kings*, trans. Yardenne Greenspan (St Martin's, 2016), originally published as מלכים ג (Zmora-Bitan, 2008).

**Eleanor Gustafson** (b. 1934) is an American Christian author. Her book *The Stones* is explicitly Christian in character but lacks apologetic features.

*The Stones: A Novel of the Life of King David* (Whitaker House, 2009).

**Allan Massie** (b. 1938) is a Scottish journalist and author who has written a number of historical novels, often set in the Roman Empire. Massie's retelling in *King David* stays relatively close to the biblical text and uses David as its narrator.

*King David* (Hodder & Stoughton, 1995).

**Francine Rivers** (b. 1947) is an American Christian author specializing in romance novels. She is best known for her book *Redeeming Love* (filmed in 2022), which is loosely based on the story of Hosea and Gomer. Her book *The Prince* retells the book of 1 Samuel from Jonathan's perspective.

*The Prince* (Tyndale, 2005).

In some of these books, Michal emerges as a woman who grows into her role, evolving from a naive teenager into a matriarch to be reckoned with. In others, Michal transforms from the young girl who falls for David's charms into a bitter woman, after suffering more than her fair share of blows in her life. Still other novels paint a negative portrait of Michal right from the start. They read the older woman's bitterness into the younger girl and insist that Michal was always the haughty princess who wanted to make life difficult for the poor shepherd boy David. I have unfortunately seen the same tendency in much confessional counseling literature: Michal, the sour, quarrelsome wife, whom no good Christian wife should seek to emulate. Well, let us take the bull by the horns and explore how we can read and understand the Bible's portrait of Michal.

## Michal's Romantic Bubble

Bible readers first encounter Michal in 1 Samuel 18:20–26. Michal, Saul's youngest daughter, is probably no more than thirteen or fourteen here, a teenager who has fallen head over heels for the charming David. David has triumphed over Goliath, and all the women of Gibeah sing his praises (1 Sam 18:7). It goes without saying that our young princess is one of the admiring women. Who would not be?

> Now Saul's daughter Michal loved David. Saul was told, and the thing pleased him. Saul thought, "Let me give her to him that she may be a snare for him and that the hand of the Philistines may be against him." Therefore Saul said to David a second time, "You shall now be my son-in-law." Saul commanded his servants, "Speak to David in private and say, 'See, the king is delighted with you, and all his servants love you; now then, become the king's son-in-law.'" So Saul's servants reported these words to David in private. And David said, "Does it seem to you a little thing to become the king's son-in-law, seeing that I am a poor man and of no repute?" The servants of Saul told him, "This is what David said." Then Saul said, "Thus shall you say to David, 'The king desires no marriage present except a hundred foreskins of the Philistines, that he may be avenged on the king's enemies.'" Now Saul planned to make David fall by the hand of the Philistines. When his servants told David these words, David was well

> pleased to be the king's son-in-law. Before the time had expired, David rose and went, along with his men, and killed one hundred of the Philistines; and David brought their foreskins, which were given in full number to the king, that he might become the king's son-in-law. Saul gave him his daughter Michal as a wife. But when Saul realized that the Lord was with David, and that Saul's daughter Michal loved him, Saul was still more afraid of David. So Saul was David's enemy from that time forward. (1 Sam 18:20–29)

Michal is the only woman in the whole Bible who is the subject of the verb "to love"—and this is even mentioned twice so that we readers really understand this incredible thing (vv. 20, 28). Loving is otherwise reserved for men in the biblical world. Her love for David, however, will only lead to sorrow.

We shall let Michal stay in her romantic bubble for a little while longer. She gets to admire her future husband from afar before reality catches up with her. Her father does not have her best interests in mind when he promises her to David. Rather, he expects Michal to remain his loyal daughter. According to Saul's plans, Michal will make an excellent spy in David's house. She can report back on David's whereabouts as a good daughter should. David, for his part, seems generally uninterested in Michal as a person. David never mentions that he is looking forward to becoming Michal's husband; he seems more concerned with becoming the king's son-in-law. There is no indication in the biblical text that David reciprocates Michal's love. Rather, she is probably just a strategic step toward the center of power.

It is unclear when exactly Michal's romantic bubble bursts. Does it burst in 1 Samuel 18:27, when David lines up the two hundred Philistine foreskins before Saul? Who wants to be bought with blood-soaked foreskins? The scenario is utterly disgusting, and I cannot help but wonder how David presents these trophies. Does David store them in a bag, only to then line them up in front of Saul and count them, one by one? The sight is extremely macabre and belongs in a horror film.

Michal gets David as her husband later in the same verse. Is it a disappointment or a dream come true? We can read what we want into the text. David's life has already started to lose its rosy glow. He is no longer Saul's favorite musician; he has instead become his favorite enemy, whom Saul repeatedly tries to kill. Being David's wife and Saul's daughter at the same time cannot be easy, but it seems that Michal's main loyalty is to David. When Saul tries to impale David with his spear for the second time, David flees to his house. There awaits a resolute Michal who comprehends that David is no longer safe there. Like a Bronze Age Rapunzel, Michal helps David escape through the window (I always imagine her using sheets to help him climb down, but the biblical text gives me no details): "David fled and escaped that night. Saul sent messengers to David's house to keep watch over him, planning to kill him in the morning. David's wife Michal told him, 'If you do not save your life tonight, tomorrow you will be killed.' So Michal let David down through the window; he fled away and escaped" (1 Sam 19:10b–12). She then takes the teraphim, apparently some sort of house god, and tucks it into bed. When Saul's soldiers appear, Michal lies to their faces when she claims that David is sick. I have thought a lot about this scene. Why do David and Michal have a man-sized house god in their home? Whose is it and what are they doing with it? Does it belong to the cult of Israel at all? Other biblical women have similar household gods, but the ones that Rachel has are small enough that she can hide them in her camel's saddle and sit on them (Gen 31:30–35). It is common among scholars to blame Michal. It seems inconceivable that David, the man after God's own heart, would have a statue of an undefined deity in his house, right? Moreover, given that God has rejected Saul, the statue must thus belong to Michal, Saul's daughter. The logic is obvious, right? However, the statue is in David's house, where Michal lives as a wife, and by the standards of the time, it should be David who decides what should and should not be in his own home.

Saul is not easily fooled, however, and shows up, probably mad as a hornet, and sees through Michal's lies: "Then Saul sent the messengers to see David for themselves. He said, 'Bring him up to me in the bed, that I may kill him.' When the messengers came in, the idol was in the bed, with the covering of goats' hair on its head. Saul said to Michal, 'Why have you deceived me like this, and let my enemy go, so that he has escaped?' Michal answered Saul, 'He said to me, "Let me go; why should I kill you?"'" (1 Sam 19:15–17). Here the biblical text is ambivalent. Is Michal lying to her father? Has she helped David of her own free will and now is slandering David to save her life? Alternatively, is she telling the truth? Did David threaten her life, and did she help him escape because she had no choice? As I said, I am leaning toward the first option, but I am not entirely sure. A man capable of procuring two hundred Philistine foreskins is not a man I trust blindly.

After 1 Samuel 19, Michal's life falls apart in the silence of the biblical narrative. David flees, and it will be ten years before she hears from him again in 2 Samuel 3:13, six wives and six sons later (2 Sam 3:2–5). I find it extremely difficult to see this as true love on David's part. At the same time, we must not forget that David manages to keep in touch with Michal's brother Jonathan without any problems throughout 1 Samuel 20–23 and mourns him properly with both words and a song in 2 Samuel 1. If David loves any of Saul's children, it is Jonathan, not Michal.

## Sibling Love

A comparative study of Michal and Jonathan shows an interesting tendency. In a patriarchal text like Samuel, I would have expected Princess Michal to accept David's love passively and Prince Jonathan to be more active. The biblical portrayal is surprisingly less one-sided, however. When David and Michal are together, Michal takes the initiative for everything that happens while David appears to suffer from inertia: While Michal loves David, rescues him, and initiates the quarrel with him, David willingly allows himself to be helped out of the window, and he seems to entrust to God to make sure that Michal has no children (2 Sam 6:23). Similarly, when David and Jonathan are together, Jonathan is the one who makes things happen: Jonathan loves, initiates covenants, saves, and supports. Again, David remains more passive, but unlike when he is with Michal, he is emotionally involved. David cries, kisses, cries some more, and grieves. In both cases, David is the object of the siblings' love, but his response to them differs sharply.

This imbalance between the two siblings has been recognized in several literary works. How does Michal feel when she realizes that she will never mean the same to David as Jonathan does? While Weil's and Brooks's respective Michals know even before marriage that she will always play second fiddle in David's life, Quinn's Michal's awakening is cruel when she understands, shortly after her wedding, that David prefers her brother's company all hours of the day. That the marriage is not working has nothing to do with Michal; she's just collateral damage, an innocent bystander who should not really be there: "Something in Michal died, burned away in that bitter dawn. Her love for David fueled the rage that her tears could not extinguish. It was a softness, perhaps her youth, that left her. In the harsh morning light, she could see her marriage to the man she loved for what it was, or at least what it was not" (296). Other retellings, especially those that use David as their narrator, blame Michal for the marital breakdown: If she had not been so distant and self-centered, their relationship would have lasted longer. Allan Massie's David, for example, is in love with Michal, and she is the main reason he fights Goliath. Massie's David describes how he repeatedly tries to draw close to Michal, but she always refuses to surrender herself completely to him. Similarly, Heller's David shrugs off all responsibility and shifts the blame to Michal. Michal is portrayed as a haughty princess who, well aware of her position in society, is not overly happy about having to marry the shepherd boy who lacks tact, style, and finesse. To further put all the responsibility on Michal, both Heller's David and Massie's David accuse her of not enjoying sex.

Even deeply conservative retellings choose to maintain that David prefers to spend time with Jonathan, while blaming Michal for the breakdown of her and David's relationship. Francine Rivers's portrayal of David, Michal, and Jonathan in her book *The Prince* is a case in point. Rivers shows no sympathy for Michal when she accuses David of neglecting her and preferring Jonathan's company. Rather, Michal is portrayed as whiny when she fails to accept that Jonathan and David have more important things to do than spend time with her (115–117, 132–135).

Eleanor Gustafson's rendering in the novel *The Stones* is also worth commenting on. Gustafson describes Jonathan as David's best friend, with whom he shares a deep and emotional connection that far surpasses the bond David shares with any of his wives (34–36, cf. 93). Unlike the empathetic Jonathan, who prioritizes David's interests in everything he does, Gustafson's Michal is a shallow and spoiled woman who uses her body to attract David sexually (31) and whose loss of David is no deeper than can be easily comforted by Palti's riches (86). When Michal observes how David looks at Jonathan, she becomes irritated and asks a little nastily if David cares more about Jonathan than about her, whereupon David whispers after Jonathan that "I do . . . I do . . . I do . . ." (36).

It is quite possible that Michal is whiny, and I might even go so far as to describe her as annoying. At the same time, she has every reason in the world to be. Her marriage is a cruel joke that no one should laugh at. Michal is so utterly alone, despairing, and neglected that I am almost unable to put myself in her shoes. It is not Michal who is destroying her marriage; it is a marriage that should never have been made. It is, therefore, strictly speaking wrong to use words like *breaking down* or *crashing* when talking about Michal and David's relationship—there is no evidence to suggest that it ever worked. It is not enough for one person, in this case Michal, to love the other for a marriage to be happy. David must do his part too, and he does not seem interested in doing that. So, if anyone in the Bible has a right to complain, it is Michal.

## Michal, Loyal Wife or Loyal Daughter?

Michal's position between David and Saul cannot be easy either. She is married to David and lives in his house. At the same time, there are clear signs in the biblical text that Saul expects Michal to remain loyal primarily to him and his family. Most retellings admit that Michal saves David at the risk of her own life, including Heller, who otherwise shows a less than charitable attitude toward Michal. At the same time, other retellings, such as Massie's book, try to hide Michal's heroism. The problem is obvious: It is difficult to associate a brave and loyal Michal with a shallow and arrogant Michal. We cannot both have our cake and eat it.

Moreover, we should not minimize the danger that Michal finds herself in after she helps David out of the window. We are dealing with a three-thousand-year-old text that reflects a patriarchal and violent society. Michal, as a woman, lacks her brother's authority to stand up to and defy Saul (cf. 1 Sam 19:1–7). While Jonathan can openly disagree with Saul, leave his father's presence, and rush out in anger, the same is not true for Michal. Her father, King Saul, still has power over her, and as we will soon see, he does not hesitate to use it to punish his daughter.

This leads to the question of why Michal chooses to stay in Gibeah rather than run away with David. On the one hand, there is nothing to prevent women from living with David during his time in the Judaean wilderness. First Samuel 25 tells us how both Abigail and Ahinoam share David's life as a persecuted refugee. On the other hand, 1 Samuel 30 in particular shows how dangerous it can be for a woman on the run, and how the presence of David's wives makes David's situation even riskier:

> Now when David and his men came to Ziklag on the third day, the Amalekites had made a raid on the Negeb and on Ziklag. They had

> attacked Ziklag, burned it down, and taken captive the women and all who were in it, both small and great; they killed none of them, but carried them off, and went on their way. When David and his men came to the city, they found it burnt down, and their wives and sons and daughters taken captive. Then David and the people who were with him raised their voices and wept, until they had no more strength to weep. David's two wives also had been taken captive, Ahinoam of Jezreel, and Abigail the widow of Nabal of Carmel. (1 Sam 30:1–5)

The question then becomes whether it is Michal who does not want to go with David or David who does not want her to accompany him. It is interesting to see how the retellings that portray Michal positively insist that Michal wants to come with David and that it is David who prevents her. In Brooks's retelling, for example, David rejects Michal's offer, saying he is faster alone. In sharp contrast, Massie describes how David does not want to abandon Michal, and how he constantly longs for her presence during his years as a refugee. Instead, it is Michal, spoiled and used to her creature comforts, who refuses to go with him. "She answered that her love was great, but that she could not see herself as a fugitive in the wilderness" (65).

We will never know what is happening in this moment between David and Michal. When evaluating David and Michal's behavior, we should take into account the power relationship between them. Although David is on the run from the king of the realm, fearing for his life, he still has considerably more options than the youngest princess in the land simply because he is a man. In a patriarchal environment, it is not a case of Michal "letting David go" with the underlying idea that she does not care. As a woman, she lacks any ability to force David to do anything against his will. At the same time, how responsible is it for David to leave Michal in Gibeah, thus exposing her to Saul's wrath? Even if we were to assume that Saul's spoiled little daughter does not like sleeping under the stars and missing her customary three meals a day, that does not actually mitigate David's irresponsibility here.

## Michal's Second Marriage

After 1 Samuel 19:17, Michal does not appear for six long chapters. We are left in the dark about what happens after Michal's encounter with her furious father Saul while we instead follow the adventures of David. The next time we meet Michal, she is already given as a wife to Palti (1 Sam 25:44), and they remain married for ten years: "Saul had given his daughter Michal, David's wife, to Palti son of Laish, who was from Gallim." This almost careless remark at the end of chapter 25 is contrasted by what has been going on throughout the rest of the same chapter, where David, once again, has been helped by the quick thinking of a woman, in this case Abigail. There are major differences between Michal's and Abigail's respective behavior that demand our attention. While Michal acts loyally to her husband, the same can hardly be said of Abigail, who goes behind the back of her idiot husband (the name Nabal actually means "idiot" in Hebrew, see 1 Sam 25:25) and opens the door to the larder wide for David, even though her husband has invited the neighborhood to a party (1 Sam 25:36). Yet readers throughout the ages have praised Abigail's prudence and resourcefulness.

There is no indication that Michal's forced remarriage is something that Michal herself wants. So far, we readers have never doubted that she still loves David and dreams of being reunited with him. By the time that day comes, however, much has happened in Michal's life. Ten years is a long time, and Michal has lost almost all her family. Her brother Ishbosheth (also called Ishbaal), one of the only surviving sons of Saul after the battle of Mount Gilboa, rules in Israel but is, by all accounts, a very weak monarch. What has Michal's life been like during these ten years? Has she come to terms with her fate and learned to live and perhaps even love her husband Palti, or is she still pining for David? If so, her dreams will soon be shattered once again. What woman wants to return to her childhood sweetheart and share him with a whole bunch of other wives and their children? I am also skeptical about David's motivation when he suddenly decides to remember the wife of his youth. Most likely, his newly reinstalled memory is connected to his dynastic expectations. A son who is both his own heir and has Saul's blood running through his veins would unite the tribes of Israel and Judah. Kings through the ages have married the daughter of their predecessor for this very reason. Henry VII of England, for example, married Edward IV's daughter Eleanor, which finally helped to end the War of the Roses (not that the situation in England was any better for it but still).

Palti is an interesting character. We know nothing about him except that he must love his wife. Although he never says it—Palti is given no lines in the biblical drama—his actions speak louder than words: "Then David sent messengers to Saul's son Ishbaal, saying, 'Give me my wife Michal, to whom I became engaged at the price of one hundred foreskins of the Philistines.' Ishbaal sent and took her from her husband Paltiel the son of Laish. But her husband went with her, weeping as he walked behind her all the way to Bahurim. Then Abner said to him, 'Go back home!' So he went back" (2 Sam 3:14–16). It is hard to doubt the love of a person who wanders around crying. At the same time, it is not at all clear how Michal feels about this. She shows no emotion at all at this stage. Is she totally paralyzed by fear of David's soldiers and therefore unable to act? Does she realize the futility of trying to resist? Does she find Palti's behavior embarrassing? Or is she actively looking forward to seeing David again? The questions pile up.

## Michal and Palti

When we look at literary retellings, we see a near consensus—in line with the biblical text—that Palti really loves Michal. Heym describes Palti as a nobody who just happens to be standing nearby when Saul needs to find someone to marry Michal. Palti has "a cast in his eye, and crooked teeth, and one shoulder was higher than the other" (63). Heym's Michal will never love this uninspiring man, but she finds comfort in the fact that at least one person seems to like her. Brooks similarly envisages a Palti whose care Michal slowly and gradually learns to appreciate. She tries to remain faithful to David at first and therefore asks Palti not to touch her. Yet when she hears about David's growing number of wives, Michal begins to doubt that David ever loved her. Her marriage to Palti is, if not overwhelmingly happy, at least satisfying and an expression of mutual affection. In contrast, Massie's smug David never wonders about Michal's relationship with Palti, presumably because he is still completely convinced that he himself is her one and only true love.

## Michal and David (Again)

After ten years of marriage to Palti, David decides that he now wants Michal back. How does Michal feel about this second enforced divorce? Is she looking forward to traveling to Hebron and being reunited with her teenage heartthrob—and his six wives? According to Heym, Michal feels excited, scared, and bitter. She also wonders to what extent David's motives are purely political: Is it Saul's daughter or the woman Michal that David wants back?

She leans toward the former, since David has waited so long to send for her. Now, as crowned king in Hebron, a shared heir is suddenly needed to show the unification between the house of Saul and the house of David. Other accounts, notably those of Brooks and Brandes, describe a Michal who, in sheer anguish, is being torn from her husband and, in Brooks's case, her children (see below).

Many literary accounts speculate further on what awaits Michal when she arrives in Hebron. Does David welcome her with open arms and make her his queen consort, or does he rather, perhaps somewhat embarrassed and filled with guilt, stow her away at a safe distance in his growing harem? Heym chooses the latter option. When Michal arrives in Hebron, David keeps her waiting for hours sitting on her donkey outside the palace to rub in who is now in power. The last time they met, Saul, Michal's father, ruled while David was the unassuming outcast; now David rules while Saul's house depends on his mercy. Despite this, it takes Michal a little while to realize that she is not wanted. Michal hopes for a passionate welcome once she is admitted to the palace, but when David appears in her room, the two have a tense conversation about who is king in Israel and about David's music. David leaves her untouched.

Brooks's account is different. Her Michal is devastated at the thought of having to abandon her children. At the same time, there are similarities with Heym's understanding of the situation. David waits several weeks before contacting Michal, but when he does, he tries to rekindle her passion. Michal, however, is unable to do so. She is emotionally paralyzed and lacks all capacity to even try welcoming David back into her life and her bed. Michal's apparent coldness, in turn, makes David relive the humiliation he experienced at Saul's court. For David, Saul's decision to give Michal to another man was a deep insult. Saul, and thus Michal, although being Saul's innocent victim rather than playing any active role in the drama, wounded his manhood and made him doubt his God-given calling. Until his escape from Gibeah, everything had fallen into David's hands and gone well for him. For David, the decision to bring Michal back becomes a symbol that restores and consolidates his own success, both as a king and as a man.

In a similar vein, but with considerably less sympathy for Michal, Massie describes how David eagerly awaits Michal's arrival in Hebron. Once there, David endeavors to show how much Michal means to him and how she is far superior to all his other wives. David is soon disappointed, however, when

Michal does not reciprocate his advances and instead remains reticent. She has always been reserved, but what she has endured over the last ten years has made her almost incapable of showing emotion.

## A Terrible Quarrel

Michal appears once again in the story of David. Michal's romantic bubble is now definitely burst, leaving behind only bitterness and anger. When David returns home, filled with joy at having danced before the ark of the covenant, Michal is waiting for him, furious:

> David returned to bless his household. But Michal the daughter of Saul came out to meet David, and said, "How the king of Israel honored himself today, uncovering himself today before the eyes of his servants' maids, as any vulgar fellow might shamelessly uncover himself!" David said to Michal, "It was before the Lord, who chose me in place of your father and all his household, to appoint me as prince over Israel, the people of the Lord, that I have danced before the Lord. I will make myself yet more contemptible than this, and I will be abased in my own eyes; but by the maids of whom you have spoken, by them I shall be held in honor." And Michal the daughter of Saul had no child to the day of her death. (2 Sam 6:20–23)

It is difficult to decide who is right and who is wrong here. I imagine David's utter despair when Michal ruins his amazing experience with God. David is forced into a bitter and worldly quarrel after having just experienced an indescribable moment of presence and worship.

At the same time, I feel for Michal. Her existence in David's house as Saul's only surviving descendant, surrounded by David's other wives, cannot be easy. David's focus on God becomes a mockery when she compares it to his constant neglect of her throughout their marriage. What good does it do her that David has a great relationship with God when she only gets crumbs of his attention? Michal knows exactly how to hurt David, and she does it with finesse. Here in the most bitter marriage scene in the Bible, Michal puts into words for the first time the pain and disappointment that has been bubbling under the surface. Both David and Michal make liberal use of both emotional and political arguments against each other. The predominant tone, however, is political, emphasized by the consistent description of Michal throughout 1–2 Samuel as "Saul's daughter" rather than "David's wife." The quarrel concerns, at least on the surface, David's behavior, or rather his attire, when he dances half naked before the ark of the covenant. According to Michal, David has humiliated himself before his people by his appearance. David's answer shows, however, that the matter goes much deeper than that: According to David, he has the right to dance before God in whatever way and however lightly dressed he feels like, as God has chosen him and his lineage rather than Michal's family. The final statement in verse 23 has to do with dynastic expectations: There will never be a monarch on the throne of Israel to unite the houses of Saul and David, as Michal and David will never have any children together. This scene clearly shows that Michal and David's marriage has turned into a festering hotbed of conflict. Michal does not have much love left for David and David, well, we do not really know what he felt from the beginning.

The quarrel of Michal and David in 2 Samuel 6:20–23 almost makes Ingmar Bergman's film *Scenes from a Marriage* pale in comparison. It is common in literary retellings to describe Michal as a spoilsport on this fateful day. Driven by her bitterness and grief, she destroys David's moment of total devotion to God. It is worth noting that until 2 Samuel 6:20–23, the Bible has presented Michal in a positive light: She remains staunchly loyal to David and suffers as a result. The question becomes why Michal, after so many years of patient suffering, now suddenly allows herself to display this destructive behavior. In other words, if she has managed to hold her tongue so far, why is her self-control breaking down now?

In Heller's retelling *God Knows*, which uses David as the narrator, Michal's behavior is characteristic of her social snobbery as Saul's spoiled princess. Thus, Michal's desire to ruin David is not a novelty but, by implication, something she has always wanted: "'She was a baneful person who spoiled my good days and rejoiced in my bad and who would never allow herself to extol or admire me'" (61). Brooks is consistently much more sympathetic toward Michal, but even she narrates how Michal's lack of self-control has devastating consequences for both partners involved. Similarly, Heym lets David speak here, emphasizing how Michal's sarcasm arouses David's anger and leads to his decision never to provide the house of Saul with any offspring. Massie moves the whole incident to David's bedchamber later that evening. David finds Michal leaning over him when he wakes up, and she hurls her accusations at him. At this moment, Massie's David understands that this is Michal's true self, and he further begins to doubt that Michal has ever loved him for who he, David, really is. In Massie's retelling, it is David, and not Michal, who is the real victim.

I personally have no great desire to take David's side against Michal, but I still think that the retelling authors are right. In this specific scene, David is undeniably the one who suffers most undeservedly. With the precision of bitterness, Michal manages to destroy something that is completely sacred to him. She could have chosen any other day to have her big fight, but she chooses this day to do maximum damage. It is not pretty, and it should not be admired, despite my opening words in this chapter. I do not think David deserves this. At the same time, I believe that David has never cared about Michal. David's sin in this case is a sin of omission. If he had ever tried to put himself in Michal's situation, this whole tragedy might have been avoided.

## Michal's Child?

The last reference to Michal occurs in 2 Samuel 21:1–14 in connection with Israel's three-year famine during David's reign. This famine is explained as a direct result of Saul's murder of the Gibeonites (v. 2). David accepts this explanation and asks the Gibeonites what he can do for them. They in turn demand that seven of Saul's male descendants should be hanged in Gibeah, Saul's city (v. 6a). Only one of Saul's grandsons, Jonathan's son Mephibosheth, is allowed to survive, either because David loved Jonathan or because Mephibosheth has a disability and thus poses no threat to David's dynasty (v. 7). We readers can choose for ourselves which interpretation we prefer.

Who are these seven innocent men, and who are their parents? To answer this question is easier said than done because of textual ambiguities inherent in the transmission of the biblical text. Second Samuel 21:8, a horrific verse in terms of content, tells us how David gives permission to the Gibeonites to kill Saul's surviving descendants.

> The king took the two sons of Rizpah daughter of Aiah, whom she bore to Saul, Armoni and Mephibosheth; and *the five sons of Merab* daughter of Saul, whom she bore to Adriel son of Barzillai the Meholathite. (NRSV; emphasis mine)

> But the king took the two sons of Rizpah the daughter of Aiah, whom she bore unto Saul, Armoni and Mephibosheth; and *the five sons of Michal* the daughter of Saul, whom she bore to Adriel the son of Barzillai the Meholathite. (Jewish Publication Society; emphasis mine)

The difference between the NRSV (Merab) and the JPS (Michal) is a matter of textual criticism. While the JPS follows the final Hebrew text (the so-called Masoretic text), the NRSV follows the Greek translation which is based on a presumed Hebrew text dating to a few centuries BCE (the Septuagint). In several cases, there are reasons to believe that the Septuagint reflects a text that is earlier than what the Masoretic text does. In this case, for example, it is likely that the Septuagint reflects the earliest text as Merab, Michal's older sister, is indeed married to Adriel (1 Sam 18:19). Nevertheless, a small seed of doubt is sown here. Could it really be that Michal has borne five sons to Palti and that David, in cold blood, hands them over to the Gibeonites to be killed?

Another of the many challenges is to determine when exactly this episode takes place in the larger story about King David's reign. The current position of the episode in 2 Samuel 21 may be interpreted to mean that the event occurs toward the end of David's life, but this is not a necessary conclusion from a narrative perspective. It is not uncommon in the Bible for events to be presented in a thematic rather than chronological order (cf. chapters 2 and 5).

## The Rest of Michal's Life

We do not know anything about what happens to Michal after 2 Samuel 6. This silence leads the reader to speculate on what her future life might be like, alone and abandoned in David's court. What does she feel when Bathsheba appears? How does she react to Amnon's rape of Tamar? Whom does she root for during Absalom's rebellion against David? We do not know and cannot know. The biggest question for me, however, is whether Michal lives to see David hand over her two half brothers and either her own five sons or her nephews to the Gibeonites for execution: "He gave them into the hands of the Gibeonites, and they impaled them on the mountain before the Lord. The seven of them perished together. They were put to death in the first days of harvest, at the beginning of the barley harvest" (2 Sam 21:9). As mentioned above, there are few reasons to doubt that Michal is forced to watch David authorize the murders of her close relatives. What does one feel in such a situation? Is it even possible to imagine this? To know that your own husband is murdering, albeit not personally, your siblings and (sibling's) children? No, it is not possible. Yet some of our retellings have tried. Brandes lets Michal almost wither away in grief. Michal's (faked) madness, as she goes around her palace lighting groups of seven candles and screaming out her grief and powerlessness, is almost real. This, in turn, becomes the prelude to Michal's revenge. Brandes allows Michal, as the sole survivor of Saul's family at Solomon's court, to become a political force operating in secret. Michal continues to feign insanity to hide how she is slowly and strategically preparing Jeroboam (who, according to Brandes, is her surviving grandson) to seize power from Rehoboam and thus return power over Israel to Saul's heirs.

Two retellings link the massacre of Saul's descendants with Michal's behavior in 2 Samuel 6. On the one hand, Brooks sees David's decision to kill Saul's male descendants as a direct result of Michal's derision when the ark is being brought into Jerusalem. Michal destroys David's moment of intense joy in God, and it makes him remember all the times Saul humiliated and persecuted him. Now, when David has the opportunity to hurt Saul's family by appeasing the Gibeonites, he takes it. Although David recognizes that this heinous act is politically advantageous to him, as it effectively eliminates Saul's remaining male relatives, his motivation lies on a deeper and more personal level.

On the other hand, Heym links the two events but in the reverse order. Heym's narrator, Ethan, suspects that David is not only ultimately responsible for authorizing the Gibeonites to kill Saul's descendants but also the one who actively orders them to suggest the idea in the first place. There is no doubt that the Saulides' deaths serve David's goal of consolidating his dynasty. Heym also points out that Michal at that point already has been forced to witness the elimination of her brother Ishbosheth for being a threat to David's throne. The temporal relationship between the event in 2 Samuel 21 and Michal's quarrel with David in 2 Samuel 6 is never clarified in the novel, but it is implied that Michal's quarrel in chapter 6 is a consequence of David's decision to kill Saul's male heirs. If this were the case, Michal's behavior toward David takes on a whole new dimension. David's joy before God becomes a mockery, knowing that the man in front of her is a cold-blooded murderer. It also adds a deeper nuance to David's words about her family and to God's choice of David's line over that of Saul. Is it really God who has given David the throne, or is it rather David himself who has usurped it at the expense of Saul's children and grandchildren?

## Narrator's Perspective

When we choose our narrator, we also choose to present our story from a particular perspective and to give that person's views the most space and authority. When, for example, Massie and Heller decide to make David their narrator, it means that we readers experience the events of 1–2 Samuel from David's point of view. The same is true when we read the Bible today. The material in 1–2 Samuel reflects, at least in part, the attempts of later writers to justify David's rise to power. The idea that history is written by the victors is an accepted concept. It goes without saying that the losers, that is, Saul and his heirs, are not given the same voice as David and his successors. David emerges victorious from the battle with Saul, and it is David's descendants, rather than Saul's, who write history. And yet, as there are always at least two sides to every conflict, the narrator's own perspective plays a major role in the descriptions of the events and the characterizations of the people involved.

Brandes's retelling *The Secret Book of Kings* is a good example of a retelling that deliberately reads the biblical text against the grain. The Hebrew title of her book, "3 Kings," plays with the idea that the novel is an alternative, pro-Saul version of Israel's history, in the same way that 1–2 Chronicles gives a thoroughly pro-David version that leaves out anything that disturbs the image of the perfect David. Chronicles never mentions Michal, for example, nor Bathsheba for that matter. Thus, Brandes's narrator, Michal, gives a very different version of David's rise to power than the one we encounter in the more "biblical" retellings that reflect David's outlook. Heym's novel *The King David Report* is another, considerably more satirical, example of how a retelling can shift the perspective to highlight a story's underlying assumptions and biases.

Brandes's and Heym's respective retellings raise the question of our responsibility as readers. In the case of Michal, the question has a double relevance: How should we read the biblical descriptions of women (who are also losers)? All biblical texts are likely to be written by men and thus reflect their views of women (there may be one possible exception, namely Song of Songs). Should we adopt their views and make them our own, or do we rather have an obligation to look for and listen to other, less normative voices in the texts?

There is no obvious answer to this question. Some of the selected retellings follow and even accept to a certain extent the Bible's own perspective, while others invite us to consider whether there may be more than one way of interpreting the characters and their actions in the David story, and how these shifting perspectives affect our understanding of the narrative as a whole.

* * *

Is Michal a role model that we ought to emulate in our own lives? Certainly not. I would not wish her lot in life on my bitterest enemies. At the same time, her fate enables us to discuss really deep questions about our relationship with God and our fellow human beings. It is easy, but at the same time terrifying, to identify with Michal. Her experiences challenge us to consider how we would have acted had we been in her shoes, and they force us to take a stand on some very challenging issues. Michal's fate leaves no one indifferent.

Firstly, how much responsibility does a person have for their lot in life? Is Michal fooling herself when she chooses not to follow David through the window that night so long ago? Should Michal have insisted on not being left behind in Gibeah? Her life would certainly have been different if she had accompanied David, even if there would never have been any guarantee that her life would have been better. Her fate alongside David in the Judaean wilderness would certainly not have been a bed of roses. Michal's fate also shows how difficult it can be to have to choose between doing what our parents want and what we ourselves want to do deep down in our hearts.

At the same time, it is important to realize that we in the West have considerably more freedom and choice than any woman in ancient Israel ever had. Was Michal even faced with a choice in this situation? The modern ideal of following our hearts at any cost is not easily translated into the biblical world. Michal is first forced to marry David. In this particular case, we know she does not mind because she loves him, but she would have been forced to do the same even if that were not the case. The same applies to Michal's second marriage. If 1 Samuel had been a romantic drama, then yes, Michal would have stood up to her father, refused to marry Palti, sneaked out into the night, stolen a donkey (horses were not usually available in Israel in the late Bronze Age), and set off at a gallop after David. This scenario, however, is a modern expectation that does not work very well around 1000 BCE. A woman at that time simply did not have that option. Michal, like any other historical princess, is bound by both her culture and her tradition and lacks the ability to choose her own life. Our modern ideal of creating one's own destiny is not entirely biblical.

Moreover, Michal's marriage to David is not something that should serve as a model for a love match either. Like Michal's relationship with her father, her marriage to David is an example of a failed relationship or rather one entered into on inadequate premises. Michal and David's quarrel is also a case in point of how not to quarrel. If the biblical text must necessarily be used as an example, then it is how not to behave. David and Michal talk past each other, they fail to stick to the point but instead mention things that appear to be irrelevant, and they deliberately hurt each other by bringing up old grudges. This text, one of the saddest in the Bible, shows in stark relief how people should not treat each other.

In a similar way, Michal and Saul's relationship invites discussion about the responsibilities of a parent toward their children and the rights of a child toward their parents. As above, the story of Saul and Michal is a textbook example of a bad child-parent relationship. When parents use their children as pawns in their political power game, it never ends well. At the same time, it is worth wondering to what extent Michal is honoring her father when she prioritizes her husband's safety over Saul's wishes. Here, however, I maintain that each person has a responsibility to prevent murder: The commandment to honor one's parents should never mean handing over another human being to premature death.

Last but not least, we must not forget David. If the story of Michal makes one thing abundantly clear, it is that we must stop seeing David as our knight in shining armor. David—the intelligent, talented, and attractive man who charms everyone with his colossal charisma and emotional expressiveness—has a ruthless side that ought to scare the living daylights out of us. It is great to have David as a friend, but it is deadly to be among his enemies. We should not allow ourselves to sweep under the carpet David's behavior toward Michal when he agrees to the Gibeonites' proposal to murder her family in cold blood. David is a fascinating mix of good and evil to a degree unparalleled in the rest of the Bible. David is not an example for us to follow.

CHAPTER EIGHT

# Jonah

## *Annoying Grouch or Rebel with a Cause?*

OH JONAH, WHAT a wonderful little book! I love this rebellious book and its rebellious main character who refuses to fall in line and be like everyone else. In all other prophetic books, God speaks most of the time; in the book of Jonah, Jonah and God get approximately the same number of lines. All other biblical prophets choose to carry out God's mission, more or less cheerfully; Jonah totally refuses, deciding instead to flee his calling, only to then, sullenly, obey God in a minimalist manner, to say the least. Yet Jonah's one-liner of a prophecy is the most successful one in the entire Bible. A whole city is converted instantaneously, yet this does not please our unusual prophet. Instead, he continues to sulk and be angry with God. The end of the book leaves readers in a dilemma as it is unclear whether Jonah accepts God's view or sticks to his own.

### Narratives

In this chapter, together with several literary retellings, we shall reflect on Jonah's calling and subsequent flight and more generally on the book's message about mercy and justice.

**Dietrich Bonhoeffer** (1906–1945) was a German Lutheran pastor and theologian. He was also an active opponent of Nazism and was a founding member of the so-called Confessing Church. He was executed for high treason against Nazism and is often regarded as a martyr who died for his Christian faith.

"Jona," http://www.otthollo.de/JONA/Bonhoeffer.html (1944).

"Jonah," in *Letters and Papers from Prison*, vol. 8 of *Dietrich Bonhoeffer Works*, eds. Reinhard Krauss and Nancy Lukens, trans. Isabel Best (Fortress Press, 2010).

**Robert Frost** (1874–1963) was an American poet. His drama *A Masque of Mercy* is a modern reinterpretation of Jonah that emphasizes the relationship between mercy and justice. The four characters represent four different views. The main character, Jonah Dove, whose name alludes to the fact that the name Jonah means "dove" in Hebrew, is in spiritual flight from God. He has lost his faith because God does not carry out the threat of destruction that Jonah was forced to deliver. Other characters are "the one who keeps track of his brother" (Gen 4:9b), Jonah's wife Jesse Bel (Jezebel), and her doctor Paul (the apostle Paul in the New Testament).

*A Masque of Mercy*, in *Collected Poems, Prose, and Plays* (Library of America, 1995).

**Gertrud Kolmar** (1894–1943), pseudonym for Gertrud Käthe Chodziesner, was a German Jewish poet and author. Born in Berlin, she was murdered in Auschwitz.

"Die Tiere von Ninive" (The animals of Nineveh), in *Gedichte: 1927–1937*, vol. 2 of *Das lyrische Werk* (Wallstein, 2003).

**Herman Melville** (1819–1891) was an American novelist and poet, best known for his great work *Moby-Dick*.

*Moby-Dick; or, The Whale* (Harper & Brothers, 1851).

**Kadia Molodowsky** (1894–1975) was a Russian Jewish author who wrote in Yiddish. Her poem about Jonah describes how Jewish identity can be experienced both as a burden and as a responsibility toward God and the non-Jewish world.

"Jonah," in *Paper Bridges: Selected Poems of Kadya Molodowsky*, trans. Kathryn Hellerstein (Wayne State University Press, 1990), 491.

**Peter Nilson** (1937–1998) was a Swedish astronomer and author. His novel *Guldspiken* (*The golden nail*) is a free retelling of the book of Jonah. The novel is inspired by real people, places, and events in nineteenth-century Sweden. Its protagonist, Elias, is a preacher trying to escape his God-given calling to preach the gospel.

*Guldspiken* (Norstedt, 1985).

**Moacyr Scliar** (1937–2011) was a Brazilian Jewish writer and physician. The protagonist of the book *The Strange Nation of Rafael Mendes*, Rafael Mendes, appears again and again throughout history in different incarnations that all show similarities to the biblical Jonah. All incarnations have in common that they try to escape their destiny (but constantly fail) because of their Jewish identity.

*The Strange Nation of Rafael Mendes*, trans. Eloah F. Giacomelli (Harmony, 1986), originally published as *A estranha nação de Rafael Mendes* (L&PM, 1983).

These literary works challenge us to think in new ways about the interpretation of the book of Jonah. They have helped me to see dimensions of the text that I would never have seen myself, with the result that my reading of the Bible has been enriched and my understanding of God's word deepened. At the same time, they challenge me by muddying the seemingly clear (and almost always preached) understanding of the book of Jonah as a message of grace from God. They force me to reflect on recognized truths and, together with Jonah, to venture into (sometimes too) deep waters.

## Background

God gives Jonah a mission (1:2). He is to go to Nineveh, the capital of the Neo-Assyrian Empire, and declare that God intends to destroy the city within forty days: "Go at once to Nineveh, that great city, and cry out against it; for their wickedness has come up before me." Jonah disagrees, however, and defies God's command. Instead of going to Nineveh, which is to the east, he travels west toward the Mediterranean coast, and boards a boat that he hopes will take him as far away from Nineveh as possible. Jonah does not want to be forced to do something he does not want to do. The question remains, however, why Jonah reacts the way he does. In short, what makes it so difficult for Jonah to fulfil God's mission?

The book of Jonah itself gives an explicit answer: Jonah, possibly because of his prophetic office, already knows how Nineveh will react to God's message. They will repent (Jonah 4:1–2), which by implication is something Jonah is unhappy about: "But this was very displeasing to

Jonah, and he became angry. He prayed to the Lord and said, 'O Lord! Is not this what I said while I was still in my own country? That is why I fled to Tarshish at the beginning; for I knew that you are a gracious God and merciful, slow to anger, and abounding in steadfast love, and ready to relent from punishing.'" Even so, this passage still does not explain what Jonah's actual stumbling block is. Why does Nineveh's repentance upset Jonah so much? Scholars throughout the ages have pondered such questions. Is it because Jonah does not want to be accused of being a false prophet, that is, he does not want to see his prophecy remain unfulfilled? It is a possible but not entirely convincing interpretation. Prophecies in Israel functioned as warnings rather than absolute predictions of the future (cf. Jer 18:7–10, see chapter 2). No one in Israel would have seen it as failure if Jonah's prophecy had led to its nonfulfillment. Rather, it would have been interpreted as a success: People turn to God, which is the very purpose of prophecy.

I like to compare this to my own experience as a parent. When my children came home from school on Friday afternoon, I asked them to put their dirty school uniforms in the laundry basket (we lived in Scotland, hence school uniforms), otherwise they would not have clean clothes the following Monday morning. My intention, of course, was never for my children to wear unwashed uniforms to school—I would have been ashamed of myself—but for the clothes to go into the washing machine. In the same way, God would prefer to see the behavior that demands punishment abstained from, so that the punishment does not need to be meted out.

Rather, Jonah refuses to go to Nineveh because he knows the destruction that Nineveh will bring to his land and people, from Jonah's perspective, a few decades later. Jonah (and the readers) know that the Neo-Assyrian Empire will destroy Israel in 721 BCE and force many of his surviving countrypeople into exile. A destroyed Nineveh would, at least in Jonah's view, preserve his country, as a destroyed empire cannot destroy other places. Jonah's logic is crystal clear: If he does not go to Nineveh, the Ninevites will not have a chance to repent, and God will consequently be forced to destroy Nineveh. The result should be, according to Jonah's logic, the survival of his own people. Jonah's choice is then between saving his own country and offering strangers a chance to survive. The choice is obvious, right?

## Jonah Questions God's Justice

Most retellings of the biblical story of Jonah are dominated by three questions: Why does Jonah flee from his calling? How does Jonah experience his time on the run from God? And what does Jonah think about God's balancing act between mercy and justice? These questions are often intertwined, and it is not always possible or even desirable to distinguish between them.

Many scholars and writers associate Jonah's flight from his calling with his conviction that God, from the beginning, has decided to pardon Nineveh. Such a pardon would further, according to Jonah, be undeserved. In other words, Jonah's flight has to do with God's (in)justice. Jonah, in his refusal to go to Nineveh, is passing judgment on God: He is demanding that God, in his role as judge of the world, should stand by his promises to repay evil with evil. Jonah does not want to obey God because he knows—but resists—that God is inclined to show compassion.

The commonly held interpretation of the book of Jonah makes it clear that God is right, and Jonah is wrong. Jonah has often been seen as a narrow-minded nationalist who refuses to let others into the kingdom of God. God, by contrast, is gracious and welcomes Jonah back when he comes to his senses. God has the right to grant salvation to whomever he wants, and Jonah should adjust his worldview to fit God's universal perspective. In this context, it should be pointed out that this line of interpretation has unfortunately often been accompanied by anti-Jewish sentiments and led to anti-Jewish polemics, which are here rejected.

Yet this prevalent interpretation is not the only possible one, and the book of Jonah, with its open ending, gives us readers the opportunity—if we dare—to side with Jonah instead of God. First, more generally, how can we humans trust God's justice when he pardons a country like Assyria, a nation known for its oppression of neighboring countries and its cruelty toward its enemies (Nah 3:19)? More specifically, how can God decide to show mercy to Nineveh, the capital of the country that, from Jonah's point of view, will soon occupy and destroy Jonah's homeland Israel (2 Kings 17)? Finally, is it really fair of God to allow a few days of repentance to lead to such unimaginable mercy, while God's treatment of Israel, whose sins pale by comparison in size and significance, is punished with destruction, exile, and Diaspora for millennia?

Several modern literary retellings of the Jonah story address these questions, using the biblical text as a lens through which we can ponder God's mercy or, more accurately, his failure to be unmerciful. The central question is the balance between mercy and justice: Can true mercy exist in the absence of true justice? Put by British literary theorist Terry Eagleton (b. 1943), Jonah refuses to obey God because there seems to be no point in traveling to Nineveh when Nineveh's salvation is already all but predetermined:

> God is a spineless liberal given to hollow authoritarian threats, who would never have the guts to perform what he promises [. . .] the point of Jonah's getting himself thrown overboard is to force God to save him, thus dramatically demonstrating to him that he's too soft-hearted to punish those who disobey him [. . .] Jonah doesn't believe for a moment that Nineveh's suspiciously sudden repentance is anything of his own doing: it has been brought about by God, to save himself the mess, unpleasantness and damage to his credibility as a nice chap consequent on having to put his threats into practice [. . .] God would have spared the city even if Jonah had stayed at home; it's just that he needs some excuse to do so. [. . .] And if God just goes around forgiving everybody all the time, what's the point of doing anything? If disobedience on the scale of a Nineveh goes cavalierly unpunished, then the idea of obedience also ceases to have meaning. God's mercy simply makes a mockery of human effort.[1]

These ideas about God's spineless justice feature strongly in Robert Frost's play *A Masque of Mercy*. Frost uses the central character Jonah Dove to ponder questions of God's mercy and, at the same time, his apparent failure to uphold divine justice. God, according to Jonah Dove, must punish the wicked in his role as the supreme God. Anything else would be an abuse of justice. Jonah exclaims: "I've lost my faith in God to carry out / The threats He makes against the city evil. / I can't trust God to be unmerciful" (393). Later in the same play, Jonah Dove continues:

> I refuse to be the bearer of an empty threat.
> He may be God, but me, I'm only human:
> I shrink from being publicly let down. [. . .]
> There's not the least lack of the love of God

In what I say. Don't be so silly, woman.
His very weakness for mankind's endearing.
I love and fear Him. Yes, but I fear for Him.
I don't see how it can be to His interest
This modern tendency I find in Him
To take the punishment out of all failure
To be strong, careful, thrifty, diligent,
Anything we once thought we had to be. (401)

The question that runs throughout the play is the balance between justice and mercy. God's mercy, according to Jonah, creates a situation where one can sin without fear of the consequences. Moreover, if God can forgive the city of Nineveh in all its cruelty, then he can forgive just about anything. Other characters in the play object and argue that God has the right to pardon whomever he wants. God's mercy is always freely given and can never be earned.

The book of Jonah offers no solution. Jonah sits outside Nineveh, and we readers will never know whether Jonah will ultimately be persuaded by God's argument and recognize that mercy is preferable to justice, or whether he will stick to his view that justice is better than mercy: "Then the Lord said, 'You are concerned about the bush, for which you did not labor and which you did not grow; it came into being in a night and perished in a night. And should I not be concerned about Nineveh, that great city, in which there are more than a hundred and twenty thousand people who do not know their right hand from their left, and also many animals?'" (Jonah 4:10–11). Frost's drama similarly ends without Jonah Dove reaching a clear decision, forcing the audience to consider the consequences of both options. Frost's Jonah dies, but it is up to the viewer to decide whether he has recognized the validity of God's approach.

The German Jewish poet Gertrud Kolmar advocates the opposite perspective in her poem "Die Tiere von Ninive" (The animals of Nineveh). This poem criticizes Jonah's inability to accept God's decision to pardon Nineveh. Kolmar uses powerful imagery to convey Jonah's refusal to hear God in the storm and to contemplate the suffering that the innocent people of Nineveh would have endured had God not changed his mind and allowed mercy to prevail over justice. The poem ends with Jonah setting off, unwilling or perhaps even unable to give in and reconsider his position:

<table>
<tr>
<td>And Jonah went.<br>And the burden of Nineveh that he<br>had seen hung over his head,<br>but he walked with a darkened mind.<br>[...]<br>It howled in the storm and it cried in<br>the wind and a voice cried out:<br>"For the sake of those!<br>For the sake of those animals, clean<br>and unclean."<br>And the messenger of the Lord was<br>stunned and looked, but there was<br>only darkness, and he heard nothing<br>but an unrelenting howling and<br>blowing,<br>that gripped his coat and pulled at<br>it and shook it, like a pleader's hand<br>[pulls] the garment of one unmerci-<br>fully running away,<br>but he did not relent; he strode<br>and held his coat.<br>(Translation by Andreas Tiemeyer)</td>
<td>Doch Jona ging,<br>Und die Last über Ninive, die er<br>geschaut, hing über seinem Scheitel.<br>Er aber wandelte in schwerem<br>Sinnen.<br>[...]<br>Und es heulte im Sturm und es<br>schrie im Sturme und eine Stimme<br>rief:<br>»Um dieser willen!<br>Um dieser Tiere, reiner und<br>unreiner, willen!«<br>Und der Gesandte des Herrn<br>schrak und sah; aber nur<br>Finsternis war, und er hörte nichts<br>als ein unablässiges<br>Wehen und Sausen,<br>Das seinen Mantel faßte und zog<br>und schüttelte wie eines<br>Bittenden Hand das Kleid des<br>unbarmherzig<br>Enteilenden.<br>Er aber kehrte sich nicht; er schritt<br>Und raffte und hielt den Mantel.</td>
</tr>
</table>

Kolmar's God speaks to Jonah in the storm, an image that is linked to the storm God sent to prevent Jonah's escape earlier in Jonah 1:4. It also alludes to God's decision in 1 Kings 19:11 to speak to Elijah by a whisper and not by a storm. In Elijah's case, God does not need to use the powers of nature to get his prophet to listen; a soft and quiet call is enough. Here God is forced to use all the power at his disposal, but it is still insufficient to make Jonah stop and think. In this way, Kolmar laments Jonah's inability to accept anyone's point of view but his own. Jonah refuses to hear God's side of the story, and he is unable to recognize that there is another kind of justice in God's concern for the innocents of Nineveh, who would have suffered if God had not canceled his plans of destruction.

Both Frost's and Kolmar's retellings stand in a long tradition of biblical scholarship that ponders the questions of mercy and justice raised by the book of Jonah. At the same time, through their poetic language and literary quality, they make us reflect anew on and perhaps even reevaluate the traditional and well-established interpretation of the Jonah story that is entirely centered on praising God's generous mercy toward the repentant Ninevites.

Frost's retelling further invites us to side with Jonah and make his questions our own. Jonah's statement in Jonah 4:2 shows his dissatisfaction with God's legal stance: What God is advocating is a situation where no equivalent suffering, no compensatory good deeds, and no atoning rituals are needed for Nineveh to be forgiven. But is it up to God to forgive the evil caused by Nineveh? Is it against him that Nineveh has sinned most grievously? Is it not rather Nineveh's human victims who in this case are reserved the right to judge? Jonah's flight from God in chapter 1 and his unfinished dialogue with God in chapter 4 thus become an example of the human struggle against injustice. This is best expressed by the biblical scholar Yvonne Sherwood in her book *A Biblical Text and its Afterlives: The Survival of Jonah in Western Culture*: Could it be that the main purpose of the book of Jonah is to test the principle of universal mercy in the most extreme circumstances and to ask a fantastic and at the same time terrifying what-if? "What if Nineveh, the 'bloody city' as Nahum puts it, the equivalent of Berlin of the Third Reich, repents?"[2] The issue is twofold. On the one hand, if the people of Berlin in 1938 had repented and turned to God, then millions of Jonah's descendants would probably have survived. On the other hand, if Berlin had been razed to the ground in 1938, even then, but for completely different reasons, millions of Jonah's descendants would probably have survived. It is a question of perspective. If we focus solely on Israel's survival, which option is preferable? Jonah seems to think the second scenario is better, while the book of Jonah as a whole appears to lean toward the first one. The question is also addressed to us: If we had the opportunity to change history in 1938, what strategy would we have favored? Which prospect would have seemed safer?

## Jonah on the Run from God

While the abovementioned authors use the book of Jonah to discuss God's (lack of) justice, an equal number of authors have made the prophet Jonah a mouthpiece for their sense of being unable to escape their God-given destiny.

Their literary retellings transform, and to a large extent also undermine, Jonah's ultimately unsuccessful escape by placing it within the broader context of humanity's relationship with God.

Jonah's attempt to escape God's will has also been interpreted more narrowly in the context of, on the one hand, God's covenant with Israel and, on the other hand, the covenant between God and the church. Jonah becomes the wandering Jew who cannot stop being part of God's own people and who suffers oppression and martyrdom as a result. He also becomes the individual Christian who seeks to escape God's calling in their life. The dialogue between literature and the biblical text ultimately becomes a vehicle for depicting the struggle to escape one's destiny. The leading theme of many of these retellings is Jonah's sense of futility, compulsion, and frustration. The Jonah story is invoked to emphasize that all attempts to escape one's God-ordained destiny will ultimately fail.

## Jonah on the Run from His Calling

The Swedish author Peter Nilson brings this aspect to the fore in an interesting and challenging way in his novel *Guldspiken* (The golden nail). The main character, the poor boy Elias, is led to believe that he is called to travel to America, the glorious land of opportunity, where the railways are nailed with gold nails. His dream is interrupted when he hears what he believes to be the voice of God calling him to go and preach in hell. To escape his calling, Elias flees on board a ship that takes him to Africa, only to realize that life on board is indeed hell on earth. God's irony is palpable, as Elias's flight, like Jonah's flight, has only brought him closer to the one place he was trying to avoid. His situation is summarized by God when he finally returns to Sweden: "No one ever escapes their destiny" (98–100, 109–133; my translation).

Nilson's dialogical reading with the book of Jonah deepens our understanding of both the novel and the biblical story. On the one hand, it stresses the futility of Elias's efforts: We all know that the biblical Jonah fails in his attempt to escape from God's call, and so we suspect that Nilson's protagonist will do the same. On the other hand, Nilson's novel challenges us to reevaluate the book of Jonah. It allows us to interpret the biblical story in a way that resonates with our own questions. The biblical prophet, portrayed as a caricature because of his wayward and grumpy demeanor, is thus transformed into a man of flesh and blood with whom modern readers can relate and empathize. Jonah is trapped by God and is forced, despite his best efforts, to do something he does not want to do.

The story of Jonah, read in this way, assigns Jonah the role of victim while God is given the role of bully, and the interaction between them sometimes feels unfair. God's decision to send a large fish to devour Jonah in order to get Jonah to fall in line and fulfil the task God has called him to has shades of excessive use of force. God and Jonah are not in the same league at all. At the same time, God's mobilization of the fish is also an expression of comedy: It really takes a giant fish to make Jonah realize that he should obey God's command.

## Jonah on the Run from His Fears

Jonah's flight from his calling has often been explained by his fear of going to Nineveh to preach. This interpretation is rather loosely anchored in the biblical text, as there are few signs that Jonah is particularly fearful. Rather, he is brave to the point of foolhardiness when he calmly informs the sailors who he is and grants them permission to throw him overboard without further ado (1:8–12). Despite this, several great literary masterpieces, most notably Herman Melville's *Moby-Dick; or, The Whale*, maintain that Jonah refuses to preach at Nineveh because of fear. In Father Mapple's sermon in chapter 9, Jonah is portrayed as a scared man who is afraid that the people of Nineveh will harm him when they hear his message. Jonah is a lonely and cowardly man, whose rebellion against God ultimately mirrors his own anxiety: "How being an anointed pilot-prophet, or speaker of true things, and bidden by the Lord to sound those unwelcome truths in the ears of a wicked Nineveh, Jonah, appalled at the hostility he should raise, fled from his mission, and sought to escape his duty and his God by taking ship at Joppa. But God is everywhere; Tarshish he never reached. As we have seen, God came upon him in the whale" (66). The sermon ends on a positive note (in contrast to the open and ambivalent ending of Jonah 4:11), with Jonah obeying God's call "to preach the truth in the face of lies" and Father Mapple urging his congregation to act likewise (66).

## Jonah on the Run from His Jewish Heritage

Other retellings emphasize more generally Jonah's sense of alienation from God and the world. The reluctant biblical prophet and his time in the belly of the fish are often transformed in these texts into a symbol of the Jewish trauma of belonging to God's own people. The feeling of being unable to renounce one's Jewish heritage is vividly expressed in Kadia Molodowsky's poem "Jonah." Inspired in part by the similarities between Genesis 4:15–16 and Jonah 4, Molodowsky combines the image of Cain marked by God with that of Jonah sitting angry and despondent east of Nineveh.

> Then Cain went away from the presence of the Lord, and *settled in the land of Nod, east of Eden*. (Gen 4:16; emphasis mine)

> *Then Jonah went out of the city and sat down east of the city*, and made a booth for himself there. He sat under it in the shade, waiting to see what would become of the city. (Jonah 4:5; emphasis mine)

Molodowsky's poem paints a figure of Jonah who in many ways represents her own fate. As a Jew, she is a person marked by God and thus unable to escape her lot in life. Her own journey took her from a shtetl in Belarus through Warsaw, Odesa, Kyiv, New York, and Tel Aviv, fleeing pogroms and other forms of anti-Jewish persecution. Jonah is fleeing from God and, in a broader sense, the persecutions and other forms of abuse that have characterized the Jewish people's experience over the last 2500 years, that is, from the time of Jonah onward. Jonah, the Jew, never escapes being part of God's chosen people:

> Lamenting, you will plead with God:
> Why am I your vessel, why me?
> I want to plant a date palm, an apple tree, [. . .]
> And a voice answers you from the storm:
> Forget your apple tree, your house and your kin,
> You are chosen for mercy and for pain,
> Go to Nineveh,
> And purify its sin.

Molodowsky creates here a dialogue with the Bible that affects both our understanding of her poem and the biblical narrative: It gives the poem greater resonance and the book of Jonah greater clarity. We experience Jonah in a new way and see his flight from God and his calling with new eyes. Perhaps

Jonah is not only a narrow-minded man who stubbornly refuses to obey God for selfish reasons but also, at the same time, a person who wants to decide for himself what he wants to do with his life.

Molodowsky's reading reflects millennia of Jewish persecution and the more recent Holocaust. Her reading of the Jonah story challenges us to reevaluate Jonah's failure to escape God's call. We are forced to explore the agony of belonging to God's chosen people. Read this way, the biblical Jonah is a victim of God's relentless calling and unrelenting demand for obedience; read this way, it is hard to hear the psalmist's words of God's care in Psalm 139:7–12 as a message of hope and comfort: "Where can I go from your spirit? Or where can I flee from your presence?" (Ps 139:7). Molodowsky's dialogue between literature and the biblical text further challenges us to identify with Jonah. Like the biblical figure, we cannot hide from God's eyes, and thus the seemingly obvious message of mercy in the book of Jonah is deconstructed. Rather than accepting God's view of the situation, we are provoked to consider alternative points of view and to wonder whether Jonah's attempt to escape from his God-given task may be justified after all. As a result, we are forced to reconsider our understanding of the genre of the book of Jonah. It becomes almost untenable to read it as a humorous little book about a man being swallowed by a fish, suitable for children of Sunday school age. Rather, we are challenged to take it with utmost seriousness and approach it with fear and trembling.

## Jonah as the Perpetual Refugee

Other retellings refer to Jonah's flight from God, his calling and his destiny, but reformulate its message so that readers encounter in Jonah a type of the eternal fugitive. This interpretation is based on the presence of several shared expressions between Jonah and Genesis 3–4. Phrases such as "to drive out," "from the face of the Lord," "to be angry," and "the east" together form a web that encourages us to read the two texts together and allow them to illuminate each other (Gen 3:24; 4:5, 6, 12, 16; Jonah 1:3, 10; 2:4; 4:1, 4, 5). As mentioned earlier in connection with Molodowsky's poem on Jonah, when Jonah and Genesis 4 are read together, Jonah emerges as a type for Cain, who is constantly forced be on the run from God but at the same time never escapes him:

> "And now you are cursed from the ground, which has opened its mouth to receive your brother's blood from your hand. When you

> till the ground, it will no longer yield to you its strength; you will be a fugitive and a wanderer on the earth." Cain said to the Lord, "My punishment is greater than I can bear! Today you have driven me away from the soil, and I shall be hidden from your face; I shall be a fugitive and a wanderer on the earth, and anyone who meets me may kill me." Then the Lord said to him, "Not so! Whoever kills Cain will suffer a sevenfold vengeance." And the Lord put a mark on Cain, so that no one who came upon him would kill him. Then Cain went away from the presence of the Lord, and settled in the land of Nod, east of Eden. (Gen 4:11–16)

This idea is concretized in Moacyr Scliar's book *The Strange Nation of Rafael Mendes*, which borrows its structure from the Jonah story. Its protagonists, all named Rafael Mendes, each act as a kind of Jonah whose behavior is consistent with that of the biblical character. As the novel progresses, the reader encounters a long sequence of Jonah's descendants—Rafael in various incarnations—that are all characterized by their rootlessness and longing for a place to call home.

One of these Jonah incarnations is living at the time of the Spanish Inquisition. He is a so-called New Christian (*cristão-novo*), a Jew forced to convert to Christianity to avoid persecution and death. After imprisonment and prolonged torture, Rafael and his companion Afonso manage to escape, only to end up on a ship run by Jew-hating sailors. Near the coast of Brazil, the weather suddenly changes. After learning that Rafael and Afonso are Jews (cf. Jonah 1:9), the sailors turn on them, holding the two "descendants of Christ's murderers" responsible for the storm: "'Divine punishment has befallen us,' muttered the sailors, 'for we are harboring two heretics, two descendants of Christ's killers.'" Tension keeps mounting, and one night Rafael and Afonso wake up to shouts and the clangor of swords: "'Save yourselves,' the captain shouted at them, 'jump into the sea'" (126). In Jonah 1:12–15, the sailors' decision to throw Jonah overboard to save themselves is presented as somewhat justified. They have tried to rescue Jonah before, but each time the storm blows up again.

> He said to them, "Pick me up and throw me into the sea; then the sea will quieten down for you; for I know it is because of me that this great storm has come upon you." Nevertheless, the men rowed hard

> to bring the ship back to land, but they could not, for the sea grew more and more stormy against them. Then they cried out to the Lord, "Please, O Lord, we pray, do not let us perish on account of this man's life. Do not make us guilty of innocent blood; for you, O Lord, have done as it pleased you." So they picked Jonah up and threw him into the sea; and the sea ceased from its raging.

Scliar's retelling transforms the sailors' decision to throw Jonah overboard into a breach of hospitality and, consequently, into murder of the already persecuted Rafael and Afonso. Rafael, like Jonah, survives the ordeal but remains homeless and continues his restless wandering in the world.

Scliar further connects Jonah 1:15 with the words of Caiaphas in John 11:50: "You do not understand that it is better for you to have one man die for the people than to have the whole nation destroyed" Inspired by Matthew 12:38 and Luke 11:29–32, both of which speak of the sign of Jonah, traditional Christian interpretation holds that Jonah's "death" in the waves of the sea foreshadows Jesus's death on the cross. According to this interpretation, which is unfortunately also often associated with deep anti-Jewish prejudices, the foreign sailors are seen as types for the Jews who wish to crucify Jesus. Scliar effectively undermines this interpretation by emphasizing that it is Jonah, the Jew, who is thrown into the sea while the sailors, who throw him into the water without regard for his safety, are gentiles. In Rafael, Scliar has created an alternative type for Jonah. Rafael, like Jonah, flees, but unlike Jonah, he lacks freedom. While Jonah actively rebels against God, Rafael's flight is merely a reaction to all the events that befall him. Nonetheless, the lasting impression is one of Jonah and Rafael who, eternally homeless and haunted by God, are constantly and vainly seeking a place to rest.

The dialogue between Jonah and Scliar's novel not only deepens our understanding of the biblical story but also challenges us to read the biblical book with new eyes. The image of Jonah sitting east of Nineveh at the end of chapter 4, not knowing whether to stay in Nineveh or go home, makes the book poignant in a way that I myself was unprepared for. Has Jonah somehow forfeited the right to his home after ensuring the survival of Nineveh? To what extent has Jonah lost either his prophetic profession or his prophetic reputation by his flight from God's command? At the same time, like Scliar's Rafael, it is impossible for Jonah to make Nineveh his new home, as he will always remain a stranger among them. Despite saving them, he is still the foreigner whose homeland will be razed to the ground by the Neo-Assyrian forces just a few decades later.

* * *

The more you read Jonah, the more difficult it becomes. At least that is my experience. Here at the end of our literary journey with Jonah, it is easy to wonder what the origin and purpose of all these different interpretations are. Put differently, what is the point of turning the book of Jonah upside down and inside out to such an extent? Why can we just not accept that Jonah is wrong and God is right?

The reason for the twisting and turning, and thus also the answer to the question, is found in the Bible itself, more specifically in Nahum. Jonah in its canonical context problematizes the conversion and salvation of Nineveh and, by extension, God's mission to Jonah. Nahum conveys the definitive version, if by definitive we mean that which corresponds to the actual historical course of events. The biblical reader and the historian agree that the historical city of Nineveh was destroyed in 612 BCE by the combined forces of the Babylonians and the Medes. This knowledge nuances the message of Jonah. Could it be that, while preaching grace to repentant sinners, the book also emphasizes that God's forgiveness is not easy to bear? Repentance must be genuine and long lasting. God's grace is completely free, but it cannot be received without serious reflection. This way of reading the Jonah story leads, at least in part, to exonerate Jonah in that his objection to traveling to Nineveh turns out to be justified: Jonah was right to refuse to travel, since Nineveh's hypothetical repentance did not lead to any lasting salvation anyway. Furthermore, God should never have asked him to travel, because it all seems to have been nothing but a cruel joke. God destroyed Nineveh regardless but only after Nineveh had destroyed Israel. To subject Jonah to three nightmarish days inside a fish is like adding insult to injury.

How can we relate to all the different messages in the book of Jonah? Should we side with God and insist that grace is for everyone, no matter what anyone has done? We are back in the triangle of God's omnipotence, justice, and love where we started in chapter 1, but the message of Jonah seems to stand at loggerheads with the message of the flood story in Genesis 6–9. The question then becomes what God requires of us humans. To return to Jonah's original dilemma, should he save his people from the Assyrian war machine, or should he give this cruel foreign power a chance to repent? If we side with God, the answer is both easy and extremely difficult. Yes, God may indeed require of you to sacrifice your people and your country to preach God's message to strangers who wish you harm. This may be the incredibly tough message of Jonah.

At the same time, the way is open for us to side with Jonah. As mentioned earlier, the book gives equal space to Jonah and God, although God seemingly has the last word in Jonah 4:11. At the same time, Jonah has the last word in that Nahum, later in the canon, gives Jonah a posthumous vindication. Nineveh's repentance was not deep enough to stop them from leveling Israel to the ground. God exclaims in Nah 2:13: "See, I am against you, says the Lord of hosts, and I will burn your chariots in smoke, and the sword shall devour your young lions; I will cut off your prey from the earth, and the voice of your messengers shall be heard no more." In Nahum, God punishes Nineveh for their sins. The extremely painful question then becomes whether God's punishment came too late. Would it not have been better if it had come a few years earlier, so that Israel would have survived?

I shall let Dietrich Bonhoeffer have the last word. This German Lutheran pastor, theologian, and resistance fighter knew the price of mercy and forgiveness in the face of incomprehensible evil much better than I do. He wrote a poem, "Jonah," from his prison cell on October 5, 1944. It is likely that by that time he had given up hope of survival and instead accepted that his execution was imminent.

<table>
<tr><td>And Jonah spoke: "'Tis I!<br>In God's eyes I have sinned. Forfeited is my life.<br><br>"Away with me! The guilt is mine. God's wrath's for me.<br>The pious shall not perish with the sinner!"<br>They trembled much. But then, with their strong hands,<br>they cast the guilty one away. The sea stood still.</td><td>Und Jona sprach: »Ich bin es!<br>Ich sündigte vor Gott. Mein Leben ist verwirkt.<br><br>»Tut mich von Euch! Mein ist die Schuld. Gott zürnt mir sehr.<br>Der Fromme soll nicht mit dem Sünder enden!«<br>Sie zitterten. Doch dann mit starken Händen<br>verstießen sie den Schuldigen. Da stand das Meer.</td></tr>
</table>

Bonhoeffer's poem, with its strong allusion to Jonah 1:15 ("The sea stood still"; ויעמד הים), gives us insight into Bonhoeffer's life. Bonhoeffer identifies with Jonah and, like Jonah, accepts his responsibility for the situation of his fellow human beings and thus also his death. At the same time, the poem highlights the biblical Jonah's moment of true heroism. Instead of letting the sailors perish because of him, Jonah grants them permission to throw him overboard. In one single, altruistic act, Jonah spares them from committing murder and mitigates the situation to assisted suicide. Thus Jonah, so often vilified for his lack of mercy, shows genuine compassion for his neighbor.

# Conclusion

## *My Biblical Friends*

What have we seen on this journey through the narrative texts of the Old Testament? My hope is that we have gained a renewed and more nuanced understanding and appreciation of the stories of the Bible. I hope that, together with a variety of authors writing from a wide range of perspectives, we have been able to enjoy and at times possibly also have been horrified by the fates of the different characters. I like to think that we are now a little better at seeing situations from their point of view and have been challenged to consider how we would have acted had we been in their situation.

The original Swedish title of the book you have just read is *Mina bibliska vänner och jag* (My biblical friends and I). It alludes to the slightly nerdy reality that I, along with a whole bunch of other biblical scholars, live much of our lives together with the people in the Bible. Sometimes they even feel more real than the people around me. Strange as it may seem, I do spend time with my biblical friends. Once, when I got stuck in an unwanted and overly long *fika* (coffee and cake break), I managed to get out of it by claiming that I had a meeting. That the said meeting was with Isaiah, the *fika* participants will never know. Besides, honestly, after escaping from the "cake orgy," I returned relieved to my Bible and my computer and continued to write, cheerfully and peacefully, on an article about some verses in Isaiah.

With this in mind, the time has come to speak openly about my own feelings regarding these nine people whose company we have enjoyed. I do not think it will have escaped anyone's notice that I am closer to some characters than others. To reiterate my words at the beginning of the book, I maintain that it is perfectly fine to have different feelings toward the various Bible characters. So, here are my very personal thoughts about my biblical friends. These thoughts are very deliberately anachronistic. By that I mean that I relate to them as a middle-aged woman in Sweden in the twenty-first century. At the same time, I am a biblical scholar from the bottom of my heart, so my fantasy will be held somewhat (but not too much) in check by my knowledge of what one may reasonably expect from a person who lived about 3000 years ago.

What would I tell my biblical friends? Let's work backward, starting with Jonah. My Jonah is a very difficult person. You can't accept that things are a certain way and then argue constantly. You also like to provoke those around you and take things to extremes. This character trait can sometimes be quite exhausting but at the same time is rather refreshing. You also often exaggerate and get angry and grumpy when things don't go your way. For example, you really mean what you say to the sailors in Jonah 1:12 when you tell them to throw you overboard. Of course, you know you'll die in the process, but it is worth it—at least you won't have to go to Nineveh. According to you, God is not playing fair when he then appoints a fish as your savior. You were definitely prepared to pay the price for your stubbornness, and now you feel cheated of your rightful destiny.

You are also not someone to waste words on things that are obvious. Your one-sentence sermon in Jonah 3:4 is concise, it must be said, and you see this brevity as a virtue. There is no point in embellishing the undeniable, or trying to soften the brutality of the message. If anything, you are consistent. You can be trusted in all weathers to tell the truth, however uncomfortable. You expect it of yourself, and you expect it of God. Concise language, plain and simple!

At the same time, I'm not sure what will become of you in the end. I am forced to leave you to your fate, sitting on your lookout east of Nineveh. Dear Jonah, since you are so often so sure of yourself, I wonder if you could change your mind? Would you be able to accept God's merciful view of forgiveness and make it your own, or would you rather prefer, in a few years' time, to come insisting that you were right all along in emphasizing the futility of visiting Nineveh? After all, the city has just missed its second chance and God must therefore destroy Nineveh anyway. Wouldn't it have been better if everyone had listened to you from the start? In any case, it would have saved both time and energy. It would also probably have saved the Northern Kingdom (Israel) a lot of suffering, as no Neo-Assyrian Empire would have destroyed it in 721 BC. I know a number of Jonahs in my own everyday life. There is usually one in every class. I can sometimes get a little mad at them when they point out what I myself, with my more laissez-faire attitude, consider to be trivialities. At the same time, I deeply appreciate Jonah and his ilk. They are needed in the kingdom of God, otherwise we would lack structure in our thinking and behavior. So, thank you, Jonah, for being my friend.

Going further back, we end up with Saul and his family. My Michal is beautiful—just like your father—but your beauty does you little good. You are also, at least in your youth, a little naive and easily led. At the same time, you are strong-willed and certainly not lacking in courage. You listen to your feelings, take your destiny into your own hands, and act on your convictions. The price you pay for following your heart is unreasonably high. Michal, if you had known what life had in store for you that day when you first saw David and fell for his charm, would you have acted differently? I sincerely wish that you may experience that at least one person puts you first in his heart. Is Palti that person? Will you get a few years of happiness and peace in your life with him? I hope you will. For most of your life, however, you are rarely more than a pawn in the power struggle around you. Dear Michal, I want to give you all the love you are not getting from your immediate family! I want to be your best friend and help you when things are hard.

I believe that you, living a long life, are forced to endure David's whole reign. I fear that you experience so much emotional pain and are so neglected. I do not want you to be bitter. But I do believe you are bitter, bordering on despairing. At the same time, I'm wondering, tentatively, if you would like to improve your situation. Would you be prepared to try to be a little more flexible and willing to compromise, at least sometimes? For example, I would advise you not to show your anger and disappointment toward David when the ark is brought into Jerusalem. If you are able to choose differently on this fateful day, you might have an easier life. Is there room in your heart to at least pretend to forgive David the unforgivable, to play a little pragmatic theater just to make things easier for yourself? At the same time, I can imagine that such horse trading belittles you in your own eyes and it is important that you can actually live with yourself. Michal, you are a bit like Vashti, who does not bargain with her principles, while Bathsheba, a woman you surely detest, is a bit like Esther, who goes with the flow when it benefits her. Personally, I have always favored the example of Michal and Vashti, but the older I get, the more I understand that Esther and Bathsheba probably live happier lives. Michal, I grieve with you.

Your older brother, Jonathan, also falls for David's charm. My Jonathan, you are impulsive and usually act on your feelings. The difference between the two of you, Michal and Jonathan, is subtle as you live your parallel lives. Despite your similarities, you, Jonathan, are so much better off because you are a man. You can rush out of banquet halls in emotional turmoil when things go against you, you can ride around the Judaean wilderness to spend some quality time with David, and you can periodically engage in heroic adventures to vent your feelings of powerlessness.

You also have a softer personality and humbler approach to life than your sister, perhaps because you have so many more opportunities than she does and receive so much more of David's love and attention. You are a very honest person who hates secrets and hates having to meet David behind your father's back. You also dislike upsetting people and resent being forced to live in the middle of a conflict that, at least according to you, is quite unnecessary. In your dream world, your father Saul lives to a ripe old age and then, after his death, David takes over the crown, while you stay on the periphery, providing support when needed.

Jonathan, you know you are one of my absolute favorite people in the whole Bible. I respect you deeply for your integrity, your wisdom, your courage to follow God's will, and your absolute devotion. At the same time, I sometimes want to shake you, at least a little, when you perhaps go too far. Do you really think you can be David's second-in-command when he takes the throne, or do you know, deep in your heart, that it would lead to civil war? There's no way the tribe of Benjamin will recognize David as king while you're alive, you get that, right? But you don't really want to be king, do you? You've seen how the royal crown ruined your father's life. You, standing between giants fighting for power, realize that in such battles there are ultimately only losers.

So, Jonathan and Michal, I hope we would have been friends in real life. As I've always loved a tragic underdog, I'd love to be by your sides. Your father, Saul, evokes more ambivalent feelings in me. My Saul, you are a person I feel great compassion for, but I do not think you are a close friend of mine. Maybe more like an acquaintance? Saul, I know that you are in a bad position and lack good advisors. It is lonely at the pinnacle of power, and you do not get the support you need from the prophet Samuel. After a few years on the throne, you are subjected to one of life's cruelest pranks. You trust God, but he stops communicating with you, and then he rejects you for things you do not think are that important. You try to do your best, but it turns out not to be enough. So you fall into the darkness of depression but manage to get up again because you believe you have found a person whose devotion you will keep for life, a young man you can trust in all weathers.

In this delicate situation, you are exposed to another of fate's more merciless whims. You are forced to realize that this person, David, will take away everything that has come to mean something to you. Even though you never wanted to be king in the first place, your kingship is now the only thing you have left to fight for. Now your reality is shattered, you stop caring, and you allow yourself to commit barbaric and completely unnecessary acts of violence against the civilian priests of Nob. The paranoia takes over, and you hunt your nemesis day and night instead of governing your country and protecting its inhabitants from external threats. Finally, you reach a dead end from which you cannot escape. In your most difficult moment on Mount Gilboa, even your commander, Abner, abandons you. Only your immediate family stands faithfully by your side, but it is no use. You and your line will die on this fateful day. Saul, I feel strongly about your fate, and I wish you nothing but peace and reconciliation.

No David without Ruth. A simple and inexorable logic. So, let me ponder a little further about my Ruth. When I first meet you, you are a widow in your mid-twenties, old enough to have experienced a lot, both good and bad. You are a warmhearted woman with a great deal of faith in God, a sense of adventure, initiative, and probably humor. I think we could have been good friends outside the pages of the Bible. I do not know why you choose to leave Moab and follow Naomi to Bethlehem. Does God give you the certainty that your destiny awaits you with the people of Israel? Do you want to support your beloved mother-in-law in her great sorrow? Do you want to feel the air under your wings, travel somewhere else, see something new, experience adventure? You challenge fate at regular intervals. I have no problem at all with seeing you as a benevolent seductress—everyone benefits when you marry Boaz, and it is not entirely wrong to help all those partners out a little. You would have protested if you had not been in on Naomi's plan. Given that you managed to convince your rather stubborn mother-in-law to accompany her to Bethlehem, you are, in my opinion, fully capable of deciding for yourself whether you should be on a particular threshing floor or not. You are, on the whole, quite pragmatic.

At the same time, you have no need to be in the limelight. Rather, you prefer to stay behind the scenes, pulling the strings and moving the pieces.

Things move quickly when you are so inclined, and you usually get what you want. When that is done, you are satisfied, retire, and revel in your success. After your wedding to Boaz, you get a whole new game plan. You are now married to the richest man in Bethlehem and, like the woman of valor in Proverbs 31:10–31, you and your household look to the future with a smile. Dressed in purple linen, you run the farm like a well-oiled machine. Everyone is happy as can be!

Moving on to Naomi, I think you too are my friend. My Naomi, you are a woman threatened to be swallowed by your own sadness and bitterness, so much so that you even change your name. Rather than being called Naomi, the sweet one, you want to be called Mara, the bitter one. Sometimes life deals us too many hard blows in a row, and we are not able to parry them. Losing both a husband and children is a terrible fate that is unfortunately shared by too many. At the same time, you are a bit of a cautionary tale, as your story shows the danger of drowning in your grief. People are often not in control of their emotions, and you can't help it when the pain and loss overwhelm you.

It takes a long time for you to start wanting to try to live and have contact with your fellow human beings again, but I think you eventually refind the joy of life. In my fantasy, I see you living in a small house somewhere along the steep and narrow streets of Bethlehem. Ruth, of course, has offered you a place to live in her and Boaz's big house, but you are happy with your independence. Obed, and later all his younger siblings, run past regularly, and you bake pita bread and prepare your special hummus according to an old recipe. A bit of an idyll, perhaps, but I think you deserve it. Besides, what else are you going to do now that Ruth is running the show and providing at such an exceptional level?

We wander further back and end up with Joseph. My Joseph, you are an energetic person whom I like a lot. I think we could have worked well together. Imagine how much you can get done if you have a coworker like that. I even think you would make a decent boss, as you seem to be good at delegating and everyone, both superiors and employees, trust you.

I also like the idea of allowing you to be happily married. You deserve it, especially after all the intrigues orchestrated by Potiphar's wife. In order for the marriage to work, however, I have to think a bit about Asenath. Here I get no help from the Bible, so I allow myself to speculate freely. Joseph, you will never work nine-to-five. Forget about it! In your role as Pharaoh's vizier and with your strong work ethic, you are not going to be home a lot. So I'll either have to give my Asenath lots of hobbies, an extensive social life, or simply a job. If she focuses too much of her life on you, Joseph, and insists that you should be more present at home, I do not think the marriage will be happy. So I'll let Asenath become a scribe. Then she can have a sensible occupation which might also involve meeting her husband at work at regular intervals. I'm not being overly anachronistic here as there is pictorial evidence to suggest that women in ancient Egypt held this occupation. Last but not least, I think that Asenath must be quite independent and intelligent, as you, Joseph, like challenges on all levels. An overly nice and compliant Asenath would probably bore you.

As I said, Joseph, you are superefficient during the day and give the impression of having everything under control. But appearances are deceptive, because at night the demons of the past creep out. You have nightmares about everything you have experienced and are torn between faith and doubt, forgiveness and bitterness. You agonize over your relationship with your father and brothers during endless sleepless nights. Dealing with an emotionally unstable Joseph with post-traumatic stress disorder is certainly no picnic. That's also why we should give Asenath all our support. It would not be healthy for her to become completely absorbed by Joseph's well-being. We need to provide her with a satisfying professional life and a good circle of friends so that she can be there for you when you need her. As I said, my Asenath is nothing but a figment of my imagination; I just want my friend Joseph to have a good life.

Joseph, I believe that you try hard to forgive your brothers for their misdeeds, but you don't always manage it. Nonetheless, you have resolved never to take revenge. This promise is much easier to keep if you do not see them very often. That's why you prefer to stay in Thebes, the capital of the New Kingdom in Upper Egypt, and rarely visit Goshen in the Nile Delta. After all, your conversation, brother to brother, is easily strained, and sheepherding has never really been your thing. Moreover, every time you feel compelled to visit the extended family, Asenath becomes all tense, as she knows from experience that every such visit tears open old wounds. Ephraim and Manasseh, for their part, are filled with terror at the mere thought of socializing with fifty older cousins who do not have much in common with the, according to them, coddled and overly fancy half Egyptians from the capital.

Before we say goodbye to my biblical friends, let's also take a closer look at my Sarah and my Noah. Sarah, I would love to be your friend. There are so many things about you that I like and look up to, but at the same time, there are things that make me a little unsure. Would you treat me like you treat Hagar? I hope not. Sarah, I think you are an intelligent yet extremely bored woman. You grew up in ancient Ur, a cultural center with plenty of opportunities for intellectual stimulation. You may be able to read and write a little, at least a few characters, and you may even have some knowledge of math, astronomy, herbology, medicine, and perhaps other subjects as well. Then, for unclear reasons, you marry Abraham and exchange your life in Ur for a life in Harran. Okay, it is not a backwater, but it is not a metropolis either. You can still satisfy your thirst for knowledge. Then God calls your husband to Canaan. There's nothing there but sheep and goats—and they are not that interesting to converse with. If you only had children, you would have something to do, but even that is denied you. Then you end up in Pharaoh's harem. You probably thought it would be interesting to visit Egypt. Perhaps you even insisted on coming along, just to stave off the boredom in the bedouin tent. Once you get there, however, things do not turn out as you expected. Your world becomes even narrower, and you feel like the walls are shrinking. You are even denied the right to your own body. If I were you, I would kick the furniture in frustration. Life gets harder and harder, and you get more and more bitter. The straw that breaks the camel's back—the first time—is when your clever plan, which may not be so clever after all, goes awry. Your servant Hagar becomes pregnant with your own husband's child, and you just want to curl up in your tent and disappear. Is there any point to your life? Yet God hears your desperate prayer, you have a son, and he becomes your absolute everything. Love overflows. What happens next is unimaginable. Your heart can't take in the horror that Abraham turns out to be prepared to perform. When you face the extent of your husband's obedience to God, your life shatters a second time and loses all its meaning. Maybe you just lie down and die?

Now there is only Noah left. Are you my friend, Noah? No, I do not think so. You are at most an acquaintance of mine. We meet regularly and try to have a conversation from time to time, but every time I feel that we do not really get through to one another. I don't understand you. You, for your part, are so confident and sure, but I don't find your conviction attractive in any way. Rather, I am taken aback when you insist that you have all the answers. Perhaps you know best; I am open to the possibility that I am at fault. However, we do not find each other properly because I, from my perspective, perceive you as single-minded. I sense that you don't like it when I go on with my endless hypothetical scenarios and my theoretical discussions about everything between heaven and earth, where I question everything and figuratively darken what you think is crystal clear. At the same time, I feel sorry for you. I don't think it was always easy for you to build the ark. I think that sometimes you dared to stop and reflect on your behavior. Should you have preached repentance, and should you have tried to intercede before God on behalf of the people around you? Then, when you go ashore at Mount Ararat and see the devastation, you realize with uncomfortable clarity the consequences of your action or, rather, your inaction. Rotting animals and human corpses lie on the ground while you stand there alive, alone with your little family. What will you now do with the rest of your days? Unfortunately, I see your vineyard project as an expression of your survivor's guilt. You plant it to seek oblivion in the intoxication of alcohol. I do not fault you for disappearing into your drunkenness and allowing your children and grandchildren to carry the blame. It may not be an active choice, and you may not be capable of acting differently. I think you thought you were doing the right thing, and maybe you were. I am not going to judge you.

In the midst of all these people and their lives, there is God. God often operates in the background of these stories, and sometimes his ways are inscrutable. Sarah eventually has a child despite having to wait what seems like an unnecessarily long time, and God, for reasons that are unclear, chooses to pardon Nineveh whether they deserve it or not. In other stories, God's hand is clearer. In Joseph's life, God rules in the background but is still a force to be reckoned with. He leads Joseph through the valley of the shadow of death to eventually allow him to be at peace with himself and a blessing to others. He also leads Ruth on her journey from alienation to community, even though she is initially unaware of God's providence. She too becomes a blessing to others, primarily to Naomi but also to Boaz and eventually, through their descendant, Jesus, to us all. Finally, Jonathan's death on Mount Gilboa is perhaps one of the most powerful symbols of self-sacrificing love that the Old Testament offers. For me, it serves as a model of Jesus's suffering and death for our sins and a new way to life.

# NOTES

## INTRODUCTION

1. John Barton, *Ethics and The Old Testament*, 2nd ed. (SCM, 2002), 29.
2. Mikael Tellbe, *Vad menar vi med att Bibeln är Guds ord?* (Libris, 2015), 98.

## CHAPTER ONE: NOAH

1. John S. Mill, "Inaugural Address," given at the University of St Andrews, February 1, 1867 (Longmans, Green).

## CHAPTER THREE: JOSEPH

1. Astrid Lindgren, *Madicken* (Rabén & Sjögren, 1983), 179. If you are interested in reading *Madicken* for yourself, it has been translated by P. Crampton as *Mardie* (Methuen, 1979).
2. Andrew Lloyd Webber and Tim Rice, *Joseph and the Amazing Technicolor Dreamcoat*, Colet Court School, London, 1968. The musical is based on the story of Joseph in Genesis.
3. Tintomara is the main character of Carl Jonas Love Almqvist, *The Queen's Diadem*, trans. Yvonne Sandstroem (Camden House, 1992). Originally published as *Drottningens juvelsmycke* in 1834 by (Johan Hörberg, 1834).

## CHAPTER FOUR: RUTH AND NAOMI

1. The books have recently been made into a musical by Björn Ulvaeus and Benny Andersson, *Kristina från Duvemåla*, Malmö Opera and Music Theatre, Malmö, 1995.

## CHAPTER FIVE: SAUL

1. Masada was a fortress where a group of Jewish resistance fighters took refuge during the First Jewish-Roman War. The contemporary Jewish historian Josephus describes the Roman siege of Masada in his book *The Jewish War*. To avoid being

captured and sold into slavery, the resistance fighters chose to commit collective suicide in 73 CE.

## CHAPTER SIX: JONATHAN

1. Astrid Lindgren, *Bill Bergson Lives Dangerously*, trans. Herbert Antoine (Viking, 1954), 136–137, originally published as *Mästerdetektiven Blomkvist lever farligt* (Rabén & Sjögren, 1951).

## CHAPTER EIGHT: JONAH

1. Terry Eagleton, "J. L. Austin and the Book of Jonah," in *The Book and the Text: The Bible and Literary Theory*, ed. Regina Schwartz (Wiley-Blackwell, 1990), 231–236.
2. Yvonne Sherwood, *A Biblical Text and its Afterlives: The Survival of Jonah in Western Culture* (Cambridge University Press, 2000), 67.

# LIST OF CITED LITERARY WORKS


Afek, Edna. "שרה היתה" (Sarah was). In *Does David Still Play Before You? Israeli Poetry and the Bible*, edited by David C. Jacobson. Wayne State University Press, 1997.

Afshar, Tessa. *In the Field of Grace*. River North, 2014.

Amichai, Yehuda. "King Saul and I." In *The Poetry of Yehuda Amichai*, edited by Robert Alter. Farrar, Straus and Giroux, 2015.

Barenblat, Rachel. "The Handmaid's Tale (Ruth)." https://velveteenrabbi.blogs.com/blog/2011/05/a-ruth-poem-for-shavuot.html, 2011.

Barenblat, Rachel. "The One Who Turned Back." https://velveteenrabbi.blogs.com/blog/2012/05/a-poem-about-orpah.html, 2012.

Bass, Samuel. "ערפה" (Orpah). Translated by Barry Dov Walfish. https://www.thetorah.com/article/the-defamation-of-orpah.

Beck, Karl. *Saul: Tragödie in fünf Aufzügen*. E. Polz, 1840.

Berggren, Mats. *Rami och Jonatan*. Opal, 2019.

Biala, Tamar. "מכתב של ערפה להוריה" (Orpah's Letter to Her Parents). Translated by Barry Dov Walfish. https://www.thetorah.com/article/the-defamation-of-orpah.

Bluwstein, Rachel. "Jonathan." In *Flowers of Perhaps: Selected Poems of Ra'hel*. Menard, 1994. Originally published in מנגד (Across from) by Davar, 1930.

Bonhoeffer, Dietrich. "Jona." http://www.otthollo.de/JONA/Bonhoeffer.html, 1944.

Bonhoeffer, Dietrich. "Jonah." In *Letters and Papers from Prison*. Vol. 8 of *Dietrich Bonhoeffer Works*, edited by Reinhard Krauss and Nancy Lukens. Translated by Isabel Best. Fortress, 2010.

Boström, Tomas. "Den åttonde sången" (The eighth song). In *Och Gud skapade människan*, edited by Magnus Sundell. Libris, 2014.

Brandes, Yochi. *The Secret Book of Kings*. Translated by Yardenne Greenspan. St Martin's, 2016. Originally published as מלכים ג by Zmora-Bitan, 2008.

Brooks, Geraldine. *The Secret Chord*. Viking, 2015.

Byron, George Gordon. "Saul" In *Hebrew Melodies*. Murray, 1815.

Byron, George Gordon. "Thou Whose Spell Can Raise the Dead." In *Hebrew Melodies*. Murray, 1815.

Byron, George Gordon. "Song of Saul Before His Last Battle." In *Hebrew Melodies.* Murray, 1815.

Card, Orson Scott. *Sarah.* Bookcraft, 2000.

Diamant, Anita. *The Red Tent.* St Martin's, 1997.

Etzioni-Halevy, Eva. *Garden of Ruth.* Plume, 2007.

Fredriksson, Marianne. *Syndafloden.* Wahlström & Widstrand, 1993.

Frost, Robert. *A Masque of Mercy.* In *Collected Poems, Prose, and Plays.* The Library of America, 1995.

Fröding, Gustaf. "Saul och David." In *Nya dikter.* Bonniers, 1894.

Gilboa, Amir. "שרי" (Sarai). In *Does David Still Play Before You? Israeli Poetry and the Bible,* edited by David C. Jacobson. Wayne State University Press, 1997.

Gilboa, Amir. "Saul." In *Voices Within the Ark: The Modern Jewish Poets,* edited by Howard Schwartz and Anthony Rudolf. Translated by Shirley Kaufman. Avon, 1980. Originally published as *Shirim baboker baboker* by Hakibbutz hameuchad, 1953.

Goldman, Anita. *Den sista kvinnan från Ur.* Litteraturfrämjandet, 1988.

Gustafson, Eleanor. *The Stones: A Novel of the Life of King David.* Whitaker House, 2009.

Hallqvist, Britt G., and Bertil Hallin. "Josef Får En Ny Rock" (Josef Gets a New Coat). In the album *Titta vad jag fann!* Released in 1973.

Halter, Marek. *Sarah: A Heroine of the Old Testament.* Bantam, 2004.

Heller, Joseph. *God Knows.* Knopf, 1984.

Hellerstein, Kathryn. "Naomi: 'Call Me Bitter.'" In *Reading Ruth: Contemporary Women Reclaim a Sacred Story,* edited by Judith A Kates and Gail Twersky Reimer. Ballantine Books, 1994.

Heym, Stefan. *The King David Report.* Kindler, 1972.

Hunt, Angela. *Dreamer.* Steeple Hill, 2004.

Huss, Abraham. "ערפה" (Orpah). Translated by Barry Dov Walfish. https://www.thetorah.com/article/the-defamation-of-orpah.

Kafri, Yehudit. "בראשית" (In the beginning). *Does David Still Play Before You? Israeli Poetry and the Bible,* edited by David C. Jacobson. Wayne State University Press, 1997.

Kafri, Yehudit. "אשת פוטיפר" (Potiphar's wife). *Does David Still Play Before You? Israeli Poetry and the Bible,* edited by David C. Jacobson. Wayne State University Press, 1997.

Kamieńska, Anna. "Naomi." In *Modern Poems on the Bible: An Anthology,* edited by David Curzon. Jewish Publication Society of America, 1994.

Klintefelt, Carolina. "Förkastad, sedd." In *Och Gud skapade människan,* edited by Magnus Sundell. Libris, 2014.

Kolmar, Gertrud. "Die Tiere von Ninive" (The animals of Nineveh). In *Gedichte: 1927–1937,* vol. 2 of *Das lyrische Werk.* Wallstein, 2003.

Lawrence, David Herbert. *David: A Play in Sixteen Scenes*. Knopf, 1926.

L'Engle, Madeleine. *Many Waters*. Bantam Doubleday Dell, 1986.

Lindgren, Astrid. *The Brothers Lionheart*. Translated by Joan Tate. Oxford University Press, 1975. Originally published as *Bröderna Lejonhjärta* by Rabén & Sjögren, 1973.

McCaughrean, Geraldine. *Not the End of the World*. Oxford University Press, 2004.

Mann, Thomas. *Joseph and His Brothers*. Translated by John E. Woods. Knopf, 2005. Originally published as Joseph und seine Brüder. S. Fischer, 1934–1943.

Massie, Allan. *King David*. Hodder & Stoughton, 1995.

Melville, Herman. *Moby-Dick; or, The Whale*. Harper & Brothers, 1851.

Molodowsky, Kadia. "Jonah." In *Paper Bridges: Selected Poems of Kadya Molodowsky*. Translated by Kathryn Hellerstein. Wayne State University Press, 1990.

Nilson, Peter. *Guldspiken*. Norstedt, 1985.

Pagis, Dan. "תפילת שאול האחרונה" (Saul's last prayer). In *Does David Still Play Before You? Israeli Poetry and the Bible*, edited by David C. Jacobson. Wayne State University Press, 1997.

Piercy, Marge. "The Book of Ruth and Naomi." In *Modern Poems on the Bible: An Anthology*, edited by David Curzon. Jewish Publication Society of America, 1994. Originally published in *Mars and Her Children* by Knopf, 1992.

Provoost, Anne. *In the Shadow of the Ark*. Translated by John Nieuwenhuizen. Arthur A. Levine, 2004. Originally published as *De arkvaarders* by Querido, 2001.

Quinn, Eric Shaw. *The Prince's Psalm*. DSP Publications, 2016.

Phillips, Erin. *A Bond of Briars*. Ethereal Echo, 2023.

Rivers, Francine. *The Prince*. Tyndale, 2005.

Rushing, Regina. *Seal Of The Sand Dweller*. Dominia, 2018.

Schmitt, Gladys. *David the King*. Dial, 1946.

Scliar, Moacyr. *The Strange Nation of Rafael Mendes*. Translated by Eloah F. Giacomelli. Harmony, 1986. Originally published as *A estranha nação de Rafael Mendes* by L&PM, 1983.

Shamir, Moshe. *The Hittite Must Die*. Translated by Margaret Benaya. East and West Library, 1978. Originally published as כבשת הרש: סיפור אוריה החיתי by Davar, 1956.

Shapcott, Thomas. "Portrait of Saul." In *Begin with Walking*. University of Queensland Press, 1972.

Shifra, Shin. "יצחק" (Isaac). In Dalia Marx, "Where Was Sarah? Depictions of Mothers and Motherhood in Modern Israeli Poetry on the Binding of Isaac." In *Mothers in the Jewish Cultural Imagination*, edited by Marjorie Lehman, Jane L. Kanarek, and Simon J. Bronner. Littman Library of Jewish Civilization, 2017.

Tchernichovsky, Shaul. "At Endor." https://benyehuda.org/read/6101, 1897.

Tchernichovsky, Shaul. "At the ruins of Beth-shan." https://benyehuda.org/read/6234, 1897

Tchernichovsky, Shaul. "On Mount Gilboa." https://benyehuda.org/read/4581, 1929.
Tchernichovsky, Shaul. "The faithful fighters." https://benyehuda.org/read/6369, 1936.
Weil, Grete. *The Bride Price: A Novel.* Translated by John Barrett. Godine, 1991. Originally published as *Der Brautpreis* by Nagel & Kimche, 1988.

# FURTHER READING

The content of several of the chapters in this book is based on my academic research. If anyone wants to read further—and enjoy considerably drier prose and a plethora of footnotes—more material is available in the following publications:


Tiemeyer, Lena-Sofia. "Reception Exegesis: How Literary Retellings Can Shed New Light on a Biblical Text and Its Interpretations." In *Biblical Reception: Models and Methods*, edited by Hannah M. Strømmen. Society of Biblical Literature, forthcoming.

Tiemeyer, Lena-Sofia. "David in Literature." In *The Oxford Handbook of King David*, edited by David Shepherd and Lena-Sofia Tiemeyer. Oxford University Press, forthcoming.

Tiemeyer, Lena-Sofia. *In Search of Jonathan: Jonathan between the Bible and Modern Fiction*. Oxford University Press, 2023.

Tiemeyer, Lena-Sofia. "Missing Jonathan: The Curious Case of the Neglected Crown Prince in Modern Dramatizations of the David Narrative." In *Historical Settings, Intertextuality, and Biblical Theology: Essays in Honour of Marvin A. Sweeney*, edited by Hyun Chul Paul Kim, Tyler D. Mayfield, and Hye-Kyung Park. Mohr Siebeck, 2022.

Tiemeyer, Lena-Sofia. "Jonah in 20th Century Literature." *Religions* 13, no. 661 (2022): 1–13.

Tiemeyer, Lena-Sofia. *Jonah Through the Centuries*. Wiley-Blackwell, 2022.

Tiemeyer, Lena-Sofia. "The Reception of David and Michal in Twentieth and Twenty-First-Century Literature." In *The Character of David in Judaism, Christianity and Islam: Warrior, Poet, Prophet and King*, edited by Marzena Zawanowska and Mateusz Wilk. Brill, 2021.

Tiemeyer, Lena-Sofia. "Retelling Noah and the Flood: A Fictional Encounter with Genesis 6–9." *Relegere: Studies in Religion and Reception* 6, no. 2 (2017): 219–239. DOI: 10.11157/rsrr6-2-706.